Jonathan Belcher
Governor of the Provinces of Massachusetts Bay
and New Hampshire 1730-41.
Courtesy of the Massachusetts Historical Society.
See page 200 for details of this painting.

FIRST AMERICAN BORN

The Life and Journal of Jonathan Belcher,
the First-Known, American-Born Freemason

David Crockett

HERITAGE BOOKS
2015

HERITAGE BOOKS
AN IMPRINT OF HERITAGE BOOKS, INC.

Books, CDs, and more—Worldwide

For our listing of thousands of titles see our website
at
www.HeritageBooks.com

Published 2015 by
HERITAGE BOOKS, INC.
Publishing Division
5810 Ruatan Street
Berwyn Heights, Md. 20740

International Standard Book Numbers
Paperbound: 978-1-55613-726-6
Clothbound: 978-0-7884-6188-0

DEDICATED TO

My wife Cynthia. For her
friendship, patience and humor.

CONTENTS

Governor Belcher's eight surviving books at Princeton University (Pg. 239-
244). The reference librarian/archivist, Margaret M. Sherry, is holding
Belcher's 1673 book, *Observations upon the United Provinces of the Netherlands*, by William Temple. Belcher may have carried this book on his tour of
Holland in 1704. The painting is of Governor Belcher, (by Moussa Ayoub,
1938), based in part on a 1734 mezzotint by John Farber after a contemporary portrait by Richard Phillips (Pg. 199). Princeton University still operates
under Governor Belcher's 1748 charter. He is considered on of the founders
and first major donor to the then named "College of New Jersey." Courtesy of
Princeton University.

PREFACE

"Ye book 'tis abt 'Em" activities and associates of a
Royal Governor in the early 1700s. The subject, Jonathan
Belcher (1681/2-1757), was born in a Massachusetts tavern
and became the Royal Governor of Massachusetts and New
Hampshire in the 1730s. He also wrote a previously
unpublished three month journal in 1704, the year he
became the first known, American born, Freemason.

Because the American Revolution is interwoven with well
known Freemasons, (George Washington, Benjamin Franklin,
John Hancock, Paul Revere, John Paul Jones, etc.) it
is thematic that a biography of this Boston centered,
first Masonic Royal Governor, will shed some light on
the pre-Revolutionary period.

We will explore Jonathan's 1704 Journal, in detail, and
his correspondence as a Royal Governor. For such emphasis
there is another reason: it has been said that history is
more than remembering dates, it is understanding the
emotions of the past.

Belcher was a tourist, in Europe, in 1704. His nearly 300
year old Journal reveals how our heritage, political
appointments and trade characteristics are anchored to
the old world.

In the 1704 Journal, Jonathan tells how he was introduced
to the Royal family. Indeed, his introduction to the
House of Hanover, at the age of twenty-two, led to his
later appointment as a Royal Governor in 1730. He
describes his thoughts when he was introduced to Sophia,
heir to the Crown of England, to George I, to George II,
to the King and Queen of Prussia and to several wealthy
merchants in Europe. Thus the 1704 Journal, along with
other documentation, indicates that Belcher's friends,
in America and England, were not only of extraordinary
social significance, at least one of them introduced
Jonathan to Freemasonry in 1704.

In answer to questions regarding the relationship between
the colonies and England, Belcher sent his son to
college in England (Oxford and Cambridge) in 1731. He
wrote over 120 letters to his son and sent many more
letters, for his son to hand carry in London, as a

technique of introducing his son and in carrying out his work as a Royal Governor. Belcher's correspondence to the Prime Minister of England, members of the King's Privy Council, the leading figures in trade and scores of others, are historically significant. Indeed, a revolution began quietly, long before the tea party on December 16, 1773.

This research will occasionally explore another area. Because Belcher is an extremely unusual Freemason, one of six in the world who stated that he was a member before the Fraternity formally organized in 1717 (see Pg. 198) and given the abundance of Freemasons later in the Revolutionary period, we will also attempt to identify his Masonic associates, hoping to shed more light on pre-Revolutionary history. Regarding the identity of Freemasons, AQC is often used, "AQC" is explained on Pg. 247 and 159.

As a final inclusive thought, there are surprising similarities between problems in colonial America and today. This book will touch on those similarities. The motives of people is also evident. Motives were not always honorable. Since the American Revolution occurred less than twenty years after Jonathan Belcher died, the second part of the book will blend the simmering problems of this Royal Governor's world, with his efforts to solve those problems. The result is a unique insight into the lessons of the past... lessons which remain relevant.

I would like to thank the Massachusetts Historical Society (Louis L. Tucker, Peter Drummey and Virginia Smith), for their kind cooperation in this research. The 1704 Journal is part of their extensive Jonathan Belcher collection. My transcript of Belcher's 1704 Journal is the first known transcript ever published. I also want to thank the Quatuor Coronati Lodge, Cyril N. Batham, Frederick Smyth, Herald E. Fernald Jr., and that remarkable octogenarian, Gerald D. Foss, Grand Lodge Historian Emeritus, from New Hampshire, for his gentle and judicious guidance. Jerry has been kind, wise and fearless in sharing his immense knowledge of Masonic research, and writing, with a new Masonic author. I hasten to add, I take complete responsibility for any errors in this research.

David Crockett
June 26, 1992
Stoddard, N.H.

This introductory note is a brief review of the "Old Style" Julian calender used by Belcher in colonial times. The O.S. calender had 365 days each year and a leap year every four years. Due to a leap year each new century, the Old style year accumulated an average of one day more than today's calender every 128 years. Our "New Style" Gregorian calender (1582) was adopted at various times in different countries (in England and America on Sept. 3, 1752). The New Style solved two problems: (1) It struck out eleven days of solar error accumulated over fourteen centuries. (2) It eliminated new century leap years not divisible by 400. The Old Style had other unusual traits: The O.S. year began March 25, about spring, March was the first month, April was number two, May was third, January was the eleventh month in America until 1752. An entry of "26-11-1681" in American records meant January 26, 1681.

Governor Belcher was clearly aware of the total eleven day difference between the New Style (used in Europe, and our Old Style, see Pg. 28), but in America he used the official Old Style system. He did use "double dating" for January to March 25: i.e. Jan. 26, 1681/2, means either January 26, 1681, O. S... or January 26, 1682, N. S. (which ignores solar error). Now consider this: The City Hall of Cambridge, Massachusetts, recorded Governor Belcher's birth on the lower half of page 535, volume one, of the 1623-1703 records. The tenth entry is:
  "Jonathan, of Andrew & Sarah Belchar / 8 / 11 / 1681". Meaning he was born January 8, 1681, O.S. calender. His birth is also noted in his January 8, 1740/1, letter: "This morning at about Two O'Clock, I enter'd the sixtieth year of my Life." (B. P. Vol. VII, Pg. 529). Meaning he was exactly fifty-nine years old at two A. M. and beginning his sixtieth year. His birth would be double dated as January 8, 1681/2...ignoring solar error.

In summary, April through December are in the N.S. year in both calenders. To estimate time, I ignore the ten or eleven day error, use the N.S. year and subtract dates. Example: Belcher's birth (N S. year) was January 8, 1682. He was twenty-two years old on January 8, 1703/4. Three months later, the date was written April 8, 1704. For those who seek more precision, convert all dates to solar corrected N.S. by adding ten days to the Old Style before 1700 leap year. After 1700, "ye Old Style began in March, April to December be common year. Solar error is eleven days and ignored in England and here." You are on your way to the colonial age of Caesar's time.

                                                      D. C.

Nicholas Withe and Lidea Fisk,   6 | 7 | 1681

Amos Marritt and Batirya Longhorn,   2 | 9 | 1681

Jn⁰. Ward and Mary Spring,   30 | 9 | 1681

Jn⁰. Mirrick and Elizab. Prousbredge,   9 | 12 | 1681½

Deaths.

Elijah Kimndrick,   aged 37,   24 | 10 | 1680

Nicholas Withe, Mason,   aged 85,   19 | 5 | 1680

Rebecah Woodward, of Jn⁰. & Rebecah,   14 | 1 | 1681½

Samuel Remington, of Jonath. & Martha,   3 | 4 | 1680

Hannah Hide, of Jonath. & Mary,   10 | 3 | 1679

Abigail Clark, wife of Jn⁰. Clark,   2 | 11 | 1681

Mitchelson Green of Jn⁰. & Ruth,   21 | 8 | 1681

Per Samuel Green 6C.

Entered by Th. Danforth R.

Mr. Jonathan Danforth   died   13 | 9 | 1682

Cambridge Births.

Hannah, of Steeven & Hannah Francis,	7	2	1680
Ebenezer, of Elijah & Hannah Kimndrick,	12	12	16⁷⁹⁄₈₀
Jerimiah, of Joseph & Mary Rusell,	21	11	1680
Hannah, of Joseph & Elizabeth Hide,	20	3	1680
Mitchelson, of Jn⁰. & Ruth Green,	14	1	1681½
Rebecca, of Gershom & Sarah Swan,	24	6	1681
Elizabeth, of Jonathan & Abigail Dunster,	22	12	1681
John, of Abram & Elizab. Jackson,	23	2	1682
Rebecca, of Joseph & Mary Symonds,	11	4	1682
Jonathan, of Andrew & Sarah Belchar,	8	11	1681
Elizabeth, of Jacob & Elizab. Bacon,	27	1	1682
Jonathan, of Will⁰ & Elizab. Robinson,	20	2	1682
Jonathan, of Jn⁰. & Mary Gove,	3	3	1682
Andrew, of Symon & Elizab. Blowers,	27	6	1682

Governor Belcher's Birth Certificate from
Cambridge, Mass., City Hall, showing the date of
his birth in the Julian Calender.

FIRST AMERICAN BORN

CHAPTER ONE: THE SEVENTEENTH CENTURY

Captain John Smith described Virginia in 1612 as "lyeth between" what is now South Carolina and the middle of Maine. The west boundary was described: "limits are unknown." Smith's description illuminates the structure of knowledge in the first English colony of America.

Two thousand immigrants arrived each year. They had reasons to leave Europe, as we will note in Belcher's 1704 Journal.

Government, except in Rhode Island, Connecticut, and Plymouth, Massachusetts, consisted of a Royal Governor and Council chosen by the King. Elected officials (selectmen, representatives, etc.) were in a minority. The "new world" was controlled by the aristocrats.

Gradually a political struggle developed between elected officials and the Royal Governor. This political struggle is part of the Jonathan Belcher story.

The Belcher family settled in Massachusetts. They began as tavern owners, twenty years after the famous Indian Chief, Massasoit, made a peace treaty with the Pilgrims at the first thanksgiving. Peace would last until Massasoit died in 1661. Ship building evolved and Belcher's father accumulated a fortune as a ship owner. The Belcher fortune provided the next generation with the education and social advantages to develop political clout. As we explore the evolution of that political clout, we will begin to reveal the subtle changes in colonial government before the Declaration of Independence.

There was nothing romantic about the seventeenth century... if you were living during that time. Society lived under a continuum of extremes. The famous Salem Witch Craft Trials occurred in the last decade of the century. Fear and superstition ruled religion. The population of Boston never exceeded 16,000 before the Revolutionary War. Most settlers owned a single room house, thatched roof, or not, a fireplace offered security in a hostile environment. Other than water power and a horse, the 1600s were ruled by survival, at any cost, using hand labor. There were bizarre regulations of English trade that were largely ignored by smugglers. Enter pirates. There was the inescapable political favoritism which was manipulated by nobility in England.

Much like today, the problems of society evolved slowly. Gradually poverty created social problems in the midst of a top heavy bureaucracy. Representatives of government confused the interests of the people because of special interest groups, not only in England, but in the colonies. Arrogance of power was unrestrained because of subversive schemes. Bribery, favoritism, and unfairness are not unique to the twentieth century. In a word, the problems of the seventeenth century, like all ages, were derived from the same source: human nature.

But there were subtle advantages. Such struggles created a bond between large families in a community. Survival, in routine daily life, created barter among all classes. The key difference between the thinking process in the 1600s and the masses of the people today, was the clear physical struggle to survive. Aside from the obvious skilled craftsmen of today, their manual skills were routine and more natural than is common today. Such skills were developed because there was no alternative. Indeed, it was a self-evident struggle to survive. Thus the romantic notions about colonial America are derived from their struggle to survive. One wonders...would they envy the twentieth century?

As we explore Jonathan Belcher's life, we will learn more about how human nature created problems. Moreover, we will concede that such problems created a United States Constitution.

The seventeenth century was the beginning of the European invasion of America. William Shakespeare died in 1616, nine years after Jamestown, Virginia was settled in 1607. A century later Benjamin Franklin was a year old. Jonathan Belcher graduated from Harvard in the last year of the seventeenth century (1699). The "new world" would be very different after he died in 1757.

As we explore Jonathan Belcher's ancestors, and his 1704 Journal, we will begin to identify the motives and achievements of the seventeenth century. Later we see how those achievements subtly led to a Revolutionary War.

The ship was searching for the Hudson River. But on November 21, 1620, after a stormy two-month voyage, Captain Jones ordered the 180 ton weakened "Mayflower" to drop anchor off Provincetown, Massachusetts. John Carver (1576-1621) was elected the first Governor of Plymouth Colony: the second important English Colony in the new world (Jamestown, Virginia, was first in 1607). Carver was among half of the Pilgrims who died in the first winter.

Subsequently, Boston was settled in 1630 by John Winthrop (1588-1649), the first Governor of the Bay Colony. Between 1630 and 1636, twenty ships a year arrived to settle New England: Strawberry Bank, Ipswich, Salem, Lynn, Charlestown, Dorchester, Newberry, and Weymouth were some of the early settlements.

Back in London, Jonathan Belcher's great-grandfather, Thomas, was a "Cloth-worker (pin-maker), bound (as apprentice) January 9, 1604, cloth-worker made free May 8, 1612, died about 1618." [1] He was the son of Robert Belcher, a weaver in Kingswood, and married Anne Solme, of Sandon, in the County of Essex on January 29, 1613. Thomas and Anne raised two sons: John (1615-1672) and Andrew (1617?-1673?). A civil war was developing in England in the 1640s.

Meanwhile, Jonathan Belcher's young grandfather, Andrew, immigrated from England and settled twenty-five miles inland, at Sudbury, Massachusetts (about 1638), where he was one of the early grantees or settlers who went to Sudbury Plantation in 1638 or 1639 ("History of Sudbury, Mass.", 1889, Pg. 26). Andrew's homestead was on four acres on Bridle Point Road, in what is now Wayland, Massachusetts. His adjoining neighbors were Thomas Goodnow and Richard Newton ("History of Sudbury, Mass."). It is believed that the first marriage in Sudbury was on October 1, 1639, when Andrew married Elizabeth Danforth, sister of Deputy-Governor, Thomas Danforth, and daughter of Nicholas Danforth, of Framingham and Cambridge, Massachusetts. Sudbury was incorporated in 1639.

---

(1) "New England Historical and Genealogical Register," July 1873.

Elizabeth and Andrew raised four daughters and one son
in the new world. Andrew is listed as a "taverner,"
and he "was a trustworthy man, occasionally employed by
the General Court to perform important duties." (2)

The Belcher family resided in Sudbury until 1646,
raising their three daughters: Elizabeth (1640-1709), who
married Pyam Blowers 1668; Jemima (1642-?), who married
Joseph Sill 1660; and Martha (1644-1711), who married
Jonathan Remington 1664. When he was about twenty-nine
years old, Andrew and his wife, Elizabeth, sold their
dwelling house at Sudbury, 23 January, 1645/6
(reserving possession of it until the following May).
After they moved to the more populated town of
Cambridge, Massachusetts, on the north bank of the
Charles River across from Boston: on New Years day,
1646/7, their son, Captain Andrew Belcher was born.
Captain Andrew, the father of Governor Jonathan Belcher,
would later build the family fortune as a mariner and
owner of a Boston warehouse.

In the intervening time, the Belcher family opened a
tavern: December 27, 1652, "The Townsmen do grant liberty
to Andrew Belcher (Sr.) to sell beer and bread, for
the entertainment of strangers and the good of the town."
On June 20, 1654 he was licensed by the County Court, "To
keep a House of Public Entertainment at Cambridge"
("History of Cambridge, Mass." Pg. 486). The location of
this "House of Public Entertainment is unknown, but it
was improved "On the first of October, 1671," soon after
their son, Captain Andrew married Sarah (July 1, 1670),
daughter of the wealthy Jonathan Gilbert (1618-1682), of
Hartford, Connecticut:

Captain Andrew, "then residing in Hartford Connecticut,
purchased of Sarah Beal, widow of Deacon Thomas Beal, an
estate (in Cambridge Massachusetts) at the northeast
corner of Brighton and Mount Auburn Streets, where the
sign of the "Blue Anchor" was soon afterwards displayed.
The original Blue Anchor Tavern, was the "most important"
tavern in Cambridge concerning its "character and

(2) "History of Cambridge Massachusetts 1630-1877";
    L.R.Paige, 1877, Pg. 486 (Town records).

permanency." ("History of Cambridge,"   Pg. 224). This
tavern, which   probably received imported wine from
Captain Andrew's ships, was first licensed in April 1672.

The immigrant family operated the Blue Anchor Tavern for
the rest of their lives. After his widowed mother died
("Aetatis sua 62")   on June 26, 1680, the young
entrepreneur, Capt. Andrew, took over the Blue Anchor
Tavern and began to develop his shipping business.
As the New England settlers scattered over the wilderness
searching for desirable land, he also began to raise a
family of his own.

"The first overland migration occurred in 1635/6 when
several churches from the Boston area walked and drove
cattle along the eighty miles to form a Connecticut
Colony near Hartford." ("American Heritage Atlas").
Captain Andrew's father-in-law, of Hartford, Jonathan
Gilbert (1618-1682), was an Indian interpreter in the
midst of the Indian Wars. and "a man of business, of
respectability, and enterprise, engaged in the trade
and coasting business of the young colonies, possessed
of great wealth for that day, and held various civil
offices, was collector of the customs at Hartford,
marshal of the colony, an office corresponding to that
of High Sheriff, a representative to the General Court
ect." ("N. E. Geneal. Reg.", Vol. 4, Pg. 229).

Meanwhile, Captain Andrew and Sarah Belcher raised
eight children. The mariner father of the future Governor
moved frequently: They lived in Hartford, Connecticut,
immediately after they married (1671-72); Cambridge
apparently (1677-78), where Captain Andrew's father
was sickly (he died about 1673);   Charlestown (1679),
Cambridge to run the tavern after Captain Andrew's mother
died (1681-82); Charlestown (1684-89), where Sarah died
after giving birth to her eighth child and finally
Captain Andrew settled in Boston (1696-1717). Andrew and
Sarah raised the following children:

Andrew (1671-?), died unmarried ("N.E.G.R.," July, 1873).
Elizabeth (1677-?), married Daniel Oliver (1664-1732).
     Daniel was a Selectman, his son, Andrew was a Lt.
     Governor of Massachusetts, and a second son, Peter,
     was Chief Justice in Mass.
Mary (1679-1699),   married George Vaughan (1676-1725).
     George was Lt. Governor of New Hampshire in 1716.

<u>Jonathan</u> (1681/2-1757), <u>first known, American born, Free-
     mason</u> and subject of this research. It is believed
     that Jonathan was born in the "Blue Anchor Tavern"
     (see "History of Cambridge," Pg. 224); see Pg. ix
     for January 8, 1681/2 date of birth.
<u>Anna</u> (1684-?), married Oliver Noyes, who was briefly
     mentioned in the twelve years of Belcher papers that
     I have reviewed.
<u>Martha</u> (1686-1748), married Anthony Stoddard in 1748, a
     minor figure in Belcher's correspondence, but who is
     titled The Honorable A. Stoddard, Esq. in a January
     20, 1734/5, Belcher letter to Warham Mather.
<u>Deborah</u> (1688/9-?).
<u>Sarah</u> (?), married John Foye, Jr., an agent for the
     town of Charlestown (see Belcher letter dated July
     26, 1742, addressed to Richard Waldon).
     (Above genealogy from "Cambridge History," Pg. 486).

The "Blue Anchor" tavern was sold in 1682 to Andrew's
sister, Martha (Belcher) Remington (1644-1711). Six
years later, on January 26, 1688/9, when the future
Governor Belcher was only seven years old, his mother,
Sarah, age thirty-seven, died. Because Jonathan formed a
life long friendship with the Remington son, Jonathan
Remington Jr. (1677-1745), it is not unlikely that the
seven year old future governor spent some of his youth
being raised in the Remington Tavern. It is also likely
because of his familiarity with shipping terms in the
1704 Journal (see July, 12, 1704, Journal entry, Pg.
25-8), that he spent some of his time, as a boy,
aboard his father's ships.

Governor Belcher's life long friend and cousin, Jonathan
Remington Jr. (1677-1745), graduated from Harvard in
1696 and became a Judge in Massachusetts, in 1715. He was
buried alongside Governor Belcher in the Belcher tomb in
the burial ground opposite Harvard College ("Sibley's
Harvard Graduates," Vol. IV, Pg. 448).

Governor Belcher's father, Captain Andrew, was a
remarkable self-educated success in the Bay Colony.
He became one of the wealthiest men in New England.
Captain Andrew is noted several times in Samuel Sewall's
diary, as a close associate with Col. Elisha Hutchinson,
Col. Penn Townsend, Captain Jeremia Dummer, Edward
Bromfield, William Pepperell (co-owner of a brigantine
vessel with Captain Andrew in 1705), Lt. Governor Usher,

and Governor Joseph Dudley. Captain Andrew was commander
of the vessel which arrived with provisions at Smith's
Garrison after the Narragansett Indian battle (Dec.
1676). Capt. Belcher's arrival after the battle was not
considered an example of courage, as much as it was of
financial enterprise. (3)   Andrew became associated
with Col. John Pynchron and Major Thomas Savage when he
was one of the Council of Safety, in 1689. They
negotiated a peace treaty with the Maquas or Mohawk
Indians in that year. ("History of Cambridge," Pg. 486).
In addition to being Commissioner of Inposts, December
25, 1691, Captain Andrew Belcher also "frequently
visited, with his vessels for purposes of trade,"
the principle shipping port of Hartford, Connecticut.
He later became a member of Governor Dudley's Council,
and was associated as an advisor to the Governor's
Council when the Councilmen examined the pirate, Captain
Kidd. Captain Kidd was captured in Boston in 1699.

Thomas Gilbert (1655-1719?), Andrew Belcher's brother-
in-law, commanded one of Andrew's ships: "The Swan, a
heavy ship, carrying an armament of twelve guns and a
crew of eighteen or twenty men, was under his command for
several years." (see Captain Andrew's deposition: "N. E.
Geneal. Register," Vol. 4, Pg. 246).

The following adventure of Captain Andrew Belcher's ship,
the "Swan," under the command of Thomas Gilbert, provides
an insight into the risks of shipping during the 1695
period. It is based on the writings of Rev. Benjamin
Colman, minister of the Brattle Street Church in Boston.
Colman graduated from Harvard in 1692, seven years before
Governor Jonathan Belcher. There are several letters
between Governor Belcher and Colman in the Belcher
Papers. Colman's account of the "Swan" is as follows:

"Rev. Dr. (Benjamin) Colman, who in July, in the year
1695, imbarqued for London (by the will of God) on board
the ship Swan, Capt. Thomas Gilbert, Commander...on the
forth day the vessel sprang a leek, and the water was
heard to pour in on the starboard tack, which alarmed the
sailers...at the end of seven weeks a Seeker made after
them, and soon came up with them. She was a privateer of

---

(3) "Sibley's Harvard Graduates," Volume IV, Pg. 434.

20 guns and 100 men, a light and fleet ship: the "Swan" was heavy laden-12 guns, and 24 men, sailers and passengers altogether. The Swan's company bore their broadsides and volies of small arms six or seven times that afternoon, defending themselves and annoying the enemy, but were taken the next morning, having their Boltspirit shot away... the French boat came on board, and the Lieutenant took all the crews money, and put them into a boat. The crew and some of the passengers were plundered of everything, even their clothing, and then dressed in a few rags of the sailers...Madam Allaire, one of the passengers, being brought on board the captor, about half a day after, entreated that Mr. Colman might be with them in the great cabin...when Madam saw him at the door, half covered with rags and cold, she ran to him and wept upon his neck, & he wept with her. Captain Gilbert burst into tears, and so did Captain Anderson... After some two months of imprisonment within the walls of Dian, they were freed by an exchange of prisoners with England." (Memoir's of Benjamin Colman, D. D., Pg. 5-13; "New England Genealogical Register," Vol. 4, Pg. 347).

Seven years after the "Swan" was captured by the French, and one month after Joseph Dudley (1647-1720) arrived from London, with his Commission as Governor of Massachusetts, Queen Ann's war with France was declared on May, 4, 1702. Dudley, who graduated from Harvard in 1665, selected Andrew Belcher for the Governor's Council. Captain Gilbert was chosen as Commander In Chief of the shipping expedition, equipped to attack the Canadian French cruisers that had been endangering Massachusetts fishing vessels (see letter of July 11, 1702, to Chief Justice of the Superior Court, Isaac Addington, from John Leverett published in "New England Genealogical Register," Vol. 4, Pg. 348/9).

Since Governor Belcher's father was a mariner in the 1700 period, let us briefly review that key colonial industry:

Vessels of Boston in the late 1600s ranged from six to 250 ton. Most of them classified as brigantines, schooners and sloops. In Belcher's day, "ships" were more in the shape of a bathtub. It would be another century before the sleek, pointed bow of the clipper ships would sail the ocean in the 1830s. A modest single decked

sloop or schooner rigged sailing vessel, with sails
pivoting on one side of the mast, were common. The
larger, multi-decked galleons, brigantines, and other
square rigged ships being more complex and expensive to
build

An eighty ton schooner could carry all of the following:
"1353 bushel of corn, 88 barrel of flour, 50 barrel of
bread 19680 staves and heading, 20 bushel of pease, 1775
Hoops and 12270 feet pine plank with a crew of 6 men to
cross the Atlantic ocean." (see "Naval Documents of the
American Revolution," 1964, Vol. I, William Bell Clark,
Pg. 1370).

Such quantities are impressive, and cargoes, according to
Belcher in the 1730s included Fish to Italy and Spain,
ships masts, spars, yards, and lumber to England. Linen
and other manufactured goods were shipped from Britain
and various cargoes such as wine from Madeira, molasses
from Jamaica, and many others between the colonies. The
struggle against the sea in those blunt nosed, well
armed rigs must have been a ride in heavy weather. A 100
ton "ship" is only about 80 foot long, and very tiny in
contrast to a modestly sized 450 foot long, 10,000 ton,
Second World War freighter.

One problem in shipping was expressed by Sir Walter Scott
(1771-1832): "Whoever commands the sea commands the
trade, and whosoever commands the trade of the world
commands the riches of the world, and consequently the
world itself." Sir Walter Scott lived in the days of
privateers. Sir Walter Scott was also accurate.

Privateers were any armed vessels commissioned by
governments, ostensibly used in time of war against the
enemy. Between the late 1600s and the 1850s, privateers
captured many commercial cargo ships transporting goods
throughout the world. With the temptation to become
wealthy in the remote ocean, many privateers were
glorified pirates. Despite the isolated destruction at
sea, pirates became public knowledge. One obvious
example in the time of Jonathan and Andrew Belcher, was
the capture of Captain Kidd, at Boston in 1699, and his
hanging in England a year later. One might recall during
this time, that England had established many "Acts of
Trade" restricting commerce to the colonies. These were

laws that were often ignored by the colonial cargo
ships. The question was threefold: Who was breaking the
law? Is that sluggish schooner heading away from England
obeying the acts of trade? Did Captain Kidd, who was
commissioned as a privateer from England, think he was a
pirate? One author who documented his career thinks not
(see "The Real Captain Kidd, A Vindication," by Sir
Cornelius Neale Dalton).

In 1700, 130 years before the development of building
clipper ships, privateers might carry as many as ten
cannons along each side and wallow along at a speed of
six to ten knots. Speed became very important for cargo
ships, not only for shipping time, but escape from a
privateer's guns.

In Belcher's day, there was a fine line between cargo
ships and privateers. If one were adventurous enough to
challenge the sea in such clumsy vessels in the
seventeenth and eighteenth century, one had best be
prepared to fight a private war. Cargo ships were fitted
with cannons to protect lives and cargo. Apparently
Captain Andrew Belcher did not take kindly to pirates,
his ship, the "Swan," was fitted with twelve guns.

Cannons were not only heavy and reduced the cargo
capacity of a vessel, they were also a tool in ship
handling. For instance, cannons were frequently lowered
over the side with a line, to reduce the draft and free
a ship in grounding. In a word, cannons were a costly,
but crucial link to survival. The difference between
bankruptcy and profit often meant more than knowing how
to sail in the unfriendly Atlantic ocean. It also meant
knowing how to shoot cannons, in a rolling vessel, at
the other fellow's rudder and masts.

In summary, from the settlement of America throughout the
eighteenth century, law and order on the high sea meant
making your own rules. If cannons and bribes were
necessary to solve a problem, in the often lawless age
of three hundred years ago, "ye" had choices: fight
the competition or be defeated. Andrew Belcher used
cannons and no doubt paid a bribe to recover his own
captain, and wife's brother, Thomas Gilbert, from prison
in France. So much for our brief review of commercial
trade in the 1700 period.

As Indian wars and piracy increased, Captain Andrew was made Commissary General (1703 to 1708) and a member of the Governors Council from 1702 until his death on Oct. 1, 1717 (see "History of Cambridge," Pg. 486). Captain Andrew shipped wine from Madeira, grain to Curacao, and various cargo to and from the colonies. His warehouse was in Boston. It is appropriate to insert at this point, that Governor Belcher was one of a company of capitalists to invest in a leased copper mine in Simesbury, Connecticut. He shipped copper ore to Bristol, England in the 1730s. It is probable that the knowledge Captain Andrew gained in Connecticut, either on his own, or from the Gilbert family, was associated with this business. (see Sept. 6, 1715, letter from Jonathan to John White). Jonathan's copper profits were not as expected, for he frequently complained about miners in Connecticut cheating him ("Belcher Papers," Vol. VI, Pg. 40, 166). There are other indications that Captain Andrew was the business person, while Jonathan was more successful in government.

In closing this research oriented toward Governor Belcher's ancestors, Belcher wrote a letter on July 7, 1748, to a Mr. Prince answering an inquiry about his then deceased father, Capt. Andrew:

"My father was as great a genius as his country could boast of but wanted an education to improve and polish it. (Gov. Dudley) who was a good judge used to say Mr Commissary Belcher would make a good minister of State to any Prince in Europe especially in the article of finances. His late farewell and blessing of me show'd his strong thoughts and great modesty. Its fresh in my memory and will be till the frost of age seals up that faculty he called me to his bedside took me by the hand and said- Son you may expect me to bless you in a better manner and style than I am able to do for God did not put it into your Grandfathers power to give me the education he inabled me to give you, but remember my last words to you are- May the blessing of the God of Abraham and the God of Isaac and the God of Jacob rest upon you and your seed for ever. Amen. Farewell. "

"Neither the Patriachs nor apostles could have done it better. Just as he was expiring the blanket was

offensive to his face so he rais'd himself a little from
the pillow and said to the late Madame Sewall who watcht
with him give me the sheet for it is my winding sheet
then he unroll'd his arms in it and said I will lay me
down and dye in peace and expir'd in a minute."

"I should not have troubled you with this acco but as
it may make some little part of an answer to what you
have desired."

"I thank you fore the sermon preacht upon the death of my
late dear and excellent sister (Belcher's sister, Martha,
died Feb. 11, 1747/8 -ed.) which has given me much
pleasure in readg.

     Revd and Worthy Sir Very much your friend and servant
     J. Belcher"
          ("New England Genealogical Register," July 1873)

The following information adds another bit of interest to
Captain Andrew Belcher:

"Rev. John Cotton of Newton, in a letter dated Nov. 7,
1717, and preserved in the library of the Mass. Hist.
Society, states that at the funeral of Hon. Andrew
Belcher, "all the ministers there had scarves and gloves.
They say 50 suits of cloathes were made. All first
cousins, Remington, Blowers, &c. put into mourning. John
Colman, Caswell, & c., all that had been apprentices to
him, were also. 90 dozen of gloves were bought, and none
of any figure but what had gloves sent 'em." ("History
of Cambridge," Pg. 135).

The giving of gloves dates from the 1600s among the
Masons of Britain. A purchase of gloves at a funeral does
not prove Captain Andrew was a Freemason, yet it is
noteworthy that in October, 1717, there were given 1080
pair of gloves at the funeral of the father of the first
known American born Freemason.

To summarize, Captain Andrew Belcher lived for seventy
years. He began in 1646/7 as the son of a tavern owner.
He lived in an age of isolated, and "unprotected
settlers, and widely separated by dense and unexplored
forests and unbridged streams, the chief communication

being by water, around the coasts." ("New England Genealogical Register," Vol. 4, Pg. 230). When the old Indian Chief and friend of the Pilgrims, Massasoit, died in 1661, Captain Andrew was a teenager. During the next forty years, as the Indian wars increased, Andrew accumulated a fortune by shipping goods between the rapidly growing colonies. At the age of fifty-eight, he sat on the Governor's Council, he had raised eight children, sent his son to Harvard, and we will soon see how he contributed to a third generation American meeting the heir to the throne of England in 1704.

Having briefly reviewed the struggles, and successes, of Jonathan's ancestors in the seventeenth century, our focus is now on Jonathan Belcher.

Jonathan Belcher, raised by rapidly prospering parents, was born on January 8, 1681/2, in the Blue Anchor Tavern, in Cambridge, Massachusetts. After his mother died in 1688, he attended The Boston Latin School, then Harvard, graduating from college second in a class of twelve in October 1699. The seventeen year old Harvard graduate would become a complex personality during the remaining fifty-eight years of his life. In a few words, Jonathan Belcher evolved from a tavern to a credible aristocrat... he understood both worlds.

Jonathan's adventurous spirit was apparent at college: at Harvard, he was the "chambermate and bedfellow of Tutor William Brattle. He spent money freely, and after the marriage of Mr. Brattle had removed a certain restraint, he provided much work for the College Glazier." ("Sibley's Harvard Graduates," Vol. 4, Pg. 435).

According to Harvard records, he proceeded M. A. at Commencement, 1702, taking the affirmative to the metaphysical question "An Creaturae Existencia sit Contingens?" (Do creatures depend on the state of existence or does the state of existence depend on creatures?).

After graduating from college, apparently a decision was made for Jonathan to sail to England, in 1704. (letter of August 25, 1732, Pg. 187-8, that he researched his genealogy in England in 1704). Belcher's genealogical research by "Robert Dale, Suffolk Herald, now in the College of Arms," with notations in 1704 is published in the "New England Genealogical Register," July 1871.

Jonathan wrote from London on July 7, 1704, to John White (1669-1721), close friend and Clerk of the Massachusetts House of Representatives (see December 27, 1704, letter to John White on Pg. 137). He also wrote a Journal of his trip through Holland and Germany between July 8, and October 5, 1704 (see Pg. 23-135). He wrote from London, to John White on December 27, 1704, saying "as I have opportunity I will write again." (see December 27, 1704, letter).

Belcher spent a total of about six years in England/

Europe between 1704 and 1730, accumulated in four voyages, and an additional three years, in his successful attempt again to become a Royal Governor, between 1744 and 1747 (Pg. 146 for his various voyages to England).

There are two areas which I explored to verify Belcher's 1741 calculation that he was made a Freemason in 1704: his Journal of 1704 in Europe, and his correspondence to John White in 1704. Both of these areas of research yielded significant historical interest.

To acclimatize the reader with terminology in 1704, we begin with an introduction to the Belcher Journal and the subsequent transcript. The Journal begins on the Thames River, at the Tower of London. At that time, the famous bachelor, Sir Isaac Newton (1642-1727), was very much alive. Sir Isaac would be fuming at the criticism of his 1704 publication, "Opticks," the result of his experiments with light and color.

Belcher began the journey in a "wherry boat," (double ended row boat used for carrying passengers down the Thames River). He mentions two friends, Lloyds and John Joe, who are certainly of Masonic interest, being his London friends in 1704. It is my speculation that Lloyd may be associated with Edmund Lloyd, who began his famous marine insurance business, Lloyd's of London, in 1688. Ship owners met in Lloyd's coffee house after their voyages, and the dangers of pirates in that age gradually grew into an insurance business. My theory is based on the fact that Captain Andrew Belcher was a ship owner who sent ships to London, (See Pg. 7-8) and it is not unlikely that he was one of the early insured owners. Let us re-emphasize, this is merely a probable theory, not an established fact.

In any case, Jonathan's Journal proceeds to describe who was aboard "Capt." Gabriel Milleson's vessel, the departure procedure aboard the yacht "Katha" (meaning Katherine), and a rather colorful description of a pirate ("privateer") threatening ships in the convoy on his voyage to Holland. Lord Portland, his wife and daughter disembarked at "Oranjepolo", Belcher continuing on to Rotterdam. Lord Portlands son, Ld. Woodstock, did not make the voyage. From the Journal it seems unlikely that Lord Portland was accompanying Belcher, however, Belcher

"commonly spent my time in walking the quarterdeck wth
my Ld, he being curious & inquisitive about the state
of N. England..." The privateer, first mentioned in the
July 12th entry, vividly illustrates the risks of
international travel at the beginning of the eighteenth
century.

Belcher was a "stranger" in Holland and "spoke no Dutch."
As an illustration of Jonathan's ability to accumulate
friends quickly, consider the following brief summary
immediately after his arrival in Holland:

He was invited by Mrs. Thomas, a passenger on the yacht
"Katherine" to stay with her family. The next day
he was recommended by "my friend in London" to see
"Vandermoulin", "found em at home, dd (dd means did
deliver) my friends Ltt (Ltt means letter) and they
treated me very civilly, I stay'd about an hour
with em & took what money I wanted, then Mr. Peter
Vandermoulin & I went to Change," (a change is a market
place for shopping) "where I stay'd about an hour and
he took me off to see the town...Next morning Mr Spranger
& Hammond came to call me...after church was done Mr.
Stone sent and invited me to dinner, where I dined with
Mr Hammond, Stone, Spranger, and some other gentleman...
after dinner I took a glass of wine with Capt. Milleson
on board the yatcht...Capt. Wadworth, who was there
Comand'r of a N. England Ship (called The Industry)..."
(see 1704 Belcher Journal, extracts July 24-28).

It is apparent that Jonathan accumulated friends rapidly.
There are five major locations that Belcher emphasized
in the three month journey: Rotterdam (July 24-29);
Amsterdam (August 1-11); Hanover (August 15-26); Berlin
(September 8-17); and Hamburg (September 19-28).

There are numerous abbreviations, and strange words for
the reader to deal with. Footnotes and explanations are
included in the text. "As ye goe hither, it might not
be amiss to bespoke a mouthful of victuals, 'tis slow
travel in 'ym dayes, 2 or 300 yr's past." The most
interesting aspect of the Journal, with a possible
connection with fellowship and the traditions of Freemasonry, is a "thankgiving" experience that Belcher noted
in Hamburg. As a brief introduction to the possible
correlation between this journal entry and known Masonic
history I submit the following comment from a respected
Masonic scholar:

"There are hundreds of English minutes (of Masonic Lodges) extant which prove conclusively that both eating and drinking and also smoking took place in English Lodges during the ceremonies... As to the Grand Lodge of England, I am strongly under the impression that drinking during labour obtained in the early years of its existence, though I am unable to adduce very strong proofs of the custom... I hold that a solumn toast may be made as dignified as any portion of our ceremonies." (one of the Founders of Quatuor Coronati Lodge, George William Speth, Fellow of Royal Historical Society, 1894, AQC, Vol. 7, Pg. 14).

In modern times the Masonic tradition of toasting continues in the fellowship of table Lodges, and Jonathan's Journal certainly includes toasting, led by a "treasurer," in the following entry. I might emphasize Jonathan Belcher's Journal has never been published and Masonic scholars have not yet examined the significance of this extract. I offer the following from the September 19/20th, 1704 entry:

"We took lodgings at the Keyser's hoof, just over against the stadthouse being told 'twas the best inn in town, After we had eat and dress'd ourselves we went to Change (4) where we saw Mr. Stratford, Foster & Watkinson to the 2 last I was recommended. (5) We rec'd there several Lttr that were directed to Hamburg. Mr. Watkinson told us that next day the English kept thanksgiving for Hochstet Victory, and that he'd take care we sh'd be invited, (6) as we were in the afternoon in ye resident's name... Next morning we went to Chh ("Chh" is abbreviated church -ed.) at 10 a Clock...The Chh is in ye English house, up 2 pair of

---

(4) As previously noted a change has nothing to do with Freemasonry. A change is simply a market place for shopping.

(5) This is the first clue, Belcher had a letter of recommendation addressed to Foster and Watkinson.

(6) This is the second clue, Watkinson invited Belcher to an "English" celebration (See point five near the end of the Journal "Some useful observations..." and letters of recommendation in Hamburg, Pg. 120).

stairs, after sermon we came down to the hall, where the
gentlemen soluted   (7)   one another, and talked some
time, there we met Mr. Colt, one of our old acquaintance,
from Hannover. From thence we went to a coffee house, (8)
and then return'd again. In the hall below was plac'd the
musick, and 6 or 7 steps up that was the room, where we
din'd, which was the first table, Here was the resident
of Denmark   and   the States the Danish admiral,   a
BurgoMaster, and four of ye senate who generally   (9)
denote that number instead of coming all, as they are
invited, some gentlemen of ye town and the English
strangers, and some of the Chief of the Hambro Compa.
were at this table. There were 2 or 3 tables besides for
the rest of the compa. We had a very noble entertainment,
the treasurer (10)   sat at the lower end of the table,
and began to everyone's health present in order as they
sat, which lasted 'till diner was done, after that the
Queen's health, and the rest of the Crown'd healths (11)
(as they call 'em) in Bumpers but we came away when
they began these, it being about 6 a Clock. Everyone
slip off when they had a mind, but they that stay'd till
the last, which was about 12 a Clock, were really well
in for it."   (12)   (see Sept. 19/20, 1704, Jonathan

---

(7)   This   token of recognition was rarely used by
      Belcher. Among 1000 pages of transcribed Belcher
      correspondence, I recall him using the term "salute"
      very   seldom. Other than ships firing guns of
      "salute", one occasion was in a letter to his close
      friend, and one time proposed Lt. Governor, the New
      Hampshire Freemason, Henry Sherburne (1674-1757).
      (see "Belcher Papers," Vol. VII, Pg. 401, and not
      included in his warm letter: Vol. VII, Pg. 548).
(8)   A separate room of the coffee-house, for the meeting
      is noteworthy (common among Freemasons in 1700s).
(9)   Apparently a variety of men met with some kind of
      "general" routine.
(10) I would call the treasurer an important clue. This
      was some kind of Fraternity.
(11) Toasting leaders of countries is certainly not
      exclusively Masonic, but it is noteworthy in this
      "English" thanksgiving that included a Burgomaster,
      Resident of Denmark, etc.
(12) The casual nature of the meeting provides an insight
      into the style of organized fellowship in 1704.

Belcher Journal Pg. 99-100).

If this record included an English group of Freemasons, although not definitive at this time, it would certainly be the earliest record of known Freemasons in Germany. Most authorities state unequivocally that Speculative Freemasonry (not operative or stone masonry) was first attempted in Germany with the appointment of the Duke of Norfolk, Grand Master of England in 1729. (see "Coil's Masonic Encyclopedia," Pg. 276). A Quatuor Coronati work states, "after one or two abortive attempts a German Lodge was established at Hamburg in 1737."("The Pocket History of Freemasonry," Pick & Knight, Pg. 262).

With sincere respect for the above scholars, Belcher's Journal establishes that: first, there was an organized company of Englishmen in Hamburg in 1704; they had previously had some kind of "Charter" (Pg. 105); the father of the wealthy, Mr Dangerfield, was their "porter," and was buried by the company (Pg. 101); Belcher was recommended to two of the "chief merchants," who invited Belcher into the company's celebration; and after "salutes," of recognition, their treasurer led some kind of celebration for a military victory. Second, no one, today, knows the identity of all the pre-Grand Lodge era Freemasons, but Englishmen who were 1704 Free-masons (such as Belcher), and who relocated in other countries, such as Belcher's associates in Hamburg, could easily organize themselves as Freemasons, just as they did in England in the 1600s. Third:

It is conceded that "authentic research" can establish few facts, of the mysterious pre-Grand Lodge era, from Belcher's September 19/20 entry. Yet, I think it is fair to state that significant information about Belcher has not been researched. For example: the 1704 Belcher Journal, his 1704 London letter (Pg. 139), his knowledge of known Freemasons (see appendix), and his bond with, the American born, Richard Partridge (Belcher married his sister. Partridge was in London, as an agent after 1701). I submit that evidence exists throughout the 1704 Journal, and in his later letters (Pg. 188), that Belcher spent some months in England before July 8, 1704. With the old evidence he was a Freemason in 1704 (Pg. 198); the December 27, 1704, correspondence to White noted (Pg. 137-8); his overture to the "chief merchants" in Hamburg from his friends in London (Pg. 120); the time he

spent in England before July, 1704 (Pg. 14, 20, 188);
and in view of a "Charter" to these Hamburg, Englishmen
(Pg. 105): I hold, therefore, that the idea of Belcher
being a Freemason before July, 1704, and of 1704 Freemasons being in Hamburg, is more credible than before.

Throughout the Journal, Belcher provides a keen insight
of society, struggles of the working class, life of
Royalty, opinions of individuals, religions, governments,
customs, and silver mines (which he ventured down into
to a depth of 400 feet). He dined with Lords, played
cards with the Electress of Hannover, met the King and
Queen of Prussia, and visited with the elite merchants of
Holland and Germany (expenses on Pg. 124-135).

It might be helpful to identify a few of the individuals
that Belcher mentioned in the Journal whom Belcher met
(appendix III, Pg. 232-8, includes a complete list of
1704 associates):

Mr. Stanhope; (died 1726) Third Earl of Chesterfield;
July 30, 1704:

Queen's Envoy Extraordinary. "thought my duty to pay my
respects to him" in Holland, at the Hague. "He told me he
took it as a particular obligation, when any English
gentleman was so kind as to call on him, and that he
would gladly do me any service in his power, so he
desired me to set and we talkt about an hour of N.
England and some other matters, and then came in one
Baron Bothman...." This Stanhope is the father of
the Freemason, Philip Stanhope (1694-1773), Earl of
Chesterfield, the later ambassador to the Hague in 1726.
Philip was a member of the Lodge at the Goose and
Gridiron and was on the 1721 list (see AQC, Vol. 25,
Pg. 27). Denslow states that Philip was made a Mason in
Lodge No. 4. Lodge No. 4 would be the Royal Somerset
House and Inverness Lodge No. 4, which met at the Rummer
and Grapes Tavern, Channel Row, Westminster, an aristo-
cratic Lodge that moved to the Horn Tavern by 1723 (see
"Pocket History of Freemasonry," Pg. 299). Apparently
Belcher was well thought of by Stanhope, after visiting
he sent his Secretary to show the young Belcher the town.

Baron Bothmar, (Hans Casper) July 30, 1704

"who is Envoy at the Hague from the Electon of Hannover."

Bothman was one of several foreign political confidants of King George I (1714-1727), a group who were often accused of selling political influence ("History of England," Feiling, Pg. 643). Bothman gave Jonathan a letter of recommendation, addressed to the heir to the English Crown, The Electress of Hanover. Belcher met Bothman at his 1704 visit to Stanhope.

Mrs. (Belcher) Willis; (Relative) July 30, 1704:

Married to the coachman of "Ld. Cutts". Mrs. Willis's father, John (1615-1672), and Jonathan's immigrant grandfather, Andrew (1617?-1673?), were brothers. Mrs. Willis's husband was more interested in his horse duties than in visiting with Jonathan. The significance of Mrs. Willis is that it indicates Jonathan was well aware of his family's relatives in 1704, and her brother was a cabinet-maker in St. Paul's Churchyard, London, the location of the "Goose and Gridiron Alehouse." The Goose and Gridiron, from "time-immemorial," was the location of the first Grand Lodge of Free and Accepted Masons in the world in 1717. The Willis family lived at the Hague.

Mr. Cockburn's son; August 9, 1704:

In Holland at the Hague; "I proposed to Mr Cockburn (son to the English minister) that I would bear his charges for his compa. he gladly embraced the offer, so left it to him to provide what might be necessary for us on the road, this day I took my leave of my friends in Amstr. asking their Command's for Hannover & Hambio..." Jonathan gave Cockburn four English Pounds in addition to paying his expenses on the three month journey.

Mr. Pooley, (in English Company who waited on the Queen Elect, Sophia, mother of King George I). August 15, 1704: In Germany at Hanover. Belcher uses a term "dd" on occasion when he gives letters of recommendation. I assume this is shorthand for something like "did deliver." Belcher writes: "& I dd him 2 LLtrs (LLtrs means letters, on one occasion in the Journal Ltt means Lieutenant) I had from Mr. Bluthwait & Mr. Chamberlin, he recd us very civilly & told us he would present us the next day to the Electress..." (The Electress means the heir to the Crown of England, Sophia). Bluthwait and Chamberlin are probably two of Belcher's "friends in

London,"   who gave him letters of recommendation. The
Governor of Massachusetts, Joseph Dudley (1648-1720), had
a patron in England named William Blathwayt, Clerk of the
Privy Council to the Queen of England, Anne (1702-1714).
Dudley, of course, was a close friend of the Belcher
family, Captain Andrew being chosen as a member of the
Governor's Council. Bluthwait might be important to
Masonic research. Pooley is later spelled Poley, and he
was "in ye Prince's (meaning George II, his father,
George I, was Elector of Hanover at this time) anti-
chamber, who as soon as he was dress'd, came out and
everybody made a low bow to him; Mr Poley presented us
to him and told him what we were... we had a very good
dinner at Mr. Poley's, Mr. Colt din'd with us and his
Secretary, who is a German but speaks good English."

Electress of Hannover, (Heir to the Crown of England)
August 16, 1704; Germany in Hanover; "Madam The respect
and good affection which the Queen of Gt Britain's
subjects (in N. England have for the good settlemt'of
your succession made me ambitious of doing myself this
honour to come and pay my humble duty to your Royal
highness." She answered. "Sir I give you thanks and
oblig'd to you for this respect."

Belcher traveled 934 miles between July 8 and October 5,
1704. Note: Old Style and New Style calender used. July
13, became July 24th when he arrived in Rotterdam. When
returning to London October 14th became October 3rd (old
style). Some of the locations from Amsterdam, include
Amerersfoort, easterly to Deventer, into Germany at
Bentheim, continuing easterly into Rheine, on to
Osnabruck, to Hannover. Then southerly to Clausthal,
north to Goslar, and then in a roughly eastery direction,
Wernigerode, Halberstadt, Brandenburg, and Berlin. Next,
working toward the northwest to Perleberg, Lenzen,
"Britzin", and Hamburg. Then to "Althenau a town in
Denmark," to "Harburg by water," to "ffeseleven a town
in sweedland," from there it is "fifteen English miles to
Raten," "ten English miles to Nuenburg," and ten English
miles to Laisey, which comes into the road to Osnabruck
homeward"

We will now explore in detail the first transcript of
Jonathan Belcher's 1704 Journal.

"Journal of My intended Voyage, & Journey To Holland, Hannover & ca: Beginning at London Saturday July 8th: O.S. 1704"

"Saturday, July 8th: This day I took a Wherry (1) at Towerhill Stairs having the honour of Mr John Joe & Lloyd's Compa. wth me to Greenwich; about 4 a clock we vent on board the Katha. yatch Gabriel Milleson Commander on whom I took my passage for Holland, as Soon as I came on board I inquir'd of the Captn. the time of Sailing, he told me he only waited for my Lord Portland and family's Coming on board;- We went on shore at Greenwich and Walkt about an hour, and then Saw my Ld. Coming in a barge; We then Return'd on board the yatch, Where I took my leave of Mr. Joe and Lloyd, & my Lord was on board in 1/4 of an hour, at his Coming the Captn. fir'd 5 guns & 5 more at my Ld. Woodstock and Lady's going off (who Came down to accompany their father) after this the Captn. made a Signal for Sailing, but Count Muffir (the Duke of Savoy's Envoy Extraordi: to the Queen of England) who was to go in the Cleveland yatch not being on board, stopt us about an hour, our Capt. thinking it not worth while to Come to Sail, in that the Convoy Could not Sail without the Cleveland, however by my Ld. Portld's Request the Capt. Came to Sail about 7 a clock and proceeded to Graves End, Where we anchor'd abt. 10, and by 12 the Cleveland was with us, at 4 in the morning We weigh'd and Came to Sail, and at twelve (the next day)"

[** Ed. Comment Follows]
The reader has many abbreviations and strange words to deal with: "Compa." is company; "wth" is with; "Katha" is Katherine; "'Em" is them; "wc" is which; "Ld" is Lord; "abt" is about, and "Ltt" is letter, but on Page 25 it means Lieutenant. Welcome to the early 1700s! Slang terms also occur frequently: "we anchored without the buoy of the nore," indicates that the yacht "Katherine" anchored outside the entrance to the harbor, "Ran that night." simply is nautical slang meaning we sailed all night. Other slang terms are more obvious insights to an early American's lingo in 1704: "the wind springing

---

(1) A wherry is a double ended rowboat for passengers.

up fresh," and "rowling and driving about the ocean."
Regarding the punctuation, spelling, and capitalization,
I decided to transcribe as Belcher wrote, as it seems
to add to the flavor of the journal. Periodically, to
illuminate the journal, and enhance comprehension for
casual reading, I interrupt the text and include a brief
summary of points of interest. "Ed. Comment Follows" are
noted to label remarks in the journal. Footnotes are used
as well to avoid excessive interruptions in the text. The
words in the journal will become easier to understand as
you read, "altho' ye must be civil abt 'Em and yer accot.
of shockt, 'tis but 112 pag's in ye 18th cent'ry:"

"Sunday, July 9th: We anchor'd without the buoy of the
nore. where lay the Bonadventure Capt. Ramsey & the Pool
Capt. (blank space -ed.) and 2 dutch Men of Warr, the
Lousdike yatch and about 40 sail of Merchantmen, which
was the whole of our fleet (there being little or no
wind) we lay 'till 6 a clock that Evening, and then the
Comadore (Capt. Ramsey) fir'd for Sailing, We Ran that
night about 12 leagues and by morning 'twas quite Calm,
and the

Monday, July 10th: Comadore gave the Signal for
anchoring, Which we did and Stay'd 'till Evening, this
day was foggy and misty, but the wind springing up fair &
fresh about 6 a clock, we Came to Sail, and kept on our
Course with a pretty breeze 'till 12 the next day,

Tuesday, July 11th: and then were again becalm'd, this
day we spent in Rowling and driving about the ocean 'till
7 a Clock, the wind then sprung up again, and we made the
best of our way till 6 the next morning,"

[** Ed. Comment Follows]
Jonathan next encounters pirates. "leagues" are often
used to estimate distances (one league, from Belcher's
other letters, is equal to three miles). The weather is
"calm," so the ship's crew rigs her small boat into the
sea and tries to tow the ship, with oars, away from the
pirate. Cannons are "fir'd," landing "athwart" (meaning
across from) her "forefoot" (the forward part of the
pirate ship where the keel meets the bow). The language
provides an accurate insight into shipboard terminology
in 1704. Meanwhile, Belcher's journal also provides a
fascinating insight into disciplined and undisciplined
emotions aboard ship in a dangerous situation: a time

when it was necessary to implement with astute judgement
the capabilities of a ships crew. If history is capturing
the emotions of the past, the July 12 entry is worthy of
consideration. In this age, Edmund Lloyd began marine
insurance from a London coffee house in 1688.

"July 12th: when we were about 4 leagues from the Brill,
(2)   the Comadore now gave a 2d. signal for anchoring,
(Excepting the Lousdike and our yatch) the whole fleet
Came to an anchor, but we being about half a league
distant from the fleet, and seeing a small Vessel about 2
miles to Lee=ward of us, and by his actions judging him
to be a privateer, We thought it best to get as near the
fleet as we Could, (it being calm) the Capt. order'd the
boat to be mann'd, to take the yatch in Tow, which being
done and the yatch's oars mann'd we did our best to get
into the body of the fleet, but finding a very strong
Currtt., and that we drove further from 'em we Came to
anchor, Notwithstanding the privateer all this time, had
his oars mann'd and made the best of his Way towards us,
he was now Come within a mile of us and we Expected
nothing but that he would be on board, so the Capt.
Call'd all hands upon deck, got ready all the small arms,
Cutlasses & ca. and posted the men Every one to his
proper place, and then fir'd a shot at the privateer,
which went just athwart his forefoot, by this time the
privateer seeing he gain'd but little ground upon us, the
tide running very strong agtt. him; he Came to an anchor;
our Capt. put 14 men in the boat, being all well arm'd
(as did Capt. Sanders in ye Lousdike, who lay all this
time Close by us) the two boats went off and Row'd as
near the privateer as they dare venture, then lay upon
their oars to make the best discovery they Could, by this
time our Comadore (perceiving us in a fight) sent his
Barge to know what was the matter, and after a little
discourse his Ltt. had with our Capt. he went on board
again, & then Capt. Ramsey mann'd his long boat with 23
men and his barge with about 20 more all well arm'd, and
they row'd 'till they Come up with ye privateer, then all
the boats lay about half an hour to make the best
discovery they Could, in which time the privateer shew'd

---

(2) As an estimate, the yacht met the privateer after a
    300 mile sailing distance from Greenwich, England.
    The yacht was located barely in sight of land,
    twelve miles (4 leagues) from Brielle, which is on
    the Meuse River in Holland. -ed.

about 60 men upon deck, he had 8 guns, spread abroad an
ostendt (3)   Ensign, and Call'd to the boats to come
on board. The officers held a Consultation and thought it
would not be prudent to attack his, so they return'd Each
boat to their Respective ships Except the Comadore's long
boat with 23 men, who was ordered on board our yatch in
Case the privateer should board us; Before I proceed I
must just hint the foolhardiness of Capt. Ramsey's men,
who would feign have gone on board the privateer only
with their boat and our's, Capt. Milleson told 'em they
could do no good but wd. needlesly murder themselves, one
fellow Reply'd   <u>Damn him, he's such a little dog, he</u>
<u>Can't kill above half a dozn or half a score of us, and</u>
<u>What's that to teach a Rogue better manners</u>. It was now
about 11 a Clock, the wind springing up fresh, the
ostender took the first of it and got undr sail, before
any of our ships and stood his Course directly for us,
which our Comadore seeing, immediately mann'd the
Cleveland yatch Capt. Desborough with about 100 men and 4
boats to take him in tow, so he came undr sail, and with
the help of the boats Came faster to us than the
privateer, tho' by this time the privateer had got within
half a mile of the Lousdike Capt. Sanders, in so much
that Capt. Sanders made a fair shot at him, which went
just amid=ships, he perceiving the Cleveland Coming so
fast to our assistance, gave three huzzas & tackt from
us, so we got rid of this troublesome fellow, who put
us all into a fright and Expectation of seeing ostendt
before next day, by this accident I must Remark the
imprudence & mismanagement of our Capt., who was over
persuaded by my Ld. Portland, to make the best of his Way
to the land as Soon as we Saw it, so he outRun the fleet,
took no notice of the Convoy, and brought us into great
hazard of being taken, (4) which had we been he might

---

(3) Ostende (Oostende is a seaport in Belgium. -ed)
(4) This interesting criticism of the English sea Captain
    by the twenty-two year old American is noteworthy.
    Although Jonathan was at ease with nautical terms as
    the son of a mariner father, he was certainly not an
    old sea dog in the English Channel. His remark also
    illustrates his occasional trait in the future: when
    he became a Royal Governor, he tended to exaggerate
    when critical of others (i.e. the yatch was close
    enough to the convoy to be rescued by row boats.-ed).

have lost his life, at least have been made for Ever incapable of seeing his Majty so that (I think) all Comanders what Ever, when under Convoy, ought strictly to observe the motions and orders of the Comadore;- about 2 a Clock we Came into Maise, which is water of a quite different Colour from the sea, looks not of so good a green--but muddy and something yellow, neither will the Sea=Water mix with it, but you may see a long for some leagues together, the difference between the water, just as if there was a fence or petition between 'Em, as soon as we went into the Maise my Ld. Portland, his Lady & 3 daughters & some of his servants went into a fishing boat to land at a place (Call'd Oranjepolo) where my Ld's Coaches were waiting for him, our Capt. discharge'd the gun's & gave three huzzas;= My Ld. had in our yatch about 30 servants, (& about 30 more in a ship he had hir'd to Carry his baggage) He is a man most stingy, without the least generosity, gave nothing to the ships Co. or any of the officers (Except the Capt.), altho' the yatch was order'd by the Queen purposely to wait on him, he generally presents the Capt. with 20 guineys which is not so much as any ordinary passenger gives considering he has between 30 & 40 of his family on board, my Ld., his Lady, & daughters are free and affable Enough, when we were becalmed I Commonly Spent my time in walking the quarterdeck wth. my Ld., he being Curious & inquisitive about the state of N England, the people, soil, trade & ca. soon after my Ld. went from the yatch the man of Warr fir'd to salute the fleet and went into Goree (Goeree is about 15 miles south west of Rotterdam.-ed.) harbor, which is the place of Rendervous for Convoys that Come for Holld., there they wait 'till they receive ordrs. of the States General, it's a good harbour about 3 leagues from the Brill; When our men of Warr are in Holland they follow the ord'rs of the States General, and when the Dutch are in England they receive ord'rs from our Ld. High Admiral. We Came to anchor at the Brill where we stay'd that night, it being between 7 & 8 when we morr'd, having little or no wind and a strong Currtt agst. us;"

[** Ed. Comment Follows]
Jonathan soon arrives in Rotterdam and will describe his uncanny ability to team up with new found friends, and explore the sights, in spite of his inability to speak Dutch. He frequently shops at the "Change;" watches his budget rather prudently; mentions high expenses as "dear enough;" the poor food, "Eating is mean;" and notes an

important person, Vandermoulin, who he was recommended
to contact. Vandermoulin, no doubt, is associated with
his mariner father, Captain Andrew Belcher, or his agent
in England. "Taking what money I wanted," on July 25th,
implies that perhaps the Vandermoulin's were bartering
money for trade with the Belcher shipping industry.
Jonathan describes the great shipping center of Rotterdam
in the July 29 entry. Money exchange rates (Strivers)
are footnoted, and all exchange rates are explained by
Jonathan at the end of his journal:

"Thurs. 24th   N.S. (note: he changed to the New Style
Calender -ed.) at 5 the next morning we weigh'd having a
fresh gale up to Rotterdam (which is about 4 leagues from
the Brill) when we Came there the yatch hall'd to the
Wharfe (Call'd the Boomtcheize) I now took my leave of
the Captn. and went ashore with mrs. Thomas, who was a
passenger with us, she Carry'd me to Her house (which is
in the Wine Street) Her husband is an English broker, a
Comical Little drunken fellow, he ask'd me to take my
lodging at his house, I being altogether a stranger &
speaking no Dutch, & having but little time to spend
there, thought it signify'd not much Where I lodg'd so I
Een stay'd there, but indeed he has but very poor
accomodations, they laid me in a Room, Where were three
beds & generally 3 or 4 Lodg'd in 'em, Which is very
inconvenient, His Eating is mean & yet dear Enough, he
was generally drunk from 10 in the morn', 'till 12 at
night their Change (5) begins at 12 a Clock, and they
who are not there buy a quarter after, pay 6 Stivers (6)
to the doorkeeper, which custom I being ignorant of was

---

(5) A change is a place where merchants meet to transact
business.
(6) 20 Strivers in Belcher's time made a Dutch Guilder,
and 22 English pence were worth a Dutch Guilder. In
the 1730s 19 shillings in Massachusetts were equal to
one ounce of silver and 10 ounces of silver were
equal to one ounce of gold. The rates increased to as
much as 27 shillings per ounce of silver during the
inflationary period of the 1730s. Belcher explains
his interpretation of the money equivalents on the
last page of his journal.

forc'd to pay 3 Stivers ye first time I went to change, being so directed by my little drunken landlord, the heighth of change is at 1/4 after 1 when you may generally see 3 or 400 people; abt. 2 I went to dinner, and after that sent to Msr:ers Vandermoulius, to whom I was Recommended by my friend in Londn for anything I might have occasion, but they were gone to Helvet Shigs to dispatch some ships lay there ready to sail. I then went on board our yatch Where I found Mr. Spranger the Chiausgeon (note: a chiaus is a turkish messenger or servant-ed.) of the yatch (who was very Civil to me in my passage) & I desir'd his Compa. with me to walk and see the town. We went first and took a View of ye Statue of Erasmus, which Stands in the Chief market place at the End of a graff, it's very finely done in Copper, being in a Scholastick garb, with a book in his hand, Turning over the leaves, (the City of Antwerp have offer'd for ye Statue 20000 Guilders) from thence we went to see the house where this great Erasmus was born, it's a low brick building Stands at the Corner of a Street not far from their gt. Church; we from thence went and View'd the Church which is very large and well adorn'd within, it's built with brick, has a very large, Square, high Tower, Carry'd up with one bigness to the Top, Which made it top heavy, and not long Since the Weight of it, made it lean so much, that they Expected Every day When 'twould tumble, but was prevented by a great German architect, who most ingeniously Righted it, by Screws and after that Carry'd up pillars of brick to Strengthen it, and it now Stands firm hardly to be shockt by the Strongest gales; This ingenious man having ingag'd in Setting it upright and put the States to great Charges in placing his Engines, and bringing the work to Some forwardness, before the thing was Effected he Run away, fearing the matter would not be Effected to his and their minds, but Contrary to that and all manner of Expectation, his art prov'd most Effectual in Securing the Towre in so much That the States (on it's being finisht) did Immediately Issue out proclomations, desiring the man to Come & accept of a noble gratuity for his unparallel'd Ingenuity, but the man went Clear of the Country and Cannot be heard of to this day, and the art is lost with him;- It being now dark we went to our lodgings; next-morning

Friday 25th. I sent again to Msr.ers Vandermoulins and

found 'Em at home, dd   (7)   my friends Ltt and they
treated me Very Civilly, I stay'd about an hour with 'Em
& took what money I wanted, then Mr Peter Vandermoulin
& I went to 'Change, (8) where I stay'd about an hour
and he took me off to see the Town, We walkt about an
hour and half to see the Stadthouse, admiralty office and
States yatchts, the Stadthouse & admiralty office are not
large, the admiralty office is built in the nature of a
Court, with a Square in the middle, the yatchts are Very
finely adorn'd with Carv'd work and gilding, but nothing
of beauty or Comeliness in the modelling, they are built
after the hackboat fashion, they never travell the Sea
with 'Em being flat bottom'd and built only for Rivers;
for the diversion of the States, they are very roomly
and Commodious within; after this I went to dine with
Mr Stone an English merchant, who treated me very
Respectfully, offer'd to do me any Service in his power,
and to Supply me with what money I pleas'd (altho' I was
a perfect Stranger & had no recommendation to him) Which
was a Civility beyond my Expectation,   (9)   Mr
Spranger din'd with us, and When we had done
dinner (being about 3 a Clock) he & I took a turn or 2
upon the Boomt Chiefl; where are the best buildings in
the town & generally many ships lying at the Wharfes,
after this we went into town and took a dish of Tea (at
shep=huad's the English Coffee house) from thence to
the Herring=fleet where lives Mr. Hammond an English
Gentleman (one of Mr. Spranger's acquaintance) he gave us
good florence, Clarret and Burgundy, We stay'd till about
8 a Clock, from thence went on board the yatch & Supt

---

(7) dd is an abbreviation that Belcher occasionally uses,
    he seems to confine the use of it to delivering
    letters of introduction. Hence I believe he means
    "did deliver". Ltt, often means letter -ed.
(8) Change, in this context, means the business
    exchange. The taking of "what money I wanted" coupled
    with the previous remarks about Vandermoulin
    dispatching ships, implies to me that the Dutch
    Vandermoulin's were familiar with Belcher's mariner
    father. The letter of introduction may be associated
    with Captain Andrew Belcher's agent, in London,
    routinely bartering money for trade for Belcher.
(9) This is another example of barter strategy.

with Capt Milleson, from thence I retir'd to my lodging
and found My Landlord in his Usual Condition; next
morning"

[** Ed. Comment Follows]
Jonathan's previous comment may be his dry humor: "and
found My Landlord in his Usual Condition," (i.e. drunk,
see July 24th entry); In the next entry Jonathan visits
an artist who works with elaborate cuttings of paper in
Rotterdam. Jonathan was fond of art, he had his portrait
done at least five times, once in London in 1729. The
famous Dutch artist, Rembrandt (1606-1669), died in
Amsterdam. There are a few expressions in the next entry
that might be helpful to explain: a "Guiney" is an old
English coin equal to 21 shillings, slightly more (one
shilling) than an English Pound. A Pound is about $1.85
in 1992. "The late Queen Mary" (1662-1694) refers to the
wife of King William III. She was very religious (see
Oct. 9th entry), and her husband replaced Protestantism
in the bloodless Revolution in England (1688); the
"Bishop of London" was an important social/political
force in England: Edmund Gibson (1669-1748) was a later
Bishop of London associated with the Prime Minister, Sir
Robert Walpole and Belcher (see appendix). There is an
interesting insight of arbitrary governmental controls
regarding house construction in Rotterdam. One might
speculate that such arbitrary rulings may have generated
interest in immigrating to America in the eighteenth
century (The population of Massachusetts, Connecticut,
Rhode Island, and New Hampshire was estimated at 360,000
by 1750. Virginia, alone, had 231,000 in 1750):

"Saturday 26th: Mr Spranger & Hammond Came to Call me,
to see the paper Works, Which are done by a private
gentleman for his own Curiosity, they are indeed very
admirable pieces of art, he has cut several fancies, as
pots of flowers, ships riding at anchor, ships in a
storm, imitation of point lace & ca. all which are so
well done, that you would almost swear they were
Realities, there is a Woman that shews 'Em to 'Tmy that
are desirous to see his Ingenuity, she told me the late
Queen Mary, was so taken wth the flower pots, he had Cut,
that she offer'd him 150 Guineys for one piece, but being
a gentleman of a good Estate thought it beneath him to
take anything for his art and offer'd it to her Majty as
a present, but she would not accept it, and he not

being willing to sell it, she went without it, (10)
from this place I went to see an instance of the
arbitrary government of Holland & the Stubborness and
folly of One of the Citizens;- One Side of a Street the
houses were all uniform, with flat Roofs, and this
man set up a house and would by no means be enough
with pers'waded to build it as the Rest, the States
Sent to him Several times, he Said his Money was
his own, and he built to please his own fancy and not
other peoples, so they let the house be finish'd all but
glazing, and will not allow him to have a Quarry of glass
in his house, which is a noble, well built house, Every
way handsome & beautiful Excepting in that, it has only
wooden shutters to the lights, he has Several times put
up glass, but they have immediately pull'd it down, and
have (I think) now laid a penalty on his putting it up
any more, by this you may See it is not So free a
government as the world Imagines for they have no laws to
Justify 'Em in this matter; - While I was here I heard
Several Instances of their arbitrariness, which I Cannot
at present Recollect, so that (I believe) the people live
undr an despotick power, While they only Imagine the
government to be a free State; after this I went to
dinner, & Spent the afternoon at Msr.ers Vandermoulin's
to discourse 'Em of the trade of Holland, & give 'Em some
short accot of N England, I took my leave of 'Em about
Sun Set and Spent the Evening at home;

[** Ed Comment Follows:]
Jonathan next begins his routine Sunday church
attendance. His rather somber observations toward the
minister are a bit different than one might expect from
a twenty-two year old American tourist today: "the
man seems to be a sober young man." Jonathan's religion
was a powerful part of his life. Among numerous examples
as Governor, see his thanks to God in the Journal at the
end of the October 4, entry.

"Sunday, 27th: Next morning I Went to hear a Church of
England parson, who preaches Just over against my

---

(10) The Queen Mary story might be a Dutch fairy tale, in
     an effort to sell art work to a wealthy tourist.
     Belcher spent ninety-four Pounds Sterling in three
     months of touring, while the minister of Amsterdam
     lived on 150 Pounds a year with a large family.

Lodging, Where the Church of England people have a small
Chamber, which they use for a Chh, the man Seem'd to be a
Sober young man, made a good discourse about family=
prayer, they told me he had allowance from the Bishop of
Londn (about 70 Pounds a year) When church was done Mr.
Stone Sent and Invited me to dinner Where I din'd with
Mr. Hammond, Stone, Spranger and some other gentleman,
when the afternoon Service was over, I Walkt to take the
air, and acquaint my Self a little more with the
Situation of the town, it's buildings & ca., in the
Evening I took a glass of Wine with Capt Milleson on
board the yatch;

Monday 28th: Next day I Walkt to the States building yard
to See some of their large men of Warr, Which indeed are
brave Warlike ships, but have not the beauty & Comliness
of the English built ships, from thence We went to the
Windmills, Which Stand on a dike at one End of the Town
fronting to the Maeze, there they grind Rape Seed, from
which they produce that, Which they Call linseed oil, I
saw one of these mills, with which they made this oil, &
polish'd marble at the Same time (by different Wheels)
Which is accounted an Ingenious piece of Work; I saw not
much more in that City than I have already noted, the
remainder of this day and the next I Spent in writing to
my friends In N England, P (11) Capt Wadworth who
was there Commander of a N England ship (call'd Industry)
This

Tuesday 29th: day I had not time to go out o'the house;
Before I leave this City I shall in Short give a general
acct of It. Rotterdam is a place very well Contriv'd for
trade and the people of great diligence & industry; most
of the merchts live by Commissions and not by trading on
their own stocks; the City is built along upon the Maese
and looks Extremely pleasant as you Come up along the
River, having Rows of trees planted before the houses
which Stand Close by the River side, It's a great place
for importing & Exporting, because there is generally
more Certainty of Convoy, It being hazardous both for men
of Warr and mercht men to go for Amerstr, the Texel being
a Very bad place to ride in, and along while before ships
Can get up the River (Call'd the Y) which begins from the
Texel (being about 12 leagues from Amstr) so most merchts

---

(11) "P" means post or mailed by ship via the designated
     ship's captain.

Choose Rather to pay the Carriage of their goods from
Amstr to Rotterdm (which is 40 English miles) & the
Commissions for shipping off, than ship 'Em directly from
Amstr, and many Mercht so trading to Holland so ordr
their business for the same Reason, this makes the Chief
trade of Rotterdm. It's a place of Refuse for a great
many English bankrupts, and very hazardous having to do
with the English merchts, most of 'Em being without
bottom or substance, yet they make shift to live with
their Commissions and some few have Estates, as Mr.
Sincerf, Reaves, Hope the Quaker & one Brown who Is
reckoned Worth 30000 Pounds Sterling. There ain't a great
many dutch merchts That are Rich, but they are generally
to be more Relied on in Way of trade & business than the
English; one Lapenan a Jew Is reckon'd a man of a great
Estate; If I think of anything more material as to this
City I shall insert it on my return from Germany;"

[** Ed. Comment Follows]
Jonathan's previous summary is almost written as if it
were addressed to his father, in answer to probable
questions about trade in Rotterdam. In any case,
Jonathan next begins a tour of the Hague, six miles
from Rotterdam, which is the heart of Government in
the Netherlands, and indeed, in the 1700s a center of
European diplomats. He misses the usual form of travel
"track skoot," which is a boat pulled along a canal by a
horse, ridden by a boy, and complains about being charged
"four times the money" traveling by wagon. But all is
not lost. After touring about (note his admiration for
William III who overthrew the Catholic James II) and
visiting with Lord Portland, who came with Jonathan on
the Yacht "Katherine," he visits the father of an early
Freemason, the Third Earl of Chesterfield, Mr. Stanhope.
Stanhope arranges an introduction to the heir to the
Crown of England. The Journal continues with a lengthy
July 30th, at the end of which he visits with a Belcher
relative. This visit adds evidence that Jonathan was well
aware in 1704 of the Belcher relatives in England and
Europe. As late as 1732 he mentions his cousin John
Belcher in St. Paul's Churchyard, London, the location of
the Goose and Gridiron Alehouse, where Freemasonry was
formally organized in 1717. The Journal continues:

"Wedn 30th: This morning about 7 a Clock, Mr.
Vandermoulin, Spranger and's Wife & I went to the Track
skoot in ordr to our going to the Hague; but Staying 4 or
5 minutes beyond the time of It's going off We mist that

boat, altho' they Saw us Coming yet they would not Stay they are so Exact as to their traveling, so we took a Stage Waggon which Cost us 4 times the money & not half so pleasant, the first town We Came to was Overskye, which Is a pretty, pleasant Village abt 3 English miles from Rotterdm, I think it has but one Street, which is the length of the town, from thence We went to Delf which Is (blank- ed.) miles more It's a very neat town, much Sweeter and pleasanter than the City of Rotterdm, here we Stay'd about 2 hours, That I might See something of the town, we went into the great Church, which is very magnificent, but adorn'd with gentleman's Escutcheons & other Curiosities but that which Is most worth Seeing is the monument of the great Nossau Wm the 1st Prince of Orange (-pltat (*) grandfather to the late King Wm. the 3d of glorious memory) (12) done to admiration in fine marble under that he lies Intomb'd, and Just before this monument you have his Statue very well done in brass, and over the whole stand 2 boys, Curiously done also in brass, holding between 'Em a plate of brass with an inscription bewailing the murder of the great Nossau, the boys are done with Crying faces and so much to the life That I Could not believe but they were living Children in brass masquerade; there is also the monument of Van=Tromp, who was Grand Admiral to the dutch fleet, and father to the great Cornelivus Van=Tromp. Several other fine Statues & monuments I saw, which are too tedious to be penn'd, from the Church I Went to the Palace, Where the famous Prince Nassau Was murder'd, It's an old low building Stands by the Chh. This glorious Prince was the first deliverer of the Dutch from Popery, he fought Several battles for them agst the Spaniards in the Netherlands, at last one day (as he was rising from dinner) a frenchman Came boldly up to him & shot him with a pistol, the fellow was Immediately taken (in the Room) by some of the Prince's gentlemen and Condemn'd to the Wheel by the States of Holland, he had of long time design'd it (as he Confesst) but Never had Imprudence Enough to Execute his Cussed Villany 'till then, 'twas

---

(*) The word ?pltat is questionable in transcribing.
(12) "William the 1st Prince of Orange," (1533-1584) was the father of the Dutch republic. The "late King Wm. the 3d" was born in 1650, and the grandson of Charles I (1600-1649).

tho't he had rec'd money from the Spaniards on this accott:;- Indeed I think he shew'd the heigth of folly and madness, not only in Committing murder and on so great, so good a man & glorious a Prince, but in that when he did it (he Confess'd) he saw no possibility of Escaping, so that he sold his life, for what he never Expected to enjoy:-Delf is a Very pleasant Town, Extremely Clean and Sweet, a place not of much trade, yet there are some merchts here belonging to the dutch East India Compa., but the Town Is mostly for merchts who have left off business & live free and Easy, It is famous for making the finest Earthen Ware, Which I had not time to go see, or hardly anything Else in the town (Staying but 2 hours) indeed I had a view of the arsenal which is very noble, had in it about 200 demi=Cannon & Several large Mortars, We now proceeded to the Hague, and in my Way I had a view (at a distance) of the place where Stands the house of Ryswick (in which the peace was Concluded) It's pleasantly Surrounded with trees being about a mile from the town of Ryswick. I had no time to Ride to it, and designing to return that way thought it might be as well to observe it more particularly then, so We went on to the Hague (which we Rid thro') to a place (call'd Scheneland) 2 miles from the Hague, it has only about 8 or 10 fishermen's houses, all that's to be Seen there Is the pleasant Sight of the wide ocean, the fishermen don't go above 2 leagues to take their fish, and you may Stand ashore & See the Dunkirkers & Ostenders take the fishermen and others and Carry 'Em away, We Stay'd about an hour here, and then went to my Lord Portland's Countrey house (call'd Susklet), His gardens are pita (? ed.) and of great Variety, the fountains play very pleasantly and the Cascades look natural, His summer house is pretty, the grotto Curious, he has no Banis (? ed.) in his garden, his Cage of bird's affords many that are foreign & Rare, the orangery is pleasant Enough but not Extraordinary the gardens are very large, full of all sorts of grdns and fruits, the walks are the worst I Ever Saw by reason of the Sand, which almost buries y'er feet Every Step you take, and for that Reason he Is oblig'd to keep men Constantly Raking the walks, His house is but a Small brick building, there we drank a glass of Burgundy, Eat a few Apricots and Return'd to the

Hague;   (13)   it being now 2 a Clock, We went to a publick house, order'd some Victuals, and While it was dressing I waited on   Mr. Stanhope, our Qn's Envoy Extraordinary to the States General, I told him I was Come from England & traveling to Hannover & Hamburg, as I was passing thro' the Hague, thought my duty to pay a respects to him, and know if any Commands in my power, to any place where I might pass and that I should be glad of the honour of being his most obedient Servant, he thank'd me, and told me he took it as a particular obligation, When any English gentleman was so kind as to Call on him, and that he would kindly do me any Service in his power, so he desir'd me to Set and We talkt about an hour of N England and some other matters, and then Came in one Baron Bothmar, who is Envoy at the Hague from ye Elector of Hannover, Mr. Stanhope told him whence I was Come and that I was design'd for Hannover to pay my respects to the Princess Sophia, upon which he rose up and Complimented me (indeed I think) with too much formality & Respect, he told me he was Sure, Her-Electoral Highness wd be Extremely glad to See one so far as from N England at the Court of Hannover and withall pray'd I would Command him, if he was Capable of rendering me any Service, I told him I shd be a perfect Stranger at Hannover, and should highly Esteem the favour & honour of a Ltt to any friend of His, he told me he would give me a Lttr to ye Princess Sophie Herself, I gave him 10000 thanks & told him I should be proud of so great an honour, after this he sate about 1/4 of an hour and took his leave of Mr. Stanhope and wish'd me a good journey, Mr Stanhope told me he was particularly Respected at ye Court of Hannover, and his Lttr might be of Service; I now took my leave of Mr Stanhope, he wish'd me a very pleasant Journey and told me he was Sorry my Stay was so short, that he Could have no opportunity of Serving me, he ordered his Secretary to go with me and shew me the town and what was to be Seen. I

---

(13) Belcher might be bias about Lord Portland. He not only was fed a "few Apricots" by the "stingy" (see July 12th entry) Lord Portland at dinner time, the worst walk "I ever saw" was owned by the same Lord Portland who Belcher named in the adventure with the privateer on July 12, 1704.

askt him first to go and dine with me,   (14)
which we did, and then went to take a view of the States
Court, which Is a fine building (I think) Envison'd
with Canals, looks Extremely pleasant, the Chambers
are noble and Richly adorn'd, the presence Chamber Where
they receive all Ambassadours & Envoys, is finely painted
and gilt, and hung with Princes pictures, the States in
the Council Chamber set all round a large table, and
Every one has his Silver Juk=Stand & Silver Sand box in a
Silver plate. Their Chairs are of Red Velvet, with
Cushions on which are well workt (with Silk) the Arms of
Holland   there is a noble elbow=chair of red Velvet,
Richly lac't with gold, with a Cushion on which Is very
Richly imbroider'd with gold and Silver the Arms of
Holland, the Chair was made for the late King Wm which he
Set in, as Stadtholder of Holland, It has now a Covering
to it and not us'd from the Court. We went to the
Spin=house, which is a place where they Confine any noted
whores, some for 2, Some 3, Some 6 years according as
their Crimes have been, It's Call'd the Spin house
because they Spend most of their time in Spinning, and
the keeper of the house looks after 'Em very Severely,
least they should be Idle, and often Whips 'Em when he
finds 'Em so, they have the greatest Stock of Imprudence
of any people I Ever Saw, for altho' they Can hardly
Speak English, yet they Can talk all manner of Lewdness
and debouchery-   perfectly, and they are not only
Imprudent in their discourse but in their actions, Even
to the last degree, they are kept with mean Eating &
drinking. from hence we went to See one of the Hospitals
of the town, which is a very good house, and the people
well provided for, with Clothing & ca, after this I went
to Visit a Kinswoman of Mine who lives at the Hague, Her
name was Belcher but is now marry'd to one Willis who is
Coachman to my Ld Cutts, he is a good Sober man near 60
years old, she was Extremely Joy'd to See me, as indeed I
was to See so near a Relation (Her father and my
grandfather being own brothers) in a Remote part of
the world; I Stay'd with Her about an hour, she told me
she was very sorry, she had nothing fit to offer me to

---

(14) If Belcher was a Freemason before this journey, he
      met the famous Lord Stanhope, father to an early
      Freemasons in this restaurant in the Hague. See
      appendix -ed.

drink, she lives but meanly, which I was sorry to see, what pleas'd me was the plainheartedness of her husband, for while I was in the house, he was in the Stable looking after his horses, so she went wth me to the Stables, & told him, one of her near Relatives was come from N England, who she ne'er Expected to See, and that I would be glad to See him, he was all this while at the further End of the Stables among the horses, so he Came towards the door and I went to him and told him, I was glad to See him, he said aye, he was glad to See me too, but he must look after his horses, but if I did not go out of town Early in the morning, he would Come and See me, so I took my leave of 'Em and went to my lodging;"

[** Ed. Comment Follows]
Jonathan's previous remark about his cousin's husband, "what pleased me was the plain heartedness..." is an insight into the tavern born Belcher's respect for the work ethic. It is probable that Belcher's wealth commonly attracted opportunists. Willis's integrity pleased him. Jonathan's scorn for the imprudence of the "lewdness" in the spinhouse is another insight toward his moral beliefs. In the next few days Jonathan explores Leiden, nine miles from the Hague, then another six miles to Amsterdam. Belcher meets "his priceless friend," Mr. Van Schaick, as he was shopping at the Amsterdam "Change." The friendship is not explained, it is reasonable speculation that Schaick met Belcher in England, and that he was an important friend of the Belcher family in the 1704 period. Schaick is worthy of further research to learn if he might be an early Freemason. On to Leiden:

"Thurs. 31st: Next Morning we Spent our time in viewing a very large hospital, which Is for Orphans, Its kept very neat, and no Care wanting in the government of and provision for the Children, We walkt a little about the town 'till 10 a Clock, and then took the skoot for Leiden, I had not time Enough in the Hague, more than to give a general acctt of it, indeed I think it the most pleasant town I have Seen, abundance of good Conversation it being the Resort of all nations, who travel on that Side of the Water, It's a place of little or no trade, but the people live mostly on the Court, the buildings are very noble and regular, (I think) I was told it had 10000 houses intending to Return that way, shall defer

any more particular observation 'till then; When we Came
to Leiden I found a dull melancholly town, hardly one
person to be Seen in the Streets, as I Came out of the
boat, a man (that waits to See, If there be any
Strangers) Carry'd me first to the Colledge, which is an
old brick building not Spacious at all, I Enquir'd for
some of the English students, but was told, they never
Study at the College, but have Every one their particular
lodgings in the town, and are at College only at Set
times When the professors attend to give lectures and
hear their disputations, the garden belonging to the
College is pleasant Enough, not large, in a gallery in
the garden are a great many Curiosities; a list of which
I bought, so shall not mention particulars, a little way
from the College Stands the Anatomy Chamber which indeed
Contains Wonderful pieces of art, I have also the
particulars in print, however It may not be amiss to tell
you, I saw an Egyptian mummy, had been done 1100 years
(as they told me) which Still was Sound and not
putrify'd, after we had Seen as much as our time would
allow us, We went to a french ordinary, and took a
dinner, and then proceeded with the Skoot for Haarlem,
from the Hague to Leiden, and from Leiden to Haarlem, you
may See Several gentlemen's Countrey Seats, which indeed
are very fine and pleasant, planted Just on the Edges of
the Canals thro' which pass the travelling trackskoots.
by that time we Came to Haarlem, 'twas Sunset, so 'ye had
not any opportunity of Seeing the town that night. We
went to an English ordinary, where we took our Lodgings,

Friday, August 1st: Next Morning we took a Walk into
town, where I Saw in the great Chh, Two large Silver
bells, which were taken by the troops of the town of
Haarlem from the Turks in the time of the Holy Warr, they
have some Small alloy of other mettal, their Sound is-
Extremely Sweet, after this we went to See the Tapestry
house, (this Town being the most famous in Europe for
that art) but being so Early in the morn', Could See none
of the work, however I took a turn in ye garden belonging
to the house, which Is pretty Enough, adorn'd with good
flowers and knots, (15) the Walks pav'd with
Small brick, in the orange house I Saw the picture of
Laurentius Costerus, who first invented printing, he was

---

(15) A "knot," as used, is an elaborate flower garden.

born in the town of Haarlem; they are also most famous in
this place for whitning linnen, and they told me
yy ("yy" may possibly mean "they yearly"- ed.) us'd about
the same yearly as much buttermilk as cost 500 Pounds
bought at 2 quarts a penny, my Stay being as short here
as at other places- I Could not make a thorrow Enquiry
into this or any other particulars of the place; between
9 & 10 we took a Skoot for Amstra (which is __ English
miles) [six English miles is given in Belcher's mileage
chart at the end of the Journal- ed] as soon as I
Came to town, I Walkt to the place Call'd the Dam, which
Is a large Square, on one Side Stands their Stadthouse,
on another Side their great Chh & a Weigh house, and the
2 other sides Rows of shops, here Is generally a great
Compa. of people; Just before 'Change, I walkt their
'till 12 a Clock, When begins their Change, Whither I
went, It's large I think longer than Londn Excha but not
So broad, on Each Side and at one End, you have pillars
which are number'd, whereby you may find any particular
gentleman, Every one using such a no. the 'Change
Is built all round with bricks and there are shops above
as in Londn, but not so fine. I think Rather a Scandal
to the City and 'Change than any thing Else, the 'Change
Stands in a Close being hem'd all round with houses,
so that It affords no good prospect to any Stranger
but is very obscure, on ye left hand as you go on to
'Change, stand a great Co. of German Jews, who are money
Changers, and as soon as I Came they Surrounded me saying
"Gelt Wisselen Mgnheer" do you want to change y'l money
Sr, they have all Sorts of Coins and are well Skill'd
In money, but full of deceit and will Charge you (if
possible) so that a man must deal with 'Em with a great
deal of Caution; on 'Change I met with several merchts to
whom I had recommendatory Lttr from my friends in Londn,
I rec'd a great deal of Civility from 'Em, and afterwards
din'd with several of 'em Mr. Van=Schaick who is
my priceless friend, hearing I was Come to town, found me
out upon 'Change, and Carry'd me to dinner with him; he
lives upon a place Call'd the New Island, which fronts to
the Sea, where you have a View of the Chief shipping port
of Amstr, Just before his door lay a sort of a ship but I
think rather a barn to look to, 'twas quite round, built
purposely to use ye trade between the Rhine & Holland,
the ship Is Sail'd with but three men, and Carryes
300 tuns of goods, the mastr, his Wife and family live
always on board, and belong to no place, being undr no-
government but neptune's, water being their Elemt they

pay no taxes to any Prince or State, they have
Extraordinary accomodations on board, four large Rooms, 2
finely wainscoated, the Mastr was Rich had abundance of
plate and China, which they us'd on board I believe at
least 200 Pounds worth, his Wife lay in on board, while I
was at Amstra and wd not Come on shore, altho', the ship
lay at the Wharfe; after dinner Mr Schaick gave me an
invitation to lodge at his house, and wd by no means
Excuse me, so I took my lodgings there, Mr Spranger Came
and took me out to walk the City and visit some of his
friends, which finisht the afternoon;"

[** Ed. Comment Follows]
Jonathan's descriptions of ships, repeatedly indicate
his more than casual knowledge of the sea. Terms of
tonnage, accommodations, seaworthy-ness, and details of
construction are periodically mentioned. It is not
unlikely that Jonathan sailed with his father in the
seventeenth century. In the next few days Jonathan tours
about and is invited to supper by the minister of the
English Church in Amsterdam, D. E. Cockburn. Cockburn's
son eventually accompanies Belcher for the rest of the
journey as a hired travel companion. Cockburn is another
interesting associate of the Belcher family in 1704:

"Saturday 2nd: Next day Mr Schaick Carried me out with
his lady and Some friends in a boat to a place Call'd
Durkordam, It's a small town, the houses built along
upon the Y, (16) it's about 3 miles from Amstr,
the people live wholly upon fishing, they take the
fish out of the River with nets made of fine silk,
the houses are mostly built with wood; from this
place we Sail'd to Sardham, where is the greatest
show of Windmills I ever saw, I believe at least 500
Stand at the back of the town, which are Several uses,
as Corn mills, oil mills, paper mills, Saw mills,
Snuff mills & ca. It's a place of much ship building, at

---

(16) The "Y" in Belcher's time was an arm of the 2,100
     square mile Zuiderzee leading into Amsterdam. The
     Zuiderzee once was a lake in the middle of a large
     swampland, and in the floods between 1100s to 1300s
     the Zuiderzee became an ocean gulf. In modern times
     "polders" (bits of land) were added to the lake by
     building dikes, pushing aside the water. The result-
     hole filled with land. It is now called Ijsselmeer.

one place where they build the dock Is fill'd up with
Earth and Stones & a fixt bridge a=Cross, so that the
ships they build wth=in that place, they are oblig'd to
hoise over, which is done by Capstanes and some other
Engines, they shew'd me a new ship of 500 tuns,
which had been Carry'd over that bridge but 2 dayes
before with those Capstanes without the least help
of Water,   (17)   which Seems almost Impossible to
Concieve off; This Small Village Stands upon the River Y
Right over agtt Amstr, they have offer'd the States of
Holland (If they will at any time give 'Em 6 months
Warning) they will be Engag'd from that time to launch
'Em a 30 Rate man of Warr Every day, for a year, which is
365-70 gun ships, which Indeed is Strange & almost
incredible Considering they have nothing of their own,
but must Transport Timber, Tarr, & ca from other nations,
How Ever their an argumant of the Curious art, great
activity & Ingenuity of mankind; I lookt into one of the
Churches of Sardham, which Is well Enough for a Country
Chh not very large or magnificent, We spent in the town
about 2 hours in all, and then return'd to Amstra being
about 5 a Clock, as soon as I Came home D. E. Cockburn
the minister of the English Chh Sent to desire my Compa.
to Supper, so I waited on him & pass'd 2 or 3 hours, then
went home, and Sat wth Mr Schaick and's wife 'till
bed=time, and then to my Chambers,

Sunday 3rd: In the morning I went to hear D. E. Cockburn,
and in the afternoon, Service being Ended about 4 a
Clock, I Walkt to the large new Chh in Amstr to See the
Calvinist's way of Worship, which is much after our
Presbyterians in England, but they have a form
of prayer, not altogether unlike that of the Chh of
Engld, they had an organ which play'd very delightfully:-

[** Ed. Comment Follows]
Jonathan next describes the practice, in Amsterdam, of
going to the English church in the house of the minister,
Mr. Cockburn. Although thrifty in church, he generally
gave about 10 English pence (see expense account at the
end of the journal), Belcher is methodical in evaluating
Rev. Cockburn's modest financial means. In the August 9th

---

(17) This may have been a type of huge fulcrum on the
     principle of a balance scale. "Earth and stone"
     countered the weight of the ship.-ed.

entry Belcher invites Cockburn's son to continue the 934
mile journey. He will later give Cockburn's son about
four English pounds (48 guilders, 22 pence per guilder),
in addition to paying his travel expenses on the journey.
On August 5th, Belcher compares St. Paul's of London, to
the stadhouse. This provides additional evidence that
Jonathan was familiar with the area of London near the
Goose and GridIron Ale house. The Goose and Gridiron,
around the corner from St. Paul's church yard on London
House Yard, a few steps from Mitre Court Passage (AQC
37/47-48), was the original Masonic meeting place for the
formation of the first Grand Lodge in the world on June
24, 1717. Note also Belcher's letters of recommendation
to Mr. Spranger, another important Belcher associate in
1704:

"Monday 4th: D. E. Cockburn has but a Small
Congregation, the Chh Is a Small Chamber in the house
where he lives, he is a Very Sober man, a good preacher,
and Carryes it with a great deal of Respect & Civility,
(18)   he was the first Minister that Ever Settld the
Worship of the Chh of England in Holland, he first settld
a Chh in Rotterdam & from thence he Came and settlt
another in Amstr (Where he now lives) the Queen allows
him 60 Pounds a year, and ye Society for Reformation 50
Pounds, the Collection from ye house's Is about 40
Pounds, and the Queen Is now Setling 60 Pounds a year;
out of this he payes for the Rent of the Chh and his own
house 40 Pounds a year and to the officers of ye Church
20 Pounds, so His salary is about 150 Pounds a year,
with which he Can but Just live, having a great family,
the remainder of this day Mr Spranger & I Spent in paying
our Respects to Mr Sweat, the Queen's paymaster general
of the army, who indeed Is a Very Civil gentleman and
lives very nobly, for the honour of his mistress;

Tuesday 5th: Next day very Early Mr Spranger &'s Wife
went away for Rotterdam, Wishing me a good Journey to
Hannover & ca, so I took my leave of 'Em, When they were
gone Mr Schaick did me the favour to accompany me to see
the City, We went first and viewed the Stadthouse, (19)

---

(18) It is not patronizing to state that Belcher was
     deeply religious. There is abundant evidence in the
     1730s from his correspondence as Governor.
(19) The Stadthouse is the Chief Executive office.

which is indeed a glorious pile, I think Exceeds St.
Paul's for fine marble and other fine work, the curiosity
of the Stadthouse can't be easily particulariz'd so I
shall not attempt it, It Stands Exactly upon a Square, I
was in almost Every Room of it, It's very well finisht
off, It has a fine pair of Chimes, one wheel of which
they tell you Cost 10000 Pounds. It's made of Copper and
Is about as bigg as a 60 gallon hogshead, the foundations
of the Stadthouse Cost as much as the Superstructure;
they tell you that It's the 8th wonder of the world, and
that they kept a particular accont of the Charge of it;
'till it Swell'd to so much, That the States ordrd the
accomptants to let the money be paid without taking a
particular accott least the mob should make an uproar,
Seeing how much It should Cost; In it they keep the Bank
of Amstr, and Several other offices and Courts of
Indicature, I Went up to the top of it, to take a view of
the City, It's built of good freestone & in Short makes a
very graceful show, Wants only a good Entrance; from the
Stadthouse we went to the new Chh, which I think Is the
largest in the City, It stands Close by the Stadthouse,
It has in't a very good & large organ ye best in Holland,
above 5000 pipes & 50 stops; the pulpit of this Chh (they
say) Cost 5000 Pounds being only of oak finely Carv'd,
they once attempted to Erect a Steeple to this Chh, but
after they had been at some 1000 Pounds Charge they
Could not Effect it by reason of the Rottenness of the
foundation; by that we had fully view'd the Stadhouse and
Chh it was 'Change time, so Mr Schuick & I went thither
and from thence Mr Spranger took me to dinner (a dutch
merct to whom I was recomended) from dinner his partner
Mr Van Rincom Carried me to view the States building yard
at Amstr, but being dark and foul Weather we had no time
to take a particular notice; & thinking to Return this
way made me not so Curious, this Evening Mr Van Rincom
and I Spent with some friends of his at a dutch
Vintness;"

[** Ed Comment Follows]
Because of the possibility of "my priceless friend,"
Mr. Schaick, being a Masonic associate, the reader might
note the next few indications of his loyalty to Belcher
as they were shopping. The tour of the "Rasp house," for
prisoners, hospital for orphans, and "The bedlam of
Amsterdam" for incorrigible morality (The spin house)
are further insights of social practices 287 years ago:

"Wednesday 6th: at 7 the next morn' Mr Schaick Carry'd me
out to show me the City, and to buy some things I had
occasion for, he Is a man of unwearied diligence, will
walk you the City over Rather than not buy you anything
at the best rate, he tir'd me so much in Walking, That I
told him I had rather give something Extraordinary than
fatigue & beat my self so much, he said It was grating
to him to See his friend give a penny more than What he
Could buy for, If he only took a little the more pains,
Which indeed was Extraordinary kind & Civil, he Is a man
of unspotted Reputation; after We had bought what I
wanted, he Carry'd me to see What the City afforded, We
went first to See the Rasphouse, Which Is a prison men
are Condemn'd to for life for the Commission of Some high
Crime, their business Is to Saw Cut, & Rasp dogwood, they
have keepers Set over to see They work without Ceasing,
many that are unruly are Chain'd to great logs, which
they are oblig'd to file to a powder before, they Can
be free, they generally work quite naked Especially
in summer; as this house Is Set up by the City for
the punishment of Criminals, and Every one pays so much
for Rasping his wood, so the City has the benefit of
their work, Which I believe more than maintains the
house. Any man seeing the Slavith miserable lives they
live would sooner Choose sentence of death than to be
put into the Rasp=house;- from hence Mr Schaick Carry'd
me to an hospital for orphans to which then belong'd 1400
boyes & girls, which I saw at supper, they are kept
diligently at work all the day are taught Reading &
writing, and well provided for with Clothing & Victuals
and a bed for Every Two, the boyes have their apartment
in one side of the hospital and the girls on the other,
they are kept 'till 12 years old and then put out to
Service, indeed It was what pleas'd me very well to see
the Extraordinary Care was taken, to keep them neat and
Clean and that nothing necessary for them should be
wanting,

Thursday 7th: Next day Mr Schaick went with me to See
another of their hospitals where was about 500 old women,
as well-provided for as the other, to that hospital
there Is a Very fine garden with good Walks & all sorts
of fruit & Roots, which Is for the benefit of those
people; from hence we went to the Spin house, of which I
need not particularize, It being much of the Same nature
of what I told you off at the Hague; the Bedlam of Amstr
is a Square building with a Court in the middle, the

people   are well Lookt after, Every one has their
particular Cell, which is very dark, I think has no light
but Comes in a little hole, made Just fit to put their
heads out, to take a little air, the building for
grandeur & beauty Is not to be Compar'd with that of
London (in Moorfields) the distemper'd people have all
of them, their Victuals and drink given in Copper basons,
which are Chain'd to the hole of Each persons Cell; after
this we went & took a View of the Jews Synagogues, which
I would willingly have Seen, but it not being their
devotion time, Could not;-   they are very noble, brick
buildings with flat Roofs, no bells, built very high, the
Entrance to one of 'Em Is very handsome; It being now
about 1 a Clock Mr Schaick & I went to dinner, and then
walkt to See the Horehouse and yard belonging to the East
India Compa of Amstr, they have docks & a yard for their
shipping, hardly inferior to those where the States keep
their Men of Warr, the house for their Stores and goods
is Surrounded with water, to prevent any hazard by fire,
It's built a great way out of the City, and took us
sometime to go to, and to view the docks, shipping, and
States yatchs as we went thither, in doing which we
finisht the afternoon;

Friday 8th: The Next day I spent in writing to my friends
in old and New England; notwithstanding I had been in ye
City 8 days and made Strict Enquiry, yet I Could hear of
no person passing for Hannover,

Saturday 9th: and being resolv'd to take my Journey on
Monday next, I propos'd to Mr Cockburn (son to the
English Minister), That I would bear his Charges for his
Compa. he gladly imbraced the offer, so left It to him to
provide what might be necessary for us on the Road, this
day I took my leave of my friends in Amstr asking their
Commands for Hannover & Hambio:,

Sunday 10th: Next day When the Services were Ended D. E.
Cockburn gave me a Supper, We had a little talk about N
England, from thence I went to my lodging;"

[** Ed Comment Follows]
Jonathan next summarizes Amsterdam, with descriptions of
the eighteenth century fear of horses vibrating the weak
soil support foundations, the common mode of boat travel
in Amsterdam ("Track skoot"), banking practices, drinking
expenses, and begins his wagon ride to Osnabrug, Germany

with his travel companion, the English minister's son, D. E. Cockburn:

"Monday 11th: Early next morning I rose to be ready for my Journey, but having about 2 hours to Spare wd willingly give some short acctt of the City of Amstr, whose wealth and trade has made it hardly 2d to any other this day in the world Except Great London, It's a City very Regularly built, the streets of a very good breadth, here are but few Coaches,- they being prohibited by the States for the Security of the City, which was a very Rotten foundation and they are fearful of It's being too much shaken by a multitude of Coaches, for this Reason, they allow no Hackney Coaches but such as are drawn-upon sledges, to which they have but one horse; there being no seat for a driver, the horse Is led by a man that walks, which Is also design'd as a preservative to the foundation of the City, a Physician's Coach is allow'd 4 wheels, but one horse; and ye number of gentlemen's Coaches Is also limited, and It's a priviledge obtain'd not with a little difficulty for a gentleman to keep a Coach, the greatest diversion of the City Is taken Either by Sailing with yatchts in the harbour or traveling in Track Skoots to their Countrey Seats, which indeed Is the Easiest way of traveling in the world; a track skoot is a boat built Large Enough for about 40 people to Set Comfortably, over it Is built a very good Roof to keep out heat or Rain, there are Canals Cut all over Holland for their passing which are about 30 foot wide and the ground on Each Side Is very level & Smooth, at the head of the track Skoot Is a Small mast or pole to which Is fastn'ed a line of abt 40 fathom, (20) and that Is fastened to a horse, which Is rid by a boy, and at the Stern Stands a man to Steer the Track Skoot, It's the pleasantest & Cheapest traveling I Ever Saw, and Holland being well adorn'd with Countrey Seats & gardens, from town to town makes it far more pleasant than 'twould otherwise be, they are so Exact in their traveling, That you may tell to a minute or Two, When you will be whither you intend, they pass

---

(20) A fathom originally was the length a man could extend his arms. It is six feet in modern times. Forty fathoms is rather long, twenty yards short of a football field.

night and day; the trade of this City Is very great the
dutch being I believe the most industrious and diligent
people in the world leaving no stone unturn'd, Whereby a
penny may gain'd. They have a Vast number of ships, and
a noble fleet of Men of Warr. Their bank Is of great Cr
in that men put in their money for 3 pct interest, the
money of their bank Is much better than their Currtt:
Coin, in that they Receive no money into the bank but
what Is the best Silver and of such a Weight; as this
City Is a place of Extraordinary trade, so It has men of
Vast Estates, and the City Itself Is reckon'd to have a
great Revenue which Is daily paid into the treasury of
the City, I was told it was at least 90000 guilders a day
which Is-- 3285000 Pounds a year, which Is to defray the
Charges of their City; they have Eleven Churches of the
Religion according to law Established (Calvinism), they
have 2 Lutheran Churches, one Chh of Engld, & one
Presbyterian meeting which was formerly Roman Catholic
Chh, but they have been for some time Silenc'd by the
States & the States have given that Chh, to the English
Presbyterians and as a mark of their Respect to them,
above the Chh of Engld and Lutheran Chh, they allow them
a bell, It's too tedious to particularize all that I Saw
in this fine City, I Can therefore tell you in short That
It is a place of great trade, (21) of great diversion,
of much Variety of Conversation, on my return I shall
Spend a few dayes here, and I shall then give you some
more particulars which now may have slip't my memory or
something that may then Come new to my knowledge of which
my time will not now allow me to inform myself. We took
boat at Amsterdm for Naasden at 8 in the morning but
might have gone time Enough with the Skoot at 10, the
post wagon of Naasden always waiting the arrival of that
boat, We Carry'd with us as much provisions as Cost us
19 Guilders; We took our places a 2 dayes before at ye
Commissary's at Amstr, for which he made us pay 8
str (22) pretending it was his due, besides 10

---

(21) If Belcher was including trade research in this
     tour of Europe for the benefit of his mariner
     father, his assessment of Amsterdam was exactly
     correct. In fact the Dutch East India Company was
     established in 1602, by 1704, Holland was one of the
     great sea and colonial powers in Europe.
(22) str means Striver, the Dutch equivalent of an
     English Pence in 1704.

guilders we pd him in part of payment, but there Is
nothing due to him on that accott, besides it's needless
to bespeak a place there, and If one would Secure the
best place he needs but write a line or 2 to the post
master at Naasden a day or 2 before. The Commissary told
us, we must be there to go with ye boat at 8, or we
should Come too late, We Stayed above half an hour at his
house before the boat went off, and drank a pint of wine
and half a bottle of spaw water, for which we were forc'd
to pay 90 str, for which reason I say let no one have any
thing out of the Common Road in any house where a boat
goes off. If you have you must pay Extravagantly for it,
I might have remembered this having been twice Serv'd so
before; (23) One payes Just as much for Carrying their
Coffers & ca thro' Muyden and from the boat When we land
up to the postmasters (to the Schipper's (24) man) as
the fstt of 'Em Comes to for a hampier or basket you may
pay nothing If not lockt; We pd the remaining post of the
Waggon to Osnabrug to the post Master at Naasden who is
a very Civil man they weigh'd only our 2 trunks and
deducted a 5 str for each. We saw the magazines and
fortifications & din'd there; the fortifications seem
impregnable and are kept in Extraordinary good repair,
the magazine is not very large or noble. The town of
Naasden is one of the frontiers of Holland, but a small

---

(23) Jonathan Belcher was one with a consistent value
     system: he was wealthy, lived rather luxuriously,
     was considerate of those in need, and like most of
     us, he became irritable when he felt cheated over
     minor expenses. Yet to read of a lone twenty-two
     year old American's frustration with wine and water
     expenses, 287 years ago, touring Europe, no doubt
     with his father's ample fortune, while Indians were
     attacking Massachusetts... it's perplexing. Jonathan
     Belcher was one of a kind!

(24) Regarding terminology, the post-master's head-
     quarters was the arrival and departure of the Post-
     wagon, a horse-drawn wagon, usually open, for
     delivering mail and carrying passengers between
     various towns. The post-wagon often was guided by a
     "postilion" on the left or "near" horse of the team
     of horses. The "schipper" was one who operated a
     small boat for transport. The schipperke breed of
     dog originated in Belgium and was used as a watchdog
     on such small boats.

countrey town; at half an hour after three we got into
the waggon, having but one passenger besides ourselves, a
Leipzig merchant, a very honest fellow and good company,
just without Naarden we were overtaken by Waggon with 3
East India Seaman going to Amersfort so drunk, That one
of 'Em was forc'd to be Carry'd thro' Mayden (as we were
told) on a Wheelbarrow, and lay as a dead Swine; When
we baited between Naarden and Amersfort, We Rencountred
Mr Musgrave and Fuller who had Come from Italy but last
from Hannover;"

[** Ed Comment Follows]
In the following August 12 entry Jonathan crosses the
border from Holland into Germany, on his way to Hanover.
He will meet the heir to the English throne, Sophia, in
Hanover on August 16. Note the important letters of
recommendation from England on August 15, Bluthwait and
Chamberlin. They feed the horse ("bait"), mention the
harsh penalty for hunting the Count's deer (August 13),
tip the man on horse back accompanying their wagon
("Postilion"-August 12), and describe the dangers of
wagon rides (August 14). Belcher's observations
occasionally provide an insight into the differences
between European and American culture: "I was surprised
to find a very good jack for roasting meat." Apparently
American rotisseries were more crude about 300 years ago:

"Tuesday 12th: We got the Waggones to bait at Loo instead
of a place (Call'd Appledore) and to Stay there 'till we
had Seen the late King Wm's house and gardens, which
indeed are very fine, the house Is built in the figure
of an N. It's well finisht within Side and the furnature
very Rich, the gardens are very large & have the finest
Cascades and fountains (It's Said) In Europe, being done
by one of the greatest Masters, We drunk some Coffee &
Tea, and gave the postilion a guilder for waiting for us
about 3 hours; at Deventeer we had a dispute about the
passage gelt   (25)   of the bridge wc: we pretended we
had paid at Naarden, but what we paid there was only for
the province of Holld as the Postmaster's son (whom we
met at Laisy) told us; The province of over Rykel Is
very large but barren, at Holderen a Village, Where we
baited I was surpris'd to find a Very good Jack for
roasting meat; They have a Corn mill, which Is turned

---

(25) gelt is a noun meaning money or gold.

with horses, which they use When there Is a long Calm,
There Is Very good hunting along a Rising track of ground
which Can hardly be Call'd a hill, Beyond that Is a
Village Call'd Goor, or Rather a tract of houses for a
mile or 2 together Scatter'd In some places and in others
Closer, at Delden in Westphalia we Eat very good ham,
and were reasonably treated there, In Coming out of a
village not far beyond Bentheim ye first Village in
Munsterland, the Waggoner thro' Carelessness had very
near overturn'd us (at noon day) down a very ugly, narrow
place, Where we had lost our limbs or our lives, but
thanks be to God We Just Escapt it; From the Province of
OverRykel, we Came to the County & town of Bentheine,
there Is an old Castle on a Rock, fine gardens within &
Two Companies for guards, It being very

Wednesday 13th: Early we Could not See it, the Comandant
not being up, about 2 mos before this time the Countess
of Bentheim a Widow, threw herself out of one of the
highest windows on a Rock; and was found on her back
naked, she was disorder'd in her head, and was watcht
for 3 or 4 dayes before by a Woman, who thinking
her pretty well that night went to bed with her &
fell a Sleep, which ye Countess observing took that
opportunity to accomplish her design, 'twas thought to
have proceeded from melancholly, the Estate being very
much indebted and she having liv'd at a high Rate for
some time at the Hague, thereby increas'd it, & being at
least forc'd to Come and live very Retir'd; her Spirit
Could not brook it; she left 2 Sons & a daughter behind
her; the Countess mother Is marry'd to the Grave
Van=Oxensten and was then at Schutterp an hour from
Benthem, where she Comes Every year to Receive her
Jointure; This Countrey Is most pasturage and pretty
good, some flax, full of wood, and a great quantity of
deer, which none but the Count may hunt undr pain of
death, yet very often they Come from OverRykel in the
night & shoot 'Em, and the night after Come and Carry 'Em
off, they are very troublesome to the Countrey people
who are forc'd to watch their Corn all night, the deer
not being inclos'd, from Schuttory we Came to Rhein a
Small town in Munsterland, from that thro' a Villa Call'd
Ipenbury, where the Steeple was thrown down in the great
Storm (which happn'd Nover: 26th: 1703) this town I think
belongs to the County of Lingen, which Is now the King of
Prussia's in succession from King Wm., the revenue of
which County I was told would amount to 100000 Guilders a
year, from that Village the way Is Extremely bad, first

going up a Steep hill, which Is as bad in the decent,
about an hour from hence we Rencounter'd Mr Cockburn &
another gentleman in a waggon they had hir'd from
Hannover. From Lingen we pass'd thro the County of
Fecklenburg, which was very pleast. between hills, with
wood & water, we had this Stage (which was 7 hours) a
Very Skilfull Waggoner, who drove us at a great Rate &
very dextrously thro' all that bad way, we Came to
Osnabrug between 8 & 9 at night and Stay'd 'till 11; The
Bishop of Osnabrug Is alternately Catholic & Luteran, the
Latter must always be of the House of Hannover, the other
they Choose where they please, the present Is of
Lorrain, a young man, not very fit for that post, much
given to Hunting, the Magistrary of the town Is Lutheran,
but the Catholics have a Chh, the Revenues of the
Bishoprick are 12000 Crowns, a mo. duly paid. Not far
from the post house Is the wine Cellar, We Supt at a
house 5 or 6 doors from ye posthouse where Except
pancakes we had nothing we Could Eat yet paid a great
Rate, as also Rhenish wine which was pretty good, and an
Extravagant Rate for spaw water, It Rain'd Just as we
went into the open Waggon or Rather a 4 wheel Cart, which
Is long and uncover'd, it Continu'd Raining very
plentifully till we got to Hannover, which Is about 80
miles from Osnabrug, at the gates of Osnabrug both the
Citizens & Soldiers keep guard,

Thusday 14th· It's dangerous to Sleep in the open Waggon
for you Ride thro' long, dark allies of Trees, whose
branches are Every now and then ready to Carry of hats
and Wiggs and sometimes may hurt you If not aware, Our
dinner Stage was at diepenan, where we Came like so many
drowned Rats, most things in our Coffers well kept, our
Cold fowl and other provisions stood us in good Stead,
they having nothing at this place to Eat or drink. From
hence we went to Laisey where we parted with our Saxon
who went in anoth. Waggon to Hamburg, about an hour from
Laisey we Cross'd the Weser in a boat pull'd a long by
ropes fastn'd to Each side of the River. We Set out about
9 a Clock & arriv'd at 6 the Next morning at Hannover."

[** Ed. Comment Follows]
Jonathan next enters Hanover, home of Sophia, Heir to
the throne of England. He remained there for eleven days.
There is an English company in Hanover, who served the
Royal Family in various capacities. This English company
may be important to Freemasonry. Belcher's letters of

recommendation indicate there may have been a 1704
friendship between the Belcher family and Mr. Bluthwait
and Mr. Chamberlin (See note 28 below). Mr. Colt is also
interesting as next month he will meet Jonathan in
Hamburg at the fascinating September 19/20 celebration.
Note the coffee house, Chapezeau's. Belcher's expense
account at the end of the journal indicates quite a party
there on August 24:

"Friday, 15th: at Delden the houses— begin to be made
after another fashion with large doors, for horses, Cows
& Swine all Enter at one door and lie mostly undr. one
roof. And the people here begin to look poor & miserable,
Neither have you anything like the Cleanliness of
Holland; you shall likewise See 5 women for one Man,
Especially from Osnabrug to Hannover; The Countrey all
along is but barren, some barley, most oats very Small &
short, yet there Is abundance of wood and they burn
nothing Else. They have great large Stoves in all their
houses Carry'd up to the Ceiling of their rooms, Neither
Men or women Comb their hair Among the Common people, but
are Nasty, go without shoes & Stockings, as soon as we
Came to Hannover we went to Chapezea's a french
Coffee man, who got us a lodging opposite to the Court,
but they made us pay 8 Gross   (26)   for staying an
hour in a Chamber at the posthouse, When we had dress'd
ourselves, we went and din'd at Chapezeau where we saw
Sr Rowland Gwin,   (27)   Mr Wind, who din'd with
us the other gentlemen not being here that day, but
Came in afterwards, they were all Extremely Civil, and Sr
Rowland offer'd in Case Mr. Pooley did not go in a day
or 2 to Hasen housen, to present us to the Electress-

---

(26) A "Gross" or groschen was a silver coin in Germany.
     According to Belcher sixteen "good grosches were
     worth a drittle, and six drittles were worth one
     Pound sterling. As an approximation, a gross was two
     and one half English pence.
(27) Belcher occasionally identifies Sir Rowland Gwin by
     his complete name, and in other entries, also quite
     correctly, as Sir Rowland. The man's first name was
     Rowland, and his last name was Gwin (sometimes
     spelled Gwynne). With respect to Belcher's tendency
     to periodically abbreviate names, one example is
     Lady Bellamont, abbreviated as "Bell," or "Bello:."

about 6 a Clock we waited on Mr Pooley, & I dd him 2
Lttrs I had from Mr Bluthwait & Mr Chamberlin, (28) He
rec'd us very Civilly & told us he would present us next
day to the Electress.

Saturday 16th: Next Morning he Sent and invited us to
Dinner, and about an hour after that he would wait for
us at Court to present us to the Prince. (29)   Before
we went out Mr Colt whose father was Envoy at Hannover
before Mr Creket, Came to Welcome us to town, about
3/4 after 11 we went to Court, where we found Mr Poley
in ye Prince's Anti=Chamber, who as Soon as he was
dress'd, Came out and Everybody made their bow to
him; Mr Poley presented us to him and told him what we
were. he Spoke only French, tho' he can Speak English,
after having Stay'd there about 1/2 an hour we went out,
and drove to Mr Poley's. 'Tis the Custome at Court to
Make a low bow to the Prince when he comes in or when he
looks on you first, then they Stand round him in hearing
and he talks with one or other all the time, and when you
have a mind to go away, you slip out Softly, when he

---

(28) Bluthwait and Chamberlin are important acquaintances
     of Belcher in the 1704 period. One clue to their
     identity is that Governor Joseph Dudley had several
     patrons in England, two of which were William
     Blathwayt, Clerk of the Privy Council to the King,
     and John Chamberlayne. If Belcher was a Freemason
     before he left England on July 8, 1704, Bluthwait
     and Chamberlin are worthy of further exploration.
     They may be associated with Freemasonry. Belcher
     wrote to Lord High Chamberlain in Dec., 1730 about a
     church matter in Boston. (B. P., Vol. VI, Pg. 66).
(29) The Prince was George II (1683-1760), who would
     Commission Belcher as Governor of Massachusetts and
     New Hampshire in 1730. The 1704 Prince would be
     King of England in another twenty-three years. As an
     aside, for those not familiar with Masonic history
     during the 1700s, Thomas Dunckerley (1724-95), was
     the illegitimate son of the Prince. His mother
     informed Dunckerley when he was thirty-six years
     old, and George II was dead. Some evidence of which
     is that Dunckerley was a gunner in the British Navy
     for twenty-six years. In any case Dunckerley was a
     powerful intellectual influence in eighteenth
     century Freemasonry.

looks Another way. We had a Coach that day because it
Rain'd, Else they do not use to take them 'till about 6 a
Clock, when they go out to Hasen house, we had a Very
good dinner at Mr Poley's, Mr Colt din'd with us and his
own Secretary, who Is a german but Speaks good English,
Before dinner I had a long discourse with Mr Poley about
the Scotch affairs he having rec'd the day before the
Resolution of their Parliament about the Succession. We
went home after dinner and return'd to him at 6 & so to
Hasenhousen. He went in his Coach and 6 & we in our
coach & 2. It's about an English Mile and an half from
the town, Where the Electress and her son the Elector of
Hannover   (30)   keep their Court, It has very large
gardens which are pretty Enough, but no great variety,
There Is a Theatre in them and an Amphitheatre, very
noble and Magnificent, with Several gilt Statues, they
have Sometimes playes acted there; there Is also the
finest orange house I have seen. We went up Stairs to the
Anti=Chamber where Mr Poley left us for a While and went
into the Electress's Chamber, after a little while he
beckn'd to us, and we came in, the Electress   (31)
stood about the Middle of the Room, and Just as we
Enter'd the door We Made a Very low Reverence to her,
then going up to her kneel'd and kiss'd her hand, after
this Ceremony was over, I told her: Thus, Madm The
Respect   and good affection which the Queen of Gt
Britain's Subjts (in N Engld.) have for the good Settlemt

---

(30) The Elector of Hanover was George I (1660–1727).
     There was a feud between George I, his son George II
     and daughter, Princess Sophia Dorothea. George I's
     wife, Sophia Dorothea of Brunswick-Celle had been
     held prisoner in Hanover since the 1695 period for
     adultery. She would remain a prisoner until her
     death. One of George I mistresses was the Duchess of
     Kendal.
(31) The Electress of Hannover, Sophia (1630–1714), was
     the grand-daughter of the King of England, James I.
     Sophia missed becoming Queen of England by a month.
     Sophia died in June and Queen Anne of England died
     August 1, 1714. Sophia's son, George I, became King
     of England in 1714. Historians consider Sophia, who
     at the least could easily converse in English, as
     more qualified as Queen of England, than her son as
     King. Belcher's Journal confirms that theory.

of yer Succession made me Ambitious of doing My Self this
honour to Come and pay my humble duty to yer Royal
Highness, she answerd. Sr I give you thanks and am
oblig'd to you for this Respect In short she Rec'd
me wonderfull kindly beyond any thing I Could Expect,
and was Continually questioning me about N England,
as the trade, people & ca; there were now in the
Chamber my Lady Bellamont; Mrs Wellden, Sr Rowland
and Several of the Electress's ladies of Honer:, We
had been inform'd by Mr Poley & Sr Rowland Both of the
Ceremonies to be us'd, and the Electress had been told by
both of 'Em of our arrival, afterwards ye Electress went
to Cards with my Lady Bellamt. & Mr Poley & play'd 'till
near Supper=time, the Elector's Bro: Duke Ernest   (32)
came into the Room, and after we bow'd to him, we talkt
with him a little in English, which he understands in
Reading very well, but Speaks it brokenly, after him Came
the Elector himself to whom we paid a very low obeisance,
and had a little discourse with him in French, While we
were talking wth: him a Servant Came and whisper'd him,
That Capt Bouche was Come Express from the Army and Just
arriv'd. He immediately retir'd and we waited half an
hour between hope and fear 'till his return, ye Electress
gave over play and went into her Closet, being a little
frightened, because of her having a Son in the army. At
length the Elector Came in again and told us the good
news, of the French and Bavarians being intirely defeated
by our Army and of Tallard's being a prisoner,   (**)
they immediately went to supper and Mr Poley because of
the good news, Stay'd that Night to Supper, which Else he
Seldom or never does. We went to town to Chapezeau's,
Where we Supt and told Mr Wind who was there the good
News, he Sent it Immediately to the English gentlemen
then at Mr Barr's, one of the principle gentlemen in
town;

---

(32) Ernest, the son of Sophia and brother of George I,
     became Duke of Brunswick after his father, Ernest,
     first Elector of Hanover, and Duke of Brunswick and
     Luneburg died in 1698.

(**) Camille due de Tallard (1652-1728), French Marshall,
     was captured along with 10,000 prisoners, by the man
     on the White horse, scarlet coat and the Garter,
     First Duke of Marlborough, John Churchill (1650-
     1722). The Duke was an ancestor of the famous Sir
     Winston Churchill (1874-1965), Prime Minister of
     England in the Second World War.

Sunday 17th: The Next day being Sunday We din'd again at
Mr Poley's, as did all the English gent. Except Sr
Rowland Gwin & Mr Molesworth who were at Hasen housen,
in the Evening we went thither, the Electress, Elector &
ca were all in the garden and all the ladies & gentlemen,
she walkt an hour or 2 and then went to Ombre,   (33)
just by the door of the orange house; they have fine
long glasses, open atop to Set on the table over the
Candles,   (34)   that the wind mayn't hurt 'Em.

Monday 18th: On Monday we didn't go out after dinner but
Stay'd to write Lttrs. to go by the post the Next day
this morning Mr Poltney Came to visit us; Mr Montague
(35) an English gentleman & his governour took there
leave of us the day before being bound for Hamburg==

Tuesday 19th: We went this Morning & return'd Mr
Colt's Visit, after dinner we went to hear the Elector's
Musick, where we had a Very good Consort 18 in compa. 8
Violins, 4 base, 2 bassons, 4 haut boyes, (36) after
this We went & Saw Mrs Weeden (possibly Welden -ed.) an
English lady who Is a Councellor's wife and Came there to
See the Electress, she Is one of the most homely women I
Ever Saw; from thence to Hasen= Where we walkt alone
with the Electress for an hour or more, there was also
the young Prince and Princess.

----

(33) Ombre is an old card game of Spanish origin.
(34) These "glasses" were probably similar to glass
     chimneys used on kerosene lamps today. The chimney
     was attributed to the assistant of Aime Argand in
     the 1700s. Argand was a Swiss chemist who invented
     the tubular wick.
(35) This Montague was unlikely to be the Freemason who
     was born in 1690, for the future second Duke of
     Montague would only be fourteen years old in 1704.
     Although the Freemason did marry a year later,
     there is no record of a continental tour in his
     extensively researched youth (see AQC 79, Pg. 70).
     It could of course be his rather loose living
     father, Ralph Montague, (1638?-1709) the wealthy and
     then Earl of Montague. Belcher does not give any
     other clues to his identity.
(36) A haut boy was a musical instrument, a coarser form
     of the modern oboe.

Wednesday 20th: Next Morning Mr Scot went with us to See
the rooms in ye Court and opera house, the Electress
Apartmt. are very fine, & particularly the presence
Chamber   (37)   which Is hung, with black Velvet lac'd
with gold & Silver with a massy table of Silver and
Stands of ye Same, there are also apartmt. for the Duke
of Tell & the Queen of Prussia, they are all full of
paintings & in going to the opera Room, there stood an
original being a st. John of _____   (38)
Valu'd at 500 Pounds str. The opera house Is
Extraordinary fine gilt from Top to bottom & all the
boxes and galeries lin'd with gilt leather, the Scenes
are also fine, The late Elector (39)   Spent a Vast
deal of Money upon O Peras and was at the Charge of
keeping a Set of players on purpose, but Since his death
there has been no operas acted, from hence we went &
viewed the Court Chappel, wc Is well adorn'd all gilt and
Sash lights to ye pews has a Noble altar and pulpit; In
the Evening Mr Colt drinkt Tea with us and we walkt round
the Ramparts, which have guns on all ye bastions and at
night Continels plaid;

Thursday 21st: Next day we paid Mr Poltney's Visit, Mr
Poley was then with him, in the evening we went out to
Hasenhousen and Supt at Chapezeau's on our Return, When
we Came home ye door was lockt and the boy gone to bed,
and though we knockt half an hour, We Could not
get in & were forc'd to go back to Chap= and sleep on
matrasses on the floor,"

[** Ed Comment]
Jonathan's embarrassment after being locked out of
his room continues and seems to have little effect
on the tavern born American tourist (see note 40).
The activities of court life gradually reveal a
casual life of entertainment, indifference to the
struggle of the common subjects, and rather severe

---

(37) Presence Chamber is the room in which a sovereign
     receives visitors.
(38) Belcher underlines a blank space.
(39) This would be the Electress of Hanover's, or
     Sophia's, late husband, Ernest Agustus Duke of
     Brunswick-Luneburg and Elector of Hanover, who died
     in 1698.

punishment to those who do not follow orders of the
Elector of Hanover (the later King George I would cut off
the fingers of a teenage oboe player). Belcher is a bit
defensive of his gambling loses in a card game with
Sophia: "We lost and no wonder, the game being new to
us." The fact that a twenty-two year old stranger from
America was able to play cards with the heir to the
throne of England didn't seem to be out of the ordinary
for the rather plucky Jonathan Belcher. The journal is
generally quite accepting of the very different culture
in Europe. On occasion, Jonathan is outspoken regarding
arrogance of power (footnote 82, for King William I in
the September 16 entry, later in the Journal). There
seems to be more criticism directed at impertinence to
authority than to inappropriate whims of authority.

"Friday 22d: Next morning all the town knew it and
laught at the Jest, Especially Mr Barr's daughters who
had Seen us out of the Windows, it being next door; to
'Em, My Lady Bellamont's Sister Sent us a Lttr to the
Abbot of Lambspring, for once we intended to have gone
thither this day & to return'd to Hannover; I gave her
man who broth. it 6 Gross who went and gave it his lady,
she bid him ask me what the money was for, such a simple
fellow was he. But It's not the custome there to give
money to servants.   (40)   We went to Mr Wind's
Chamber in the Morning and in the afternoon to see my
Lady Ann Bellamont, We Return'd her the Ltt she had
given us, because we had Chang'd our Resolution and
deferr'd our Journey 'till we went for good and all,

Saturday 23d: We went Next Morning to pay our respts to
Mr Poley, but he was not dress'd, then we went to the
Prince's levy and at 2 a Clock to the Consort of Musick,
it being twice a week. One of the haut boyes a young boy
& the best player had run away Since Tuesday, which was
the 4th time he had done so, the 3rd he was taken, he was
kept 15 dayes in prison & fed on bread and water, and now

----

(40) At this point, Belcher had been humiliated by being
     locked out of his lodging and forced to sleep on a
     mattress on the coffee house floor (Chapenenzeau's).
     After indiscreetly tipping the servant of a card
     playing associate of the Electress, many would be
     eager to continue their journey as planned. Jonathan
     Belcher is tenacious in his purpose.

the Elector Sent him word If he would promise to Run away
no more, he'd only Cut of 2 of his fingers, his answ:
was hewd. Run away a thousand times If he did not hang
him, The haut boyes are all Slaves, the Elector buyes
'Em from one at Cassel, who breeds them up and sells
'Em afterwards, as soon as the Consort was over, we
went to Hasen housen to wait on my Lady Bell: (41)
she was not in her lodging, but her niece was whom I
talk'd with a little last time we were in ye garden,
she is a Very free, Sociable temper & pretty handsome,
We Sat with her an hour or more, & then went up to my
lady, who was at Cards with some of the ladies of
honer., at 6 the Electress went into the gardens, and
after we had Walkt a little with her she gave us a Lttr.
she had rec'd that day from Prince Maxillian (her Second
Son) to read giving an accott: of the action of Hockstet,
that Evening we had the honour to play at Cards wth: her
at Lantiloo,   (42) which is entirely different from the
English way, as they play it there. There were at play
Her Royal Highness, my Lady Bell: Madm Bennison, Mr
Cockburn & I, When one gives the Cards to the Electress,
you rise & give them with Ceremony, but they that play
often, do it only the first 2 or 3 dealings, We both
lost & no wondr., the game being new to us, after play,
we supt with my Lady Bellomtt., who Is very kind and
good natur'd and Wishes well to Everybody;

Sunday 24th: Next Morning Mr Colt Came to our Chamber and
went wth: us to the gt. Chh, where they were to Sing the
Te Deum   (43)   for the Victory the most of their
Service before Sermon was Palms & Hymns Sung by Voices in
the organ loft & sometimes by the people, There were
also Violins, Trumpets, flute, & haut boyes. The Te Deum
was Sung by all the people after Sermon, It was also
Sacrament day, they gave the Communion at the altar, one
Minister the bread and another ye Wine, Each that Recd,
Came up to them & took it kneeling; from Chh we went to
the Ramparts & Saw the guns fir'd thrice Round, they
began Just as the Te Deum, began in the Court Chappel,
We din'd at Mr Poley's that day. after dinner we took a
Coach and had Mr Wind's compa. to see the Count deplat's

---

(41) Belcher occasionally abbreviates Lady Bellamont.
(42) Name of a card game, possibly lansquenet, Belcher
     lost about two Pounds and twelve Shillings.
(43) Te Deum is an ancient Latin hymn of praise to God.

house, which Is near the town, both the house & gardens
are Very fine, We Saw only the Count's Apartmt. which are
ye first Story, the Countess being then in ye other
above, They are full of pieces of paint, Several
originals Especially in his Closet, (44) the hall or
Room you Enter first, Is very glorious and magnificent,
painted from top to bottom. Near the house he has a
manufactory of whitning wax for Candles, They have an
Engine by which they break it in Water into small pieces,
'tis afterwards laid out to Whiten in the sun 'till It's
Enough, they never Cover it but in Windy weather, they
then melt it and make ye Candles which they Smooth
afterwards with a Roller on a Table & hang the Candles
out again. From thence We went to See the fall of Water,
about half a mile further, It's artificial, occasion'd
(I suppose) by their altering the Course of the River to
bring it thro' ye town, it falls but from a little
heigth, yet makes a great Noise and Is pleasant Enough.
We drove back to town and at the usual time all three
to Hasenh=, It was then Mr Winds fortnight turn of
Waiting, he being one of the Electress's Gentlemen,
He handed her down to the garden, we paid what we lost
the night before (45) and gave the Electress's
to the valet De Chambre Tis the custome here Never to
give the Money you loose the Same Night, but the first
after, or when you Come in a ps. of paper. I walk'd this
Evening with the young princess, Daughter to the Elector,
she Is of a Very Sweet Temper, and very Comely. (46)

[** Ed Comment Follows]

---

(44) "Closet" in this context is Count Deplat's private
     chamber for council or devotion.
(45) This refers to the Cambridge Massachusetts born
     Belcher, gambling at cards with the heir to the
     English throne.
(46) Princess Sophia Dorothea later married Frederick
     William I (1688-1740), a man George I, despised (See
     August 16, entry for Belcher's description of the
     "16 or 17" year old "rough hewn" Frederick
     William I. Princess Sophia Dorothea was the mother
     of the Freemason, Frederick the Great. Frederick the
     Great (1712-1786) once sent a note to another
     Freemason, General George Washington: "From the
     oldest General in Europe to the greatest General in
     the world."

The following brief entry is a remarkable example of Belcher's notorious routine ability as a polished social gentleman. Jonathan actually inspired George I to speak English for the longest time in three years! Belcher was described by Thomas Hutchinson, the last Royal Governor of Massachusetts, as "elegant, graceful, and hospitable." ("History of Massachusetts Bay," 1765, Pg. 281, Mayo Edition). Thomas Hutchinson, also noted of Jonathan: "By great freedom in conversation and an unreserved censure of persons whose principles or conduct he disapproved, he made himself many enemies...some never ceased pursuing revenge until they saw him displaced." In a word, Jonathan was socially at ease in any company and apparently rather outspoken. The following entry illustrates his remarkable social skills with the future King of England:

"a little after this the Elector did me the honour to talk English with me, and was very pleasant & Smiling he understands it pretty well, but Speaks it very indifferently, Sr Rowland Gwin told me that he had not spoke so much in three years before.

Monday 25th: Next day We We (as written-ed.) went to the Prince's Levy, he address'd himself to Us as Soon as he Came out, we told we were going away and ask'd If his Highness had any Commands for Berlin. This Is all the Ceremony of taking leave, he told us we had Spent but little time here, sd. he believed we found nothing diverting, so he Wish'd us a good Journey. We gave the English gentm. a dinner (cost a florin a head besides wine). We return'd Mr Molesworth's Visits this Morning, who had been twice to see us. their Visits here are Court Visits, they Take a turn or two abt the Room, or Sit half a quarter of an hour & so adieu. You Never go further than your Chamber door wth. a Visiter Except a person of great quality, The first time you Send your footman to know If they'r wth: in but after a little acquaintance Come wth: out Ceremony. In the Evening we went to Hasen housen, there were None but Mr Barr's daughters with the Electress, Mr Wind handed her Highness down to the gardens, and we them, and walk'd with 'Em the most of ye time. While we were there an abbess of a lutheran Monastery Came to see the Electress, who rec'd her with a great deal of kindness, & made a fashion of taking her in her arms while she stoopt and kiss'd her hand and her petticoat, all Strangers kiss the Electress's hand, tho not quite kneeling, yet with the knee bended. she play'd at Ombre with the Electress, my Lady Bell: always making the third, the Electress orderd the sloce (?-ed.) to Invite us to Supper, when the Electoral family Is Sat the Chamberlain shews Strangers their places. They keep but one Table, While they Stay at Hasen housen the Maids of honour and the gentlemen Eating with them. There were Then at Table Her Royal Highness, the Elector, Duke Ernest, one of the Duke of Wolfeinbuttle's Generals, the Abbess, Mr Cockburn & I & 7 gentlemen & maids of honour, There was but one Service which Consisted of 14 dishes, and nothing Is remov'd 'till the Compa Is gone out, one of the Pages Sayes grace before and after meat, Tis not the Custome to drink to any of the Electoral family, If they, you drink to, do not look towards you, you Send the page, who Stands at your back, to tell 'Em you drink their health, and then you bow to 'Em, as soon as they rose, We went before 'Em to the presence Chamber, to wait 'till they Came thro' Where we took our leaves. The Electress gave us a Lttr. to the Queen of Prussia, We kiss'd her hand kneeling as the first time, and made a low bow to the Elector and Duke Ernest & so come to my Lady Bellamont's apartmts. Where Mr Wind waited for us, both he and she Supping there that night, because there Was no Room at table, Else she Constantly Eats at table & he in his waiting time and other times When there Is room, We took our Leaves of my Lady Bellamt. & her Niece & went home."

[** Ed. Comment Follows]
In the next lengthy August 26th entry, Jonathan provides a rare contemporary account of the Elector (the later King George I), his mother, Sophia, and other members of the Royal family. He includes their entertainment, management style, income, personalities, interests, and a summary of the living conditions of the less fortunate in Hanover. Note the "picture" (painting of Sophia) given to Jonathan as a present from her to New England. It is probable that Sophia's present was based on the expectation that she would become Queen of England when Queen Ann died. A diplomatic gesture to key individuals in an English colony. It indicates that Belcher's American associates were known to include the Governor of Massachusetts, Joseph Dudley, and also the self made New England ship owner,

Jonathan's father, Captain Andrew Belcher, (1646/7-1717)
who was on the Governor's council in 1704. Dudley was
appointed Governor in 1702 by Queen Anne (1665-1714).
Sophia (1630-1714) died a month before Queen Anne.
George I became King of England:

"Tuesday 26th: Next Morning we took an Extra Waggon to go
for Lamb-Spring. We got Another Ltt from my Lady Ann
Bellomt. to my Ld Abbot there, and one from Monser. Barr
to ye Intendant of the mines at the Hertz, Mr Bouche. We
put up our things, pd. our ordinary, din'd at
Chapazeau's, took our leave of the gentlemen and Set out
from hence about 3 a Clock for Heldesheim. We took our
servant with us 'till we should come into ye post Road
from the Hertz. In the Summer time the Electress and
Elector live at Hasen housen and the young Prince &
Princess keep their Court in the town, When they don't
go to Hasen=, they play in the Evening and Compa. resorts
thither, Before they go to dinner there Is a Set of
trumpeters play to give the Servants Notice that dinner
Is ready, The guards are Chang'd betwixt 11 & 12 a Clock
the Haut bois (who have a livery) play all the way before
'Em, and While they Stand in the Court & Exchange the
Centinels- No horse guards there or at Hasen== Besides
the Musicians, who have Some More sons less Salary the
Elector keeps a troop of french Comediacy who (when the
Court Is in town) act once a week and in the Carnival
time twice or thrice.- The Elector Is a good Manager
and looks after Every thing himself, He has no favorites,
Nor has any of the family, He has a Council, which meets
once a Week, there Is also a Chancellour. His Revenues
are Reckon'd 300000 Pounds Str. a year, the profit of the
Mines alone amounting to 100000 Pounds of it, When the
Duke of Tell dies that dutchy falls to him which will
make him a great Prince. The troops of Tell and Hannover
in the Service of the allies are 15000 Men, they have
lost Several good officers in the last battle. He never
plays and Seems to be of a thoughtfull temper, yet I
don't See but that he talks free Enough, so Sophie haves
of him, That he's a man of little talk. He Is reckon'd
a Wise Prince, an Instance of Which he gave at the
beginning of this Warr, When the Duke of Wolfembuttle who
rec'd a Monethly pension from France, for the raising of
Men, Just as the Elector of Bavaria did, and he had
already got about 12000 Men on foot, the Elector of
Hannover undr. pretence of Changing his garrisons,
order'd all his troops to march in one Night, and to meet

at Wolkembuttle, Where they arriv'd Early in the Morning
Surrounded the town and brought away the 12000 Men
prisoner's to Hannover, Where all the officers were kept
'till that Duke gave Security for his good behavior and
the Soldiers Were Sent into the Service of the allies,
Thus the Elector in so short a time quash'd the design
that duke had been so long forming to raise a body of Men
to be Joyn'd by the French, which would have given a
great diversion to the allies. The Emperour might Easily
have Served the Elector of Bavaria at the Saucekolt, The
Elector's youngest Bro Duke Ernest Is a mighty Sweet
Temper'd man, Very familiar free & pleasant. He is
design'd for the Bishoprick of Osnabrug, and for that
Reason Is very Studious. The Electress looks something
old in her face, yet Is hale and Strong, has a good
appetite, Walks 2 or 3 hours together, she Speaks
English, high & low Dutch, French, Italian and Lattin
all those languages very well, she has been in France,
all over Germany, in Holland, Italy & (I think)
Constantinople, she Is very affable & inquisitive in
Conversation, Is kind & motherly to all English Even
almost to a Royal fondness, The young Price is brisk and
full of life, Speaks most French Never English, unless
Sometimes with Mr. Scot an English gentleman of the
Elector's; bad Lugus (?-ed.) be (illegible-ed.) neither
does he affect much talking with the English, indeed some
of the English have behav'd themselves, as to give great
offence and make 'Em to be despised, Especially my Ld.
Manlesfield & his compa the most Rakish, Scandalous
Embassy that Ever was heard off, Which was when he was
Sent by King Wm. to Complimt. the house of Hannover upon
the Settlmt of Succession and to Carry the Elector the
George (47)and garter; My Lady Bellamont has Apartments
in the Court while at Hasen: and When she doth not Eat at
Table, has her Meat dress'd particularly in the kitchen
for Her; The town of Hannover Is but Small, there are not
above 4 or 5 families of note in it, they have a Strange
way of building their houses, for Its only the first
Story wc: Is to be dwelt in, the Rest which are some
times 3 or 4 More Is only made for granaries, No Windows
but long Slits, they Say It was Contriv'd to keep Corn,
in Case of a Siege. The houses are generally very Large

---

(47) The George is a jewel showing a figure of St. George
     forming part of the insignia of the highest order of
     British knighthood, the Order of the Garter.

but little room in them, one great door at which Enter
Coaches, horse, Swine & ca. The Women here Walk the
Streets in White sheets instead of black Fales they Use
in Holland, things are pretty dear and If one has any
thing to do with a Tradesman, It's best to make the Bargain aforehand, our dinners Cost 12 Marien grosch (48)
a ps., Red wine 18 M: G: & Burgundy 24, but Mr. Colt
an English Gentleman took a Method Cheaper & better in
that Where he lodges he 'Companies him with- Strangers,
Where he Can improve his French & German Tongue, and
have all the News That passes, Whereby the other English
Gentlemen keep together, and thereby Can not improve in
any foreign language; We gave 2 Crowns (49) a Week
for our lodging, 8 good grosch a day to our footman he
providing himself with all Necessaries, & 12 Marien
groseh for Coach going to Hasen= & 12 Returning, tho' If
you Stay Supper It's more, If you take a Coach, by the
day 2 Crowns. 1/2 a day, one. They are made only for a
fosome (four people-ed.) as for the English gentlemen
there, they were all very Civil & obliging, Spend most of
their time in Reading indeed there Is little Else to do,
a Court life, being very Idle; Dressing and diversion Is
all their Care & Concern and they live in an Entire
oblivion of Religion and will (I fear) insensibly fall
into atheism, they Never go to any Chh nor mind Sunday
any more than any other day. Mr. Poley, Mr. Scot &
Colt go sometimes to the French Chh. Mr. Poley Is a
very Civil gentlemen, of good Sense, talks very Calmly,
lives Regularly & Seems to be Sound in his principles,
which I fear the Rest are not, yet I Must do 'Em

---

(48) A "marien grosch" was a low alloy grosch, with the
same stamp and appearance of a "good grosch." The
confusion must have been a problem, whereas 16
good grosch made a drittle, it took 24 marien grosch
to equal a drittle. A marien grosch equaled about
one and two-thirds of an English pence. Belcher
states at the end of the journal that one English
Pound equaled six German drittles.
(49) An English Crown equals 5 shillings. For general
reference, the English Crown was probably first
known as such when an Oxford Crown was issued during
the reign of Charles I (1625-1649). It was silver
except when a gold coin of similar value was issued
in the mid 1500s.

this Justice that they all live Soberly, not given
to drinking or any debauchery That Ever I heard off; Sr
Rowland Gwin keeps 3 or 4 Servants, a Coach, 4 horses &
a Chair, dines often at Hasen: Else goes out Every after
Noon, and reads to the Electress some English book (at
present Earl of Clarendon's History) (50) 'till about
the time she goes to Walk, When returns home, They
are all Except Mr. Poley and Mr. Colt, whom I never
heard on that head, mightily devoted to ye interest
of the Hannover house, and don't Care how soon they
Could have the happiness to accompany the Electress
into England, they fancy the Queen Is very unhealthy
& that she cannot live long, But that the Electress
will outlive her. The Electress did me the honour of
her picture to Carry with Me as a present from her
to New England, (51) but it not being quite
finisht, When I Come away Mr. Wind promis'd to Send it
to me to Amstr. The Chief Clergyman at Hannover Is
one Abbey Lockum, who Is Superintendant, they have
Nunneries for Women, but I think no Monasteries, Neither
do the Nuns take the Vow; but often Come out and Marry.
On all their altars they have Silver Crucifixes &

---

(50) Edward Hyde, 1st Earl of Clarendon (1609-1674) was
     Lord High Chancellor of Great Britain in 1658.
     He began his history after fleeing England with
     the then Prince Charles during the 1640s Civil
     War. He died in exile after opposing Charles II's
     divorce. His granddaughter, Anne, was Queen of
     England (1702-1714), while Sophia was reading the
     great "History of the Rebellion", finally published
     by Clarendon's sons in 1702.

(51) The painting provides a clue to the Electress's
     perception of Belcher's letters of recommendation.
     First of all Belcher's father, Captain Andrew
     Belcher, was not only a very wealthy Massachusetts
     merchant, at this time he was a member of Governor
     Joseph Dudley's Council in Massachusetts. He was on
     the Governor's Council from 1702 until his death on
     October 31, 1717. Dudley was aligned with Queen
     Anne, for the Queen appointed Dudley immediately
     after King William died in 1702. This would add to
     the evidence that Belcher was recommended by
     individuals in London of high political position,
     with a strong support of Belcher's position in New
     England. Sophia was quietly preparing to be Queen.

pictures Round, which are histories of our Saviour and of
his passion & ec. the Women Sit all in the body of the
Chh. the Men under the pillars and in the galleries, the
poor Scholars who all ware Cloaks go about on sunday from
door to door, singing in a body, which Is their Way of
begging; the houses have nothing of the newness of
Holland, the flies are very troublesome and bite one's
legs Most intolerably by reason of the horses daily going
thro' their houses; The Elector's Stables are not far
from the Court, We told 150 horses When We Were there,
and there are Stalls for above 200, the arsenal
Is Just by the Stables, all the Wood that Is burnt at
Court Is brought from the Mountains in the Hertz, Instead
of a Rattle which they have in Holland, they blow a
horn at Night Every hour. We did Not See a beggar in
all the town, tho' It's but a poor place, without almost
any trade. It Seems there Is Care taken to Maintain 'Em.
They have ye Same Custom as in Holland of Coming about
with a Velvet bag and a bell to it in time of Sermon for
the poor, and the Common people put on their hats
too, tho' Not so much, the Women Sit on their tales,
While the Minister prayes before preaching, but all kneel
when he Sayes the Lord's prayer; There Is an old fountain
of Rockwork with Several Statues round it before the New
Chh. It has been pretty Enough, but now in decay Neither
does the Water play any more. The ladies here all affect
to have black hair & ey=brows and for that End are forc'd
to grease it they that do so Never use powder. I told my
Ld. Bell: that the Indian Women in our Country do so too,
and she very imprudently told the Electress of it, who
lookt Very grave upon it and wd. Not own they did so
there. Why Sayes she do ye think the ladies grease their
hair here, O Lord Madm. sayes my L. Everybody knows that,
this gentleman observ'd it the first Night he Came here,
few or None wear patches, Nobody takes snuff in the
Electress's presence, If they do they turn about. all the
family have the Title of Highness, the Electress that of
Royal Highness sometimes, tho' in discourse, Sr. & Madm.
are oftner' us'd than any other Title. The Elector has 2
Turks that wait about Court, one of 'Em he took in
Hungary. He always wears the garter. He has No guards
When he goes out only a few servants. We Came to
Heldesheim betwixt 6 & 7 at night the way being good
from Hannover, at the gates one of the Soldiers Comes and
asks you, Whence you Come, Whither you go & What Countrey
Men you are, the first thing Everybody Must observe

here, Is the badness of the streets, for Worse Never were, I don't believe they have been Mended for some hundreds of years, you are Jolted to death and In danger of being overturn'd, the town Is much larger than Hannover, but Miserably poor. The Jesuits have a Convent here and give teaching to poor Scholars gratis, one Can't Walk the Streets but he'll be attack'd by 100 of these poor boyes begging with O Do mine, Dom: We went to a Convent of Benedictines, having seen the abbot at Hasen hausen some dayes before, 'tis Call'd the abbey of St. Michel, he made us welcome, We sup't there and he gave us a glass of Wine, the Monks were very Merry & laughing aloud and very heartily in another Room, one of the Brother's Came in to Conduct us in, he was a young, Smug, Wanton Ey'd fellow as ever I saw, (52) they are about 29 besides Servants and lay Brothers; the Bishoprick of Heldesheim Is worth a great deal more than that of Osnabrug but the town Is govern'd by it's own magistrates, who are Lutherans, the Chh: are also divided betwixt ym. and the Papists. The Elector of Bavaria's Brother was at the Same time, Elector of Cologn, Bishop & Prince of Liege & Heldesheim & Bishop of Ratisbon & a- and Now he has Nothing of these Revenues being In arrest by the Emperour, The abbot Sent a torch home with us Else we had broke our Necks in such dreadfull Way, We Lodg'd Near the postmasters Where they put us between 2 feather beds which Is a strange way of lying in hot Weather, how Ever I slept well Enough in 'Em, but Mr. Cockburn didn't like 'Em. We got up"

---

(52) The evidence of Belcher's dress and appearance is found in various parts of his journal, particularly his account of expenses at the end of the journal. It must have occurred to the "young smug" monk that Belcher was going to be unaccustomed to his accommodations that evening. Possibly that was what the laughter among the monks was based on. Belcher wore a powdered wig, carried a sword, purchased a cane for five guilders, and hired washer women, footmen, barbers, and various other luxuries. It is doubtful that the monks were frequently hosts to such boarders as the impeccably dressed and formally mannered, twenty-two year old, Jonathan Belcher... of New England.

[** Ed. Comment Follows]
Jonathan next starts off by wagon to Lambspring where
we note the activities of the refuge settled English
monastery after the thirty year religious wars in
Europe (1618-1648). Monastic life, in Lambspring, was
perhaps easier than some might think today of the early
eighteenth century: They had twenty-seven members and 100
servants; could whip and imprison and deliver criminals,
and "I thought the maid of the house, where the father
carried us to drink a glass of wine, was very free
and familiar with him." Jonathan was a sort of moral
policeman in Boston, he held the office of tithingman in
1714. The brief mention of Charles II (1630-1685) refers
to the 1651 period. Charles fled to France, two years
after his father, Charles I, was beheaded as King of
England. Charles I (1600-1649) was King when Belcher's
grandfather, Andrew, immigrated to America in 1638. The
political notions of the Catholic monastery is evaluated
by Jonathan: "Tis a good arguement that Charles I was no
Papist... if they (the monks) did, they'd not only have
his picture, but Cannonize him for being Martyr'd by
Hereticks." Note letter that Belcher carried for Austin
Belson:

"Wednesday 27th: Next Morning by 4 & set out by 5 in
another post Waggon to Lambspring. We had very bad way,
we passed thro' a Small Village Call'd Saltzerdal, from
their making of salt, they have salt springs there; of
which they make it, they have no Chimneys in this
Village; but the Smoke Comes out at their doors &
windows, If they have any.-We Came about 8 to Lambspring,
which lies Extremely pleasant on the brow of a hill, and
Surrounded by 2 or 3 more Cover'd with wood. We lighted
at a house Near ye Convent and went there a little after,
and Saw my Ld. Abbot, Capt Knightly his brother and 2 or
3 of the monks, the Abbot and his brother were Just going
to Heldesheim, they were very Civil and Kind & Made us
Several Compliments, We dd   (53)   Capt. Knightly the

_____

(53) The abbreviation dd (possibly meaning "did
     deliver") is again used with the commonly used
     letter of recommendation. Lady Ann Bell: means
     Lady Bellamont who Belcher met eleven days before
     with the Electress of Hanover.

Recommendatory Ltt. We had from my lady Ann Bell:, after
that we went to Dinner wth: 'Em and then they went away,
My Ld. Abbott Recommended us to one of the Fathers, to
take Care of us in his absence. As soon as they were
gone this fathr. Carried us, first thro' all the gardens
which are large & full of fruit trees, abundance of pruin
plums, by wc: they make money, a Small red fruit they
Call a Cornelian, English apples & ca., In my Ld. Abbot's
garden Is a little Oratory,   (54)   built by the last
abbot, who resign'd it to this prest., at the End of the
other garden; which Is the Monks, there Is the spring
that gave Name to the place, It was first built for a
Nunnery by the Count of _____"s (as written-ed.)   only
Daughter, who was the first abbess and indued by him
largely with all the land about it, in the year 847 or 8,
but these wanted good water, the Story goes that the
Abbess was playing with a lamb, she had brought up, which
upon a shepard's going by (if I remember right) jump'd
out of her lap; and Where it light, there Sprung out
Water, Whence It has the Name of Lamb=Spring, the Spring
Is now Cover'd with an arch and Is pretty good Water. It
Continu'd a Nunnery 'till the Sweedish Warrs, When the
Nuns were forc'd to fly and all things Seiz'd on and
destroy'd, It was how Ever restor'd at the treaty of
Westp=halia, and (upon application of the English Monks
(who had no Refuge) given to them; The archives were
preserved by an old Woman, by putting them in a Chest
wth: flax over 'Em, which was not Regarded. They are
Superiours of the Village and all the land about the
house Rents are their's, but they pay Taxes to ye Bishop
of Heldesheim. They Can whip and Imprison but inflict no
further punishmt., but deliver the Criminal over to
Heldeshein, They only have the privilege of hunting,
which Is very good, great herds of wild swine. They have
above 100 head of Cattle, 1000 sheep, great flocks of
geese, ducks & ca. they kill about 80 hogs yearly, the 0
economist take Care of all these things and of tilling
the ground, When the Corn Comes into the granary & the
Meat into the Kitchen, they are undr. the Inspection of
others. They have 100 Servants belonging to ye house and
are not above 27 fathers and Bro: but they have Several
young Men and boyes, who are boarders at the Rate of 20
pounds a year, some always Coming & going, some few lay
Brothers and one or two Seculars. They that Enter have

---

(54) An oratory is a chapel for private devotions.

their probation years, and are askt in that time,
solemn'ly 4 times, If they Continue their Resolution, but
many times quit before It's at an End. They are Most of
'Em younger Brothers, some of good families, who have not
forgot how they liv'd in the world, they often travel,
and go in to England. They are oblig'd to be up at 4 a
clock to go to mass 'till, after that they Study 4 hours
'till high mass.— Besides they'r being tied to their
hours, I see no other Mortification they Can pretend to,
but that they live as Much as their Ease & take their
pleasure & diversion as much as any that live in the
world, Excepting women, only I thought, the Maid of the
house, Where the father Carry'd us to drink a glass of
wine, was very free and familiar with him. they told us
yy (Belcher's abbreviation, "yy" may mean something like
"that they" in this case –ed.) were often Merry among
themselves & have dancing and other diversions, Neither
have all of 'Em forgot God's Study, God bless my soul
& ca. on occasion. They live Retir'd from the world,
but for ought I Saw, their Concern & Care for it, Is
as great as If they liv'd In it. In their gardens
they have large fish ponds, which furnishes ym:
on fast dayes. From the garden the father's Carry'd
us up to the Library, where they have a pretty
Collection of books, (55) all that I lookt to,
were given by My Ld. Mosdant. He shew'd us a shirt,
which King Charles the 2d. had on when in disguise after
Worcester, It was as Course as any Meal Sack, when the
King came to_____'s (56) house a priest,
who was there found him very Un Easy, and upon the King's

<hr>

(55) Belcher was a sizable book collector for the early
     eighteenth century in America. He not only is
     credited with a leading part in founding Princeton
     College, he left 474 volumes of books to that
     college from his estate in 1757.
(56) Belcher used coded names in much of his
     correspondence as Governor. The interception of his
     bold writing was apparently on his mind. In this
     case, since Charles II led the most immoral
     reign in the history of England, he was not a
     favorite of the adventurous, but still prudish
     Belcher. Either Belcher could not recall the name
     after the day's events, or perhaps this was
     Belcher's, pre-Victorian, method of protecting the
     innocent family name of such a dolt.

Complaint, bought him a shirt of his and Sent this for a present to ye Monastery. In looking over the books of devotion the father fell out agt. the Pietist's at a most prodigious rate & told us Several Stories of their Madness and folly (as he call'd it) I found none of the best of that kind here but he told me Most of those books were in private chambers. from the library, we went to their Chh which they built new about 30 years agoe, It's pretty neat and fine, adorn'd with many pictures drawn by alay=Brother of the Convent. There are 7 altars in all, They have a fine, large organ; the Sacrist shew'd us all my Ld Abbott's robes, which are most of 'Em Rich and fine, his Crosier of Silver, his Mitres very rich, one of which was presented by King James the 2d. wrought all over wth: gold Wire Another Was wrought by an English girl wo: liv'd Sometime in the Convent and Is now a profess'd Nun in a german Nunnery. The Church lies low and Is very damp which spoils ye pictures, they designed a Steeple but the foundation would not bear it. After this We went and took a glass wine, and talking of the Strangers at the Convent, the father Mentioned Mr. Austin Belson, (57) for whom I had a Ltt. thinking to have found him at Amstr. and had his compa. to Hannover, We desired his Compa., he told us he had been there three Weeks. We Supt with 4 or 5 Monks Among whom was my Ld. Frederick Howard (uncle to ye prest. Duke of Norfolk)- As we guest by his Carriage & discourse having more life & Air & Courage in his talk than the Rest. We lay in a Chamber in the Stranger's apartmt. where were the pictures of King Charles ye 2d. King Ja. 2d., his Queen, the Pretended Prince of Wales & his sister. Tis a good argument (I think) That King the Charles 1st was no Papist, That they themselves did not look on him as such, If they did, they'd not only have his picture; but Cannonize him for being Martyr'd by Hereticks. The Conditions Requir'd of those that Enter there, are, That they Must be English, Educated to & have a genius for learning, of a good family, tho' that they do not so much stand on, If other qualifications are not Wanting, they Equally admit with or without Money. When

---

(57) Mr Austin Belson is worthy of further research. He may be associated with the Belchers, or friends of Belcher in London. We now know that D. E. Cockburn accompanied Belcher, and Belson was expected on the trip from Amsterdam.

they take the ordrs. they Make a Will and dispose of what
they have Either to Relations or to the Convent. They had
procur'd us a waggon to bring us to Sasin, so We Set out
this"

[** Ed. Comment Follows]
For those intrigued by the methods of manual labor nearly
300 years ago, the next few days provide fascinating
descriptions of silver mining. The terminology of water
"wheels," drawing up buckets of ore, the "wildman," the
"beaters," and the eventual oven provide knowledge of
mining with the manual struggles of the "good old days."
Jonathan's adventure into the mines may be motivated by
his Simesbury, Connecticut, copper mines, which he
eventually gained control of from the heirs of his
maternal grandfather, Jonathan Gilbert (1618-1682):

"Thursday 28th: Morning after We had breakfasted for
that place. We Stay't No longer there than till we got
fresh horses and a Waggon, Which brought us to Clausthal
ye Chief town in the Hertz, thro' the Worst way that
Ever man travell'd. Tis all Mountainous yet Very pleasant
to the Eye, Covered with tall Streight firr and green
plots of grass, a great deal of the woods Is cut down
for, the Service of the Mines at the Wild Man, which
Is the first town in the Hertz. The Water Runs out from
the Mines, at Clausthal which is a mile distant- I mean
6 English miles,   (58)   so that one Can go all that
Way undr. ground in a post Waggon, We Came to Clausthal
between 4 & 5 a Clock in ye afternoon and lodg'd in the
Council house Just by the great Chh (which is Cover'd
with lead). We Went Immediately to Monser De=boucha who
lives in a palace, as great as a Prince, We delivered
him Monser De=barr's Ltt., he rec'd us civilly, ask'd
some questions, and order'd one of his gentlemen officers
to shew us the Works.=====

Friday 29th: Next Morning the gentleman Came to go with

---

(58) The only explanation for "a mile" being "6 English
     miles" is some connection with Belcher's familiarity
     with leagues as a sea measure. A league varied from
     about 2.4 to 4.6 miles at different times and in
     different countries. A League is generally called
     5.56 kilometers, possibly this was his meaning.

us, He first Carry'd us to the Mint, Where we Saw 'Em
coin both great and Small pieces & Edg'd the great ones
with these Ltts. <u>Om hertz der Thaler Klingt Das Landt</u>
<u>die rugte bringt, in the mines the dollars clink, pick</u>
<u>fruit the earth yields</u>. from thence We went to the
Mouths of Several Mines, a great large Wheel
a good Way undr. ground turn'd by the Water,
draws up the buckets wth: oar from the bottom, they
go down by ladders, at another whole, They have
Another Machine to draw up ye Water from the bottom
& throw it into Canals, that Carry it out at the
Wildman, the Wheel that Moves this Engine Is also turn'd
by Water & generally at a great distance from the Mouth,
But in Many of the Mines they are forc'd to draw up the
oar by Horses, for Want of Sufficient Water, there Is
great difference in the oar, some being Much Richer &
finer than others, some have Silver (lead) some Copper
(59)   & some all three. From the Mines We Went to the
Mill which they call Bugwyrken, This Work Is all done by
the boyes, Where the oar Is beat to powder, It is thrown
In Small quantities Undr. the beaters or pounders the
Water Constantly falling down & driving it forward thro'
a Sieve of Brass, from Whence a long Several Channels,
'till it Settles all along, that which Settles soonest Is
the best being the heaviest. They take it Up out of these
Channels & throw a Small quantity of It into a Kind of
Square Tub with Water, ye one beats with a Stick and
Stirs round 'till he throws it all out, from which It
Runs down a board Sloping Cover'd with Cloths all along,
to which the oar Sticks as it Runs along, and What Is
light Is Carry'd by the Water, then they take the Cloths
& Wash the oar from 'Em in tubs, Which Setling Is then
fit for an oven, Where it's only so much heated as to
Cake together, from that oven, It is carry'd to a
furnace, where It is Melted and as it Melts, runs down
into a hollow, from that they let it into anothr in the
ground, the dross on the top Is like the Scim or Cream of
milk Its good for Nothing they take it off by Iron forks,
and the Mettal they take Up in an Iron ladle & put it
into Molds of a Round form. These Cakes they throw into
An Anothr. oven, Where you See the Mettal, boil & Melt

---

(59) Belcher ran a copper mine in Simsbury Connecticut at
least as early as 1715. The mine was leased among a
company of investors. (see letter to John White
1715).

like lumps of pease, this has 2 bellows, One to blow the
fire and another, Which Makes a Terrible Noise to blow
the lead from the Silver, Which falls to the bottom, but
I could not Rightly Understand yt. operation Whither the
lead was blown, the officer that Went with us Speaking
only German, and you May Sooner as Understand Chinese
than One of these Workmen, The Miners & ca. having a
language of their own. The Silver Is afterwards Refin'd
and Markt according to It's fineness & Sent to the Mint,
Whence It's Carry'd to the Treasury Weekly. In all these
ovens and furnaces they throw in great quantities of wood
to Increase the heat, with the oar & mettal. & some of
the fires are frightfull and terrible to look at, it
brought to My Mind the fire of Hell, and <u>who can dwell</u>
<u>with everlasting burnings</u>. These were all the Several
operations We Saw, which I Could not perfectly Understand
for the reason aforesd. Neither Could I ask such
questions as I would have been glad to know, and Which
might have given me a perfect knowledge of them. Who Ever
goes to See ye mines here, had need have a mine of Silver
to Satisfie all those that Crave Money of one, the boyes
running after one Continually, besides what one gives at
the several houses.   (60)   Mr. Bouche did us the
favour to order one of those they Call Sworn Men to go
down to the Mines with us

Saturday 30th: Saturday morning they Never going down
that day, Mr. Cockburn did not Care to go down, but I
dress'd My Self in Miner's habit & went down above 400
foot   (61)   and was in Several passages Where they
were digging. They bore holes in Several places in the
Rocks with Iron instruments, and put gunpowder therein
and by a train (a trail of powder- ed.) blow it up, but
they Must be very Carefull in this, Else It very often

---

(60) To those that might have missed it, this is
     Belcher's dry New England humor: if you want to see
     the mines, you had better be rich enough to pay all
     the beggers.
(61) What follows is evidence that Belcher was not a
     contemptuous Brahman with a Master's degree from
     Harvard. This is a premeditated brazen adventure,
     illustrating his hunger for information. It is
     equivalent to climbing a twenty story building, on a
     wooden ladder by the light from a torch.

does Mischief also very often Vast pieces of Rocks fall
in & Sometimes kill the Workmen. All the Way you go down
is Supported by Vast quantities of wood & great trees,
When you go down there Is one before and Another behind
you with lights to guide your Steps, and If the Candle
happens to go out Its's a great wonder If you don't
perish, the passages in the Mines being so Many and
different. They begin to Work about half an hour after
five, but before they go down, they Meet all at four &
have one to read prayers to 'Em and a Chapter or two in
the bible, because they may Chance never to Come up
again. They told me I was but half Way down but I dare
not Venture any further, They Work abt. 6 hours and are
then reliev'd by others, they blow up about 11 a Clock
and in 2 or 3 hours after break It in pieces. They Carry
Each an half glass to know the time by. Every passage has
it's Name and Every place Where they Work, so that they
have towns and Streets below as well as above ground and
Every Mine has a name also, In some places Where the oar
Is Very good, they Work night & day on Saturday all the
men are paid off their Weeks Work in the Council house.
This Is also Market day for all manner of things being
pay day. Many of the Miners drink and play away their
Money before Monday Morn', notwithStanding they labour so
hard for it, and In daily danger of their lives, There
are about 2000 Men belong to the Mines. Several officers
keep their Coaches & dress well. At the refining as they
told us, there had been brought in above 2000 oz. of
Silver that week. The Elector of Hannover has the Sole
advantage, as a Prince of four of the best Minetowns in
the Hertz, the other three are in partnership with the
Duke of Wolfembuttle of which the Elector has 4/7.
Besides his share as a Prince, he has a great Interest as
a Proprietor and Several other advantages. Mr. De Bouche
Is intendant over all the Hertz and all the Mines
belonging to the Elector, but the Duke of Wolfembuttle
has an Intendant for his part. There Joins to Clausthal
another town Call'd Saltzerdal Which Is in partnership.
They Reckon 2000 houses & 10000 Inhabitants In Clausthal.
The men here generally Marry Very young at 14 or 15 and
Commonly before 20, Especially those that Work in the
Mines, because they are afraid they should die 'Ere they
Tast the pleasures of Matrimony. They have a great Many
Children and you shall see 6 or 10 people in a little
house. There Is good pasturage about the town a great
Many Cows, and some goats, which give Very good milk, the

Water Is very bad, beer not good, but they have good
Rhenish Wine, the Seasons here are Very late, they were
but Making their hay the latter End of this moneth. We
eat good Strawberries at Mr. Bouche's, the gentleman
who shew'd us the Hertz din'd with us twice, & presentd.
us with a Chart of the Hertz done by Himself.

Sunday   31: Next day Mr. Bouche Invited us to Dinner,
Which was very good, There were some of the officers
there who paid him the same respect, as If he had been
the Elector, he gave us a glass of Excellt. Champaign.
He is absolute here for all depends on him, he lives in
great State, When he went to take the air in his Coach
and 6, he had four Servants riding before & after him.
We went to the postmaster after dinner intending to go
that afternoon, but he told us his Waggon and his Coach
were broke, and that he Could not give us one 'till Next
day, besides some other Excuses, We thought he had
only a mind to put us off,   (62)   and so we went
to Mr. Bouche desiring he would ordr. us a Waggon that
night. He Sent for the post Master and gave him such a
Reprimand as made the poor fellow tremble Come hat
in hand to us. But We Could not get away, for he
had not got his Waggon Mended, and We should have
been benighted, and Were therefore oblig'd to Stay
'till Next Morning. The Hertz are Worth one's Seeing,
'Tis another kind of living there and It's Worth
observing the great difference there Is in the Conditions
of Men. These poor people are at a prodigious labour, but

---

(62) This is a minor point, but it demonstrates
Jonathan's life long trait: in spite of the
consequences, he often refused to accept limits from
those he perceived as subordinates. He was
unsuccessful in this case, but as usual he made
his point for the future. It is complex to justify:
Belcher was very generous with his close allies, he
gave one quarter of his fortune to one of his three
children (13,000 Pounds) to go to school in London
for ten years, thus he could not understand those
who were not loyal to him. In this case Jonathan
had spent over two Pounds Sterling seeing the mines,
(plus tipping beggers and postilions) he might have
had a mild attack of disloyalty and felt he deserved
better service. However you read it, Jonathan
Belcher would be reckoned with.

It is for others not ym: Selves tho' they have the Silver
in their own ground, & dig it with their own hands, yet
they must be beholden to others for it, and have Nothing
but what they have them. And What Is as strange, the
little they have they Spend it as foolishly, as If they
had it all, Cards and dice Is their pastime as well as at
Court, and here in they agree with the greatest and
Debauchees, in that they Spend all the time they have to
themselves in gaming and drinking so that many times
they'r oblig'd to live on bread and Water all the week.
'Tis also something strange to See with what prodigious
labour Silver Is got and with What profuseness it Is
spent, nothing Is harder Come at and nothing Easier
parted with, yet 'twould Make a Man a Miser to be A Mo.
or so at the Mines."

[** Ed. Comment Follows]
Jonathan next travels 160 miles in seven days, with time
and energy for touring in between. There are a few
problems, "stinking duck" for dinner, and "ye people
are uncivil." At any rate, he arrives in Berlin (a major
stopping point) on September 7, 1704. According to my
calculation, the wagons traveled about three miles
an hour. We are talking about eight hours a day on the
road for a week. Jonathan rarely complains, although
at the end of the journal he states: "you'll find your
teeth so numm'd with the cold that they seem to be loose
in your head, and your gums are so sore, that you
can't bear to put your teeth together but as the fun
& the heat increase, they recover." He also mentions
clothing in the cold: "boots lined with fur, & coats
lin'd with it also, and for their head a thick cap
with a neck to it, that comes down to their shoulders
and covers most of their face before... some travel with
masques (face mask- ed.), with glass eyes to 'em." (see
Pg. 118). The Journal continues:

"Sept. Monday 1st: This Morning We left Clausthal at 6 a
Clock, and came to Goslar about half an hour after 9. the
Way Is bad, but we had been us'd to so very bad Way, that
We thought Every thing Else Easy. Goslar lies at the
foot of the hills and Is an Imperial free City, Lutheran,
but in the Bishoprick of Heldesheim We went after dinner
to See the Dome Chh, Where in the Quire, is the Altar of
a Saxon, heathen God call'd Crodo, and Just behind it Is
the Statue of our Savior Sweating blood, In a Chest the
Statue of Matilda Daughter to the Emperour_____

(63)   who was bury'd there. In the body of the Chh a large Crucifix of the altar, with the 2 thieves on Each Side, the Centurion and the Soldier piercing our Savior's side, this Is done so much to the life that It is really affecting. Near the altar Is a former Emperour's Chair of Stone, with a brass back, at the coming in there Is painted on the Wall the picture of a most prodigious man, with a great oak for his Staff, whom they Call the great Christopher; They told us also a Story of a great Devil's speaking thro' a hole at the further End of the Chh, but I Could not Rightly Understand it; from hence We went to the Town Cellar to drink a glass of Wine, which we got, very good. The houses here are mean and low, & yet here are some people of fashion. There are mines near this town but not depending on them, for they have no ground almost belonging to them without their Walls. There Is a great deal of Copper in the oar here & some gold, but they are not near so considerable as at Clausthal, the Way of Working Is Intirely differt. too. but We having seen those at Clausthal, We thought it not Worth While to be particular as to these. We stay'd in this town 'till Tuesday after dinner, because we intended to travel by the ordinary post, wc. goes not from Halberstat 'till Wednesday, so that by being misinformed at the postoffice at Clausthal We lost four days, Which were Murder'd in being spent in such pitifull places.

(64)   This night

Tuesday 2d: We Came to Wernigoroda thro' a pleasant Villa about half way Call'd Islenburg, Where the Count of Wernigoroda Resides, tho' he has a great house at that place, because they of the town are not well affection'd to him, We lodg'd at a house, Where the man was Buagomaster, Ampthuan, & postmaster General, made such by the King of Prussia, who has Seiz'd on the County of Wernigoroda, so that the Count has but a Small part left him, he was Cousen to King William, & to the King of Prussia.

---

(63) As written, Matilda was probably the daughter of the King of England, Henry I. Matilda (1102-1167) was promised the English Crown by the weak King Stephen (1135-54), civil war erupted and eventually Matilda's son Henry II (1154-1189) became King. "The Emperour" in this case is probably Henry I.

(64) Time wasn't wasted for four days, it was "murder'd."

Wednesday, 3d: The next day about 6 in the Morning We
set out for Halberstat Which Is but 2 miles further, on
the Right hand We Saw the Castle of Regenstein on a
Mountain, the Count of that Name dying wth: out Issue
his lands were divided between the King of Prussia & the
Duke of Wolfenbuttle at _____ (as written- ed.)
A Mile from Halberstat, We saw another Instance of the
danger of having too powerfull a neighbor, There Stands a
great house, in which formerly liv'd a gentleman, who had
lent 50 or 60000 Crowns to the Count of Regenstein, and
had from him that house and the Superiority of the Burg &
ca. 'till he sh'd be repaid the Money. But When the King
of Prussia took possession of his inheritance, he told
the gentleman he had had these things now as many years,
as that he had Rec'd the money again, and so turn'd him
out of all, but he gives a 1000 Crowns a year to his son
during life. When we Came to Halberstat We found the post
Waggon had gone away the night before, which put us to a
Confounded Nonplus. But We Resolv'd to take an Extra
Waggon to Magdeburg. There We Went & Saw the Dome Chh,
Where are Several fine tombs, and four great pillors that
have Each other Small ones round 'Em, That Sound
Musically like so many Chimes, all different notes. There
is a Woman there that paints very well, they Call her the
English Woman, but she was born in Portugal, her father
Came to England with Queen Katharine and she Marry'd a
german painter that Setl'd at Halberstad, she Is a Widow
& Rich. It was this day the Monethly fast throughout all
Brandenburg. We Saw Several a gentsel (probably means
gentry- ed.) people here, and there are a great many
french, after dinner We Set out for Magdeburg Where we
arriv'd about 8 a Clock, by the Way We Saw Several
gentlemens houses. at a Village about a mile from
Halberstat the King of Prussia has a house and in the
chappel Is the first organ of all Germany. We Were
Examined at the gate of Magdeburg Where Stood a guard of
24 horses.

Thursday 4th: Next Morning We went and (illegible- ed.)
the dome, Where are a great Many Curiosities, but
there being a printed list of 'Em, shall Refer
to that. Just by the Dome the King has built a new
house of Two stories, It is not yet finish'd, but
the Second Story Is furnish't tho' not Very Richly.
He Is Making new fortifications about the town and a
Cittadel on the other Side the River, In the New town or
Suburbs Is a Catholic Nunnery, rebuilt lately and not

quite finisht, We heard their Vespers, there were not above 12 or 14 of 'Em, they pronounc'd the lakue Very distinctly, almost the half of the Inhabitants are french, the town lies Convenient Enough for improvemt on the Elb Which Runs up to Hamburg, and here Is a great Corn Trade, that day We were there above 100 waggons loaden therewth: Came into town, It is ships of from thence to Hamburg and so to Holland.

Friday 5th: the Next Morning We took place in the lacad Coach as they Call it (that Is a Waggon for goods & passengers Cover'd over) because the post Waggon did not go 'till Saturday Night, We baited first at Horeseaufts, Where We Could not but admire the humour of the people who though poor Enough, would not Sell us any plums, tho' their trees were ready break with 'Em, because they would not be at the pains, or were not us'd to Sell 'em. We lay that Night at Siesa, Where we Cookt a Very good Supper for ourselves, and the people Were very obliging, at

Saturay 6th: three Next Morning we were in the Waggon again & Come to Bradenburg about 10, we had a Miserable dinner there, the Master of the house, had been in England & spoke a little English, yet he had the Imprudence to give us only a Stinking duck, one that was half putrify'd. We Came this Night to a little Village Call'd Wostermart, Where the house they brought us to Was so bruitish, that We all remov'd to another and lay there, and indeed all this road ye people are more Uncivil and brutish, than any that I traveled."

[** Ed. Comment Follows]
Jonathan next arrives in Berlin, where he remains for ten days and writes extensively. Here Jonathan lodges at a recommended French "ordinary," eventually meets the English Envoy, Lord Raby, and various others of the English "company." The wealth of the King of Prussia provides an early insight into the beginning of Prussia's enormous rise to power. Prussia was the leading Kingdom of Germany in 1704, and included almost all of Germany's sea coast. The Queen is introduced to Belcher, and the casual nature of Court life is apparent. The Queen is the daughter of Sophia, who Belcher met in Hanover. The Queen's son, Frederick William, "a tough, unhewn, clumsey youth," married George I's daughter, who Belcher also met in Hanover. Frederick William's son was the famous Frederick The Great, who was a Freemason.

The story from the famous Leibnitz (September 11),
is an insight of "scientific" thought in 1704:
imprisonment of a "'prentice" by the King in an effort
to promote his own wealth. The 'prentice was converting a
"groach coin" into gold! There are several footnotes to
explain the antiquated terms used in Berlin. Next stop
the curious fellowship in Hamburg, September 19th:

"Sunday 7th: Next morning about 4 we proceeded on our
journey & Came thro' Spandow, which Is fortify'd and at
the other Side of the town a fort or Cittadel, very neat
and surrounded with Several broad ditches fill'd
by a River that Runs by the town. It's made use of
as a prison for State pris'ners. Not as far from
it on the Right hand Is Cottl. Bulan's house given
him by the King. he Is governour of ye Cittadel and a
little Way further you Enter a Wood, which brings you
almost to Berlin, in the middle of it Is the Queen's
Residence a fine house. Berlin affords a Very fine &
agreeable prospect on that Side We entered it. We Came
to town abt. 11 a Clock, and after having Stopt at 2 or 3
places, were Set down at the Custom house=yard, Where
all our things Remained 'till 4 in the afternoon, and
then the Vissiter Came and lookt into our trunks. The Way
from Magdeburg to Berlin Is generally Sandy, but nothing
so bad as represented to us. Neither deep 'till near
Berlin. the Waggon we Came in Is a Very Slow and dull
kind of traveling, yet It has this advantage it keeps
you from rain & Wind & Cold Weather, Which you are
Expos'd to in the other & you have 4 or 5 hours
to Repose to in the night. We went to lodge at Mousieur
Vincent's a french ordinary to Which we were Recommended,
Where we din'd in our Chamber being Very Sharp Set,
having been a'long time without Victuals. We sent
to my Ld. Raby's our English Envoy,   (65)   who
had Compa. at dinner that day who Stay'd 'till
Supper also, so that We Could not See his Lordship. My
Ld. Huntly a Scotch roman Catholick Sent to know our
Names, as soon as he heard there Were Strangers arriv'd,

Monday 8th: and Next Morning sent his gentleman to
Compliment us on our arrival, We went about 10 a Clock
to wait on my Ld. Raby, but he was not up, and in the

---

(65) Lord Raby invites Belcher to dinner Sept. 10.

afternoon again, but he Was not Return'd from dinner. We saw Mr. Tilson his Secretary & one Mr. Powel my Ld's. nephew, and in the Evening Mr. Tibson Came and Sat an hour or two with us. That afternoon we went and saw the arsenal There are about 300 brass guns and mortars, some of them taken in battles & some of them presents from other princes and many of 'Em Cast by the late Elector.   (**)

Tuesday 9th: Next morning We Sent again to know If we Could Wait on my Ld: Raby, but he Made his Excuse, being post day, and desir'd our compa. to dinner on Wednesday. We waited on my Ld. Huntley who offer'd to go with us to Lutzemburg to present us to the Queen, Since my Ld. Raby Could not that day. This afternoon We went to See the King's (**) palace, which he Is rebuilding, and will be very Noble When finish'd the Kings apartments which are the 3d story are almost done and so Richly furnish'd that I was amaz'd to see so much Riches, and It put Me in Mind of the Queen of sheba, who when she had Seen Solomon's glory, it Is Said there Was no More Spirit in her, In one of the Chambers was a bed presented him by the States of Holld cost 5000 Pounds Str. There are a great Many fine pictures all along particularly In a gallery, and one piece of our Savior's face Which they tell you Was done by St. Luke, While he Was alive, It has indeed something divine in it's looks and Strikes one with an awfull Reverence they Can trace the age for 11 or 1200 years, yet looks as fresh as any picture there, the Pope has lately offer'd the King 100000 Crowns for that piece. from hence We took a turn in the garden's which are always open for people to Walk in, but are Nothing fine or Extraordinary, there Is in the middle a jet d'eau that throws up the Water very high, and Will much higher When the tower that Joins the palace Is finisht, but they are so bad architects, that tho' It's Not half finisht, they were afraid of It's falling, & Were forc'd to Raise Supporters at Each Corner, Which are Carry'd a good height; from the gardens. we went to the library, Which Is also in the

---

(**) The "Late Elector," Frederick William (1620–1688), was "Great Elector" of Brandenburg, the heart of the Prussian Kingdom. Frederick William was the father of Frederick I (1657-1713), the first Prussian King mentioned by Belcher.

Court, It is pretty large and has a great many good books
but few of Ancient Editions of the Classick Authors, In
the Chamber adjoining are the Manuscripts and Many other
Curious books, for antiquity, Rich bindings & ca. Many
draughts of Chinese & Japan dressing very fine, among
other things, a little Small book written by an English
lady, in above 50 quite different hands being the heads
of so many Chapters of the bible in Patine Verse, done
also by herself and some of them Very good, and the
finest writing you shall see. There was Luther's
Translation in dutch written wth. his own hand, An octavo
bible in English that belong'd to King Charles the 1st:,
a little book, about half as big as one's thumb, Which
Was short prayers in high dutch printed, a latine bible
written on parchment by one of the Emperour's daughters,
one of the first printed books on one side only, a fair
greek Manuscript of the New Testament, More legible than
print, Several books and Manuscripts of the Chinese, and
a little Cabinet with all their characteor & ca. -About 6
a Clock my Ld. Huntley came to our lodgings & We went
with him to Lutzemburg Which the Queen has lately built,
but not yet finish'd, It being post night, It was pretty
late 'ere she Came out of her Cabinet. My Ld. Told her of
our being there, and her Chief Lady of honour was our Sr.
Charles, I deliver'd the lttr which the Electress gave
me to her in my favour, but she was inform'd before hand,
for the Electress had wrote her by 2 posts and given her
an Accott: of our Coming, and Several other particulars
as We found by her discourse afterwards. she Was
Extremely kind, & free & easy in discoursing after she
had talk'd about half an hour, she presented the Princess
of Hesse Cassel & the Prince's of Anspach to us, and We
Made them our reverence and after that she Went to Cards.
We stay'd not Much longer that Night because My Ld. Was
Willing to be soon home. There Is little or No Ceremony
Us'd at the Queen's Court, but they live with a great
deal of freedom and Easiness.

Wednesday, 10th: Next Morning My Ld. Raby sent again to
Invite us to dinner & to tell us the King was to dine in
Town and that he hop'd to See us at Court, but the King
did not dine in town, We went to the palace & after we
had stay'd about an hour, the King Came out and went down
Stairs, a little after him Came the Prince Royal his son
& then follow'd all the Court, They Stood a pretty while
at the bottom of the Stairs, & my Lds. Raby & Huntley

talk'd sometime with the King, after that the King went
into his Coach & we addre'd my Lord Raby, at half an hour
past 12 we went to his house & I deliver'd him the Lttr
of recommendation which I had from Mr. Poley, he gave us
a very good dinner. there was at dinner my Lds. Raby &
Huntley, my Ld. Raby's Secretary a French Officer, Mr.
Cockburn & I, In the afternoon Mr. Powel went with us to
the Amphitheatre, Which Is upon the Walls of the town
made for the fighting of bears and other wild beasts.
They have there 2 beasts they call orexes, which are as
big as a large bull, & much like one; a very big head,
and the forehead, very thick of long hair, Which Smells
like the Sweetest Musk, you Can pull it off Easily, they
live wild in the woods of Prussia, I very narrowly
Escap'd having my arm broke by one of 'Em, for putting my
hand in to feel their Skin, he turn'd his head Suddenly
to Strike me with his horn, but hit against the wall,
which being Close to it, Sav'd me. This afternoon we did
not go to Lutzemburg and Mr. Powel Sat with us all the
Evening."

[** Ed. Comment Follows]
Jonathan's previous bull-like animal sounds like an out
of place Musk Ox, or perhaps a domestic Yak, a cross
between the wild Yak of Asia and Mongolian cattle. After
a brief tour and playing billiards (Jonathan gambled at
Billiards and lost on Sept. 23, see expense account on
page 131), the next account relates to the famous German
scholar, Leibnitz (see footnote 66 on Lebneitz). He
repeats the story of an "apothecary's 'prentice" buying a
manuscript, at a low price ("3 or 4 marden grosch", about
six English pence), which explained the secret mythology
of the "philosopher's stone" (i.e. an imaginary stone
or chemical composition which was believed to have
the power to convert base metals into gold). The
famous scholar was captivated with how the "prentice"
began consuming the apothecaries supplies for his
experiments, was fired, later rehired, and his eventual
fate after his questionable success:

"Thurs 11th: Next day we went with my Ld. Huntley to
the Tennis= Court, from thence to the King's Stables
Where we Saw about 200 horses, but Could not then See the
Rust=Kamen, which Is above them, so we went to the
Chamber of Medals and Antiquities, We had only time to

See the Silver Medals, which are in a Cabinet by themselves both Ancient & Modern. My Ld. Huntley din'd with us at the ordinary. after dinner we went to Billiards, and then to take Another View of the library, Where we met with one Mr. Leibnitz, (66) with whom we had an hour or two's Conversation. He Is Mighty Civil & obliging. He Is president of the Academy of Sciences, which the King has lately Erected in Imitation of the Royal Academy of Paris, as he Strives to Imitate the King of France in Everything. We chanc'd to fall upon the Subject of Chymistry, and he told me a Story that lately hapned at Berlin. An apothecary's 'prentice bought of a Soldier for a Small matter (3 or 4 marden grosch) a Manuscript in high Dutch, Which he had brought from Switzerland which was a Treatise of the Philosopher's Stone, the Apothecary sometime after finding, Several Materials in his shop Spend Very fast, upon Enquiry found 'twas his 'apprentice and turn'd him out of doors, he Continu'd Still working with what Money he Could get, but was poor, and after a year or so, his Master took him again and he Stay'd his time out, in which he at last found the Secret, & sent 100 ducats (or 500 I don't know which) to his Mother, and wanted Not Money himself. When his time was out, his Master Invited one of the Ministers and some others to sup, When he had thank'd his M:er for all his favours, he told him, he would shew them a piece of art, they laugh'd but were willing to Comply so as far as to be present with him, he made a fire and all things ready, and there being nothing at hand the Ministers gave him 5, 2 grossh pieces out of his pocket, which he put into his Crucible; & something else to it, & brought it out a lump of gold, which he presented to his mistress. He then took his leave of 'Em and went to Magdeburg, where (I think) his friends liv'd, but this thing taking air, ("taking

---

(66) Gottfried Wilhelm, Baron Von Leibnitz (1646-1716) was a famous German scholar and Mathmetician. He is credited with Sir Isaac Newton with the notion of differential calculus. Leibnitz died in poverty, in spite of his founding the German Society of Sciences. Belcher's favorable impression of Leibnitz may be a result of the great mathematician's monad theory: everyone is unique and their existence is in harmony with God.

air": the word spreading -ed.) and the apothecary's
wife presenting the King with the piece of gold, he sent
for him and at last brought him away by force but he soon
after made his Escape and fled to Saxony, Where being
also known in a little time; the King of Poland order'd
him to be taken up and Set him to Work, but he made his
Escape there also, but was prisn'd & taken and Closer
kept at Dresden, Where he now Continues, Nobody Is
allowed to See him, and the walls of the garden that
belongs to the house he Is in, are rais'd up a great
heigth on his accott. 'Tis about three years Since this
happened; Mr. Leibnitz told me, he had been at great
pains to inquire into this matter, wc. puzzl'd him a
little, Since such a thing had been done & so the Matter
of fact undeniable. The King of Poland Said to Some that
ask'd him about It That he did indeed make gold, but not
Enough for him. While we were there the Queen & ladies
of honour took a Turn or two in the garden in a thing the
French call a Boudin, It has No Seat, but their legs hang
over it, holds about 5 or 6 on Each side, she had the
Margrave   (67)   the Kings Brother, to be her Coachman
who was bareheaded, he for the Most part drives her When
she goes out, and did last Casuwal (?-ed.) quite to
Hannover. (which Is 150 English miles). We went in the
Evening to Lutzernburg the Queen kept her Chamber that
night and Sent for the Music, there Sung first an Italian
lady, and then the 2 Princesses Hesse Cassel an Anspach,
they all Sang Very fine, but the Princess of Anspack
Charmingly. We did not Stay 'till Supper, there being
little or no Compa. & my Ld. Raby and Huntley, Having by
another door gone into the Queen's Chamber We were alone;

Friday 12th: Next day we Saw the Rest of the Medals &
Antiquities, there Is a Very large Collection of Medals
ancient and modern, One of the latter Weighs 500 duckets,
Another 200, a third 100. There Is also a Cabinet of
Medals of brass and Copper; after them We Saw a Cabinet
of Very precious Stones. In this Chamber are some busts
of the Ancients as Seneca, Plato, Socrates, Cleopatra
& ca. In another are a great many sorts of urns & lamps

_____

(67) Margrave was originally a military keeper of marches
     or borders in Germany. It is also known as the
     English equivalent of the German hereditary title of
     nobility.

lately dug up at Lutzernburg When the Queen built her
palace among other things there Is also two busts of a
King and Queen done in a sort of Clay bogld (68) of
a dark brown Colour, the Eyes are of the Natural Color,
which makes it look very lively, and in my mind
preferable to any of Stone or Marble, but that art Is
Entirely lost. We went from hence to the Rust=Kamer above
the Stables, to which you go up, not by Stairs, but a
Continual assent for taking up their slayes. The first
thing we saw there were those Sleyes, which are very
fine and Richly guilt, are made for one lady to Sit In,
and the gentleman Sits astride behind, who holds the
horses Reins. The trappings for the horses Is full of
Silver bells all along one Side are wooden horses with
Rich trappings some Set with Rubies and Emeralds, One or
two taken from the Turks. There are a great many fine
Equipages, most of 'Em made lately by the King, yt. which
was made for his Coronation Is very glorious. the bridle,
Saddle & ca. being Set with Brillion (69) Starrs,
and fixt with gold buckles & ca. On another Side of the
building are one of a kind fine arms, and one the other
swords, bows halberd's (70) & ea. Among which are
a great Many Very Curious things. There Is an ancient
Sword with an inscription like greek but which no body
Could read, 'till within some few mos. a grecian Bishop
who pass'd that way, taking it in his hand, read it very
fast, and then kiss'd it with a great deal of reverence,
and Said the Inscription declar'd it to be the Sword of

---

(68) This word is uncertain, possibly a form of bogy,
     which is an object of superstitious fear.
(69) I believe the intent of this word is derived from
     brilliantine: A dress fabric, of mohair and cotton,
     glossy on both sides, resembling alpaca but of
     superior quality.-ed.
(70) A halberd was used in the days of knights. It was an
     axe shaped blade with a steel point on the business
     end and held by a six foot wooden handle. One had
     the option of chopping or spearing. We might
     speculate that Belcher observed (see note 73), some
     of the earliest muskets, introduced in the 1500s.
     They were about fifty pounds and six or seven feet
     long, requiring two men to aim and fire.

Constantine the Great, (71) There is the sword which was Tamerlane's, (72) and they have also his armour which the late Elector procur'd at a great Charge. It's Soft and plyable, nothing of Iron or Steel, Seems to be of Wire and Woorsted, Is very light, yet shot=proof, as they have try'd it Several times. It would be End less to name all the things here, but in general this Chamber Is very well worth Seeing, among the fire arms, there Is the musket which the Janizaries (73) wear, It is so heavy, that It is as much as one Can do almost to lift it, If they be so much Stronger than other men I Can impute it to nothing, but their drinking only water and No Wine, and their taking of opium; after Dinner We went to the Kunst Kamer, Where are many Curious pieces of art, There is the King's Efigies in wax dress'd in the Same Clothes he us'd to Wear & Sitting in a Chair, Is very like and look as if 'twere alive. some Cabinets very fine, a great Many things in amber & Ivory, an Ivory Consle Table (74) and Stands, a little ship that Moves on a Table & Turns about Several times of it Self and furls It's

----

(71) Flavius Valerius Aurelius Constantinus, Constantine the Great (272-337) was a Roman Emperor, 200 years after Julius Caesar. The story is that Constantine saw a vision of a cross in the sky after a battle, with these words: "By this sign thou shall conquer." The arch of Constantine in Rome is 1675 years old today. It is a fine preservation of the ancient Roman tribute to Constantine's reforms.

(72) Tamerlane (1336?-1405) was a decendant of Genghis Khan, a conqueror from the Persion Gulf deep into Russia. Tamerlane's conquests were violent, but as a ruler, if you were prudent enough to be an ally, he was considered less autocratic than most in the fifteenth century.

(73) A Janizary was a professional Turkish soldier between the 1300s and 1826.

(73) This term probably means console table, where the table top is carried by one or more decorative styled brackets.

Sails,   (75)   several Curious things from China, There
Is also kept a dye which a Man that Was to throw for his
life, broke in the Middle in throwing & so threw a 6 & a
1 and ye other having Cast but 6 before him, the man who
Cast 6 & 1, sav'd by life and the other was Executed,
this dye the King keeps as a great Rarity. There are also
Two Silver Cups thicker than an English Crown, Which this
present King of Poland (Augustus) Squeez'd together, one
with his hand, another with his thumb only, and another
of the Same thickness, thro' which (at some distance)
he Struck with an arrow only with Casting it wth: a
good force out of his hand.   (76)   A knife of 8
inches long, which a fellow now living at Hall in
Saxony, Swallow'd and had it three years in his Stomach,
in wc. time it was 2/3 Consum'd, and by magnetick
plaisters   (77)   drawn from his Stomach & taken
out of his side. likewise some Natural Curiosities, as
shells, buds, several birds of paradise, and What Is very
Strange a Stag's head in the middle of a tree, which has
enclosed and grown 'round it, and the horns Stand out at
holes in it. In this and the Chamber of Antiquities, all
ye things have fine glass before 'Em, all the Chambers of
the King's apartments looking glasses in the Windows and
the largest glasses you Shall See, all made at Berlin, In
one window the looking glasses at the Sides are so
dispos'd, as to reflect 20 or 30, If only 2 or 3 Stand
together; about 5 a Clock my Ld. Raby Made us a Visit in
his Coach & 6 attended by 8 footman & 2 horses rid by his
coach=side;"

[** Ed Comment Follows]
In the entry of Sunday, (September), 14th, Jonathan
mentions a "long discourse on religion." We might

---

(75) With respect to the self propelled model ship, Peter
     Henlein, a lock smith of Nurnberg, Germany is
     supposed to have invented the first watch in
     approximately 1500. By Belcher's time, spring
     operated devises were well developed.
(76) Perhaps Augustus also liked to intimidate his
     vigilant neighbors with fairy tales.
(77) This may be a true story, over a century before
     Belcher was in Germany, Ambrose Pare (1509-1590)
     became one of great surgeons of France. He served
     four different Kings and wrote a treatise on gunshot
     wounds.

speculate on his conversation by referring to a letter
he wrote as Governor to Joseph Williams, an English
organizer for the "Society for Propagating the Gospel
among the (American) Indians." May 25, 1731: "I agree
with you, Sir, that great is the decay of the spirit of
piety & vital religion... we seem to have lost our first
love, and the spirit that drew our forefathers into this
desert. Luxury & vanity too much swallow up the thoughts
of the present and rising generation..." In the August
16th entry Jonathan is invited to see the King's Crown:

Saturday, 13th: Next Morning Early We went to
Ozarijenburg, one of the King's palaces, which
he is building. There Is little or nothing remarkable
there; but a Cabinet of China, which ye King has
taken a great deal of pains in the Setting up They are
full to the top, In One Room Is a pyramid in the middle
of very large Jarrs. In the other are a gt. many dishes
and things of agate, amber & ca. some of gold, some
set with precious Stones, Engraven very richly The
gardens are very large Standing on one Side of the house.
There Is a tower built not far from it for raising up the
Water for the Waterworks, at the bottom of the Stair Case
to the house Is a pipe which Is to throw the Water to the
top of it. There Is a fine Chappel piepacing (? -ed.) in
one End of the house. We returned about 5 & went this
Evening to Lutzemburg, Where we Supt with the Queen &
two Princesses, Mr. Leibnitz was also at table, the
Queen was very pleasant, and free in discourse.

Sunday 14th: Next day we Went to the french Chh, We
din'd again at my Ld. Raby's, and had a long discourse
about religion. We went this night also to Lutzburg, but
were disappointed, for the Queen was gone to schoon
hausen to sup with the King.

Monday 15th: Next Morning We went to See my Ld. Huntly;
where we met Mr. Powel who went afterward wth: us to the
new Stables, Call'd the Dasen's Stables in the new Town,
above which Is ye academy for painting, drawing,
architectury & ca., Where all that Come are taught for
Nothing. The King gives a pension to a Rector and four
Masters, besides Substitutes who are oblig'd to attend
twice a week for teaching gratis any that incline to the
art. There Is one great Room with Several Statues in it,
and Where they also draw after the life a man or woman
Standing Naked all the While, he that shew'd us the place

said they had no difficulty to get Women to Stand,   but a
great deal to get Men. But one that had gone there for 3
years, told us, he Never Saw a Woman there, only Men once
or twice a year, there Is a preemium given, and Every one
does   a   piece   in   the   part he applies to. We spent ye
afternoon in writing and wth: Mr. Tibson & Powel, having
nothing Else to do, and went at night to Lutzburg, Where
We Stay'd 'till Supper time and took our leaves of the
Queen as she rose from Cards, she Wisht us a good Journey
to Hamburg, and Sd. she was glad If we had met   (78)
thing acceptable to us here. We also made our Reverence
to the Princesses & took our leaves of'Em. the Margrove
that night lost 1400 duckets   (79)   with the Queen in
less than 1 1/2 hour. We stood that Evening almost all
the While by ye Princess of Anspach, and made her laugh
once very heartily at a Jest on her maids of honour, one
of which was very tall and another a little woman.   (80)

Tuesday 16th: the Next Morning Early We took our places
in the Waggon for Hamburg, and my Ld. Raby Sent us word
yt. the King had Sent the Key of his Cabinet to town and
accordingly We went with Mr. Powel to Court Where the
grand Chamberlain who had the Key attended us, as We
Enter'd the Cabinet, we had on Each side 'us 8 guards
with a Standard flying, on a Table in the Middle of the
Room, Stood the Crown, It is Vastly Rich, having about
200 large diamonds, and Several fine pearls in the shape
of a pear, one of Which Is valued at 60000 Crowns. It's
perfectly oval and smooth, The sceptre is also very Rich

---

(78) Belcher occasionally omits words. On a few occasions
     he duplicates the same word, in what must have been
     a time consuming journal. Between the word "met"
     and "thing" he crossed out a few letters, in this
     case he may have been attempting to use a few words
     spoken to him by the Queen.
(79) A ducat of Europe was either gold or silver, about
     twenty dollars at todays gold rate of 360 dollars an
     ounce. The Kings brother (margrave), according to
     Belcher's rather bland remark, lost 28,000 dollars
     in less than ninty minutes.
(80) The reader might recall that Belcher was favorably
     treated by the Elector of Hanover, George I, on
     Sunday, August 24, 1704, after visiting with his
     daughter for a hour. The same pattern repeats itself
     with the King.

having Many Jewels, and two large rubies In it. He has 2
Coats the buttons of Which are large Brillion & Cost for
Each coat 800000 Crowns, one of them we Saw as also a
large diamond In his hat Cost 20000 Pounds Str. He has 2
large diamonds in heritage from ye house of orange, they
are Called Le Petit fancy the largest of Which they tell
you Is near as big as the famous one of the Duke of
Telarence, but my Ld. Huntley wo has Seen 'Em both told
us, It is not half so big. There are also in this Cabinet
a great many things of gold, some Enamell'd, some Set
wth: precious Stones of great Value. We Saw also several
necklaces of large pearl, this Cabinet Is valued at 3
million of pounds sterling. A great many people took this
opportunity of Seeing the Crown, for the King keeps the
key of it himself, and Never Sends it to town but as a
particular respect he would show to the English. I had
forgot to observe that almost apposite to the Court upon
a bridge the King has lately Set up his father's Statue
on horseback of brass. It was done with a great deal of
Ceremony, with blowing of trumpets and the guards passing
by made a low reverence to it; We went before dinner and
took our leaves of My Ld. Raby; My Ld. Huntley dine'd
with us at the ordinary, and took his leave after dinner,
and We went directly to the posthouse Where we went off
with the Waggon at 4 a Clock. Berlin is a fine town and
will be Much finer, for the King makes Everybody build
good houses, their houses are built with brick and
overlaid with a kind of Mortar, Which they Whiten and
Make it look Just as free Stone; (81) The new town Is

----

(81) Freestone is hand cut and shaped stone work re-
     quiring more skill to fit than rough masonry. There
     are many huge sandstones, forty cubic feet in size,
     in the 4800 year old Cheops pyramid that fit
     together without motor. They are so well shaped that
     a knife will not fit between them, yet the devision
     is clear and precise. Those are rough stones
     compared to the polished work that once covered
     Cheops. Many Masonic scholars believe that the word
     "Freemason" is derived from freestone, however, the
     prefix "free" had different meanings for various
     generations of Freemasons over the years (see Pick &
     Knight, 1983). The noteworthy point is that "the
     modern revival" of Freemasonry was on June 24, 1717,
     and that Jonathan was a member of the Fraternity
     in 1704.

very fine with walks in the Middle and rows of
trees, there they take the Air in yer Coaches
in the Evening, there are three or 4 towns Joyn'd
together, It's very populous, A great many french,
who have a great incouragemt. from the King, and he
imployes Many of 'Em instead of his own people;   The
Keeper of his library, Medals, Kunst & Rust Kamers are
all Frenchmen- he has also taken Care to Settle Many of
the Refugees of Orange in his Countrey reckoning himself
their Prince, my Ld. Raby has the Managemt of the Money
rais'd for them in England & Mr. Tilson Is one of the
Committee appointed for the distribution of It among
them. The whole Country here is Sand (? ed.) and full of
woods, and one would think Could produce little or
Nothing, Yet they have here plenty of all sorts of
provisions, and reasonable, but other things are dear
being brought from Leipzick and Hamburg. there Is very
fine Steel Work, but dear, They Make Wine here too, which
they Say Is pretty good. The King Is the Vainest,
proudest Man in the world, and Strives in Everything to
Imitate the King of France. He Is daily buying Jewels and
Making rich furniture and Is building so Many houses that
he will scarce be able to finish one of 'Em, If any
gentleman has a house which he likes, he obliges him to
Sell It, & he presently begins to rebuild it. This Is one
piece of his Vanity, To Say That No King in Christendom
has so Many houses as he; He Is not so deform'd as some
Make him, but looks old. He has been Earnestly desiring
That My Lord Raby, Might have the title of Ambassadour,
Which he has at last obtain'd and My Ld. Is to Make his
Entry as such, as soon as he Can get his Equipage ready,
which Is to be very Splendid, This he thinks will be a
president for the States & others to do the Same. As the
ffather (as written-ed) Sets up for initating the King of
France, so does his son as much admire the King of
Sweeden, The Prince Royal as they Stile him, Is abt. 16
or 17 years old, a Rough, Unhewn, Clumsey youth,
Careless in his dress, having all the Niceties & fineries
of Courts, his Genius Is wholly to Warr & arms, & he may
prove a troublesome neighbor, When grown up.   (82)

---

(82) The "16 or 17 year old" who may prove to be a
     "troublesome neighbor, when grown up" is Frederick
     William I (1688-1740). Belcher was right, Frederick
     William I raised an army of 80,000 men, a famous
     giant regiment, for he loved tall soldiers.

The King tells people he buys jewels, because his son takes delight in 'em, at which his son laughs, & doesn't Care a farthing for 'Em, and had as live see so Many pebbles, but that he pretends to admire 'Em to please his father. The King thinks it below him to Speak to Any Undr. a Lord; and sometimes asks Whither the King of France will speak to Any English gentlm. undr. Quality. This Makes English gentlemen ne'er go near the King's Court, but Constantly to the Queen's Where there Is a great deal of Easiness & freedome without Ceremony, Much More than at Hannover. The Queen is a fine Woman, but gross, (large woman-ed) of a great deal of sense & learning, Speaks Many languages, Is a great Reader, she's a great admirer of Rabelais, (83)   Montague & such authors, and has a great Esteem for Mr. Toland. The King allows her 6000 Pounds a year for her Table & 2000 a year for building, 8000 Pounds a year for Clothing, besides Several other great allowances, he Comes once a Week or so and dines or sups wth: her, but has not bedded with her there 10 or 12 years. Indeed their Way of living Is very different, for he goes to bed at 7 or 8, & Rises at 4, Whereas she goes to bed at 4 & rises at 12, (84)   she loves gaming, dancing and Musick, and he hates all such things. There are frequently OPeras at Lutzemburg, Acted by the ladies of the Court, some of Which are very pretty Women. The King of Poland's Comedians are also at Berlin and act in the Winter. The King's only daughter by another Wife is Married to the young Price of Hesse Chassel. She Is a Very homely Women, of a Sower down=looking Countenance; and of a morose temper, she Speaks very little to anybody, but the Princess of Anspach who was at Court when we were there, Is of an Extraordinary Sweet temper affable In Conversation of an agreeable humour, not a beauty, but handsome Enough, Especially after Somedays Acquaintance, she having a great deal of Sweetness in her face, Which Makes Everybody love her. They Say she Is to be Marry'd to the King of Spain, since ye Inf???tio? (ed.) of Portugal Is dead, but she must turn Roman Catholick. The Queen has Very much of Duke Ernest's face

----

(83) Francois Rabelais (1494?-1553) one of the great French humorist's and satirists mocked moral behavior, and emphasized free living.
(84) The calculation seems to be they would be awake together between noon and seven at night, for a "weekly visit."

(her brother) (85) she has 2 Turks in her Service, one
of them Marry'd to his own Country Woman, speaks very
good English, Italian, ffrench & Dutch. The King (as
all ye princes of Germany are) Is very absolute & has no
law but his own will, and as he Is very Extravagant in
his Expenses, so he Makes his poor subjects pay for It,
and taxes them heavily, When he wants Money His yearly
Revenue Is Reckon'd 7 millions of Crowns about 1500000
Pounds a year Sterling, he has Constantly 50 or 60000
men In pay, most of 'Em in Service of Luged (?–ed.) the
Emperour and the States, Who are Reckon'd very brave
Troops. His Court Is very Splendid, some who had
been at both, told us but little Inferiour to that of
France for all persons of any figure are oblig'd to be at
Court When the King Is in town. they go Very Rich & fine
here but not near so genteel as the ffrench. their
Wigs are but indifferent. The grand Chamberlain Is the
Man who has all the power here, the King Is Manag'd by
him and his lady, and unless they are for a thing It will
not do. There were No English at Berlin while we were
there, Except the Envoy's family; my Ld. Huntley & Mr.
Burnet a Scotch Man, then sick a Very Comical Sort of
gentleman, When he's well, he Stayes at Lutzenburg, and
the Queen keeps him there to have diversion with him. My
Ld. Raby is as Civil a gentleman as Ever I saw fit
for that Court, loves dancing & ca. he Is well belov'd
there and Respected by the King, but as Most other's
places all his heaven & happiness in the pleasure &
diversion of this life, and I'm afraid thinks but little
of another. Mr. Powel & Tibson are also very Civil and
obliging My Ld. keeps a Very good table, and Is very free
& Merry, and Excepting the King Makes the greatest figure
at that Court. He Is grandson to the Earl of Strafford,
Who was beheaded. We did Not go to See any Chh here, for
they look'd but Mean, and We were told, there was nothing
in them worth Seeing. The Post from Berlin to Hamburg
goes very swift, but Is very troublesome, because at
every Stage you Change Waggons, as well as horses &
postilions In all the Kings dominions the posts are
Regulated. Besides the postage, you pay to Every
postilion 6 grossh which Is allow'd him for the
Maintenance of his horses, the King gives him besides a

---

(85) The Duke of Ernest would be the Electress of
     Hanover's (Sophia 1630–1714) son, brother to
     George I (1660–1727).

New Coat Every year, Which has the King's arms on it, and a New Waggon Every 2 years, & 100 Crowns a years, but he Must both buy and Maintain his horses himself.

Wednesday, 17th: We took our provisions along with us, for Nothings to be had on this road.

Thursday, 18th: We pass'd thro' the Duke of Macklenburg's Countrey & Saxe Lawenburg, the Duke of which Is Extinct, and It now belongs to the house of Lunenburg. We should have Come into Hamburg on thursday night, but Could not by ye Slow driving of one postilion. And were forc'd to lodge at a sad pitifull house without the gates and got into town Next Morning."

[** Ed. Comment Follows]
The following two days are the most curious entries in the Journal for Freemasonry. This section was detailed in the introduction to the Journal. Footnotes outline my interpretation of this unusual gathering in Hamburg: the "thanksgiving for Hochstet Victory." There are several ideas that need further research: The "Porter" (see note 93); the "Charter" (see note on Pg. 105); and the possible identity of the various Englishmen in this company. There may be a clue to pre-Grand Lodge era Freemasons in this aspect of the journal:

"Friday 19th: We took lodgings at the Keyser's hoof, Just over against the Stadthouse being told 'twas the best Inn in town. After We had Eat and dress'd ourselves We went to Change (change is the shopping area-ed) Where We Saw Mr. Stratford, ffoster & Watkinson to the 2 last I was recommended. (86)   We rec'd there several Lttr that were directed to Hamburg. Mr. Watkinson told us, that next day the English kept thanksgiving for Hochstet Victory, and that he'd take Care We sh'd be invited, (87)   as We were in the afternoon in ye Resident's name. (88)   Mr. Strickland

---

(86) Note Belcher had recommendation letters from his friends in London and elsewhere addressed to Foster and Watkinson.
(87) This English "thanksgiving" may include English pre-Grand Lodge era Freemasons.
(88) The "resident" would be an English diplomat residing in Hamburg.

our English Esq. and his governer din'd with us at the
ordinary, they lodging at the same house, Next day
We went to Wait on the Resident, but being post day, We
Could not See him, Which we knew before hand. After that
We went & took a turn on the Ramparts in a Coach.

Saturday 20th: Next Morning We went to Chh at 10 a Clock,
Where we heard prayers and sermon and the Te Deum sung.
The Chh Is in ye English house, up 2 pair of Stairs,
after Sermon We Came down to the Hall, Where the
gentlemen Soluted (89) one another, and talked some
time, there We met Mr. Colt, one of our old acquaintance,
from Hannover. from thence we went to a Coffee house,
and then return'd again. In the hall below was plac'd the
Musick, and 6 or 7 steps up that was the room, Where we
din'd, Which was the first Table, there was the Resident
of Denmark and the States the Danish admiral, a
BurgoMaster, and four of ye Senate, who generally depute
that number instead of Coming all, as they are Invited,
some gentlemen of ye town and the English Strangers,
and some of the Chief of the Hambro Compa. Were at
this table. There were 2 or 3 Tables besides for the
Rest of the compa. We had a Very Noble Entertainmt, the
treasurer (90) Sat at the lower End of the table, and
began to Everyone's health present in order as they Sat,
Which lasted 'till diner Was done, after that the Queen's
health, and the rest of the Crown'd healths (as they call
'em) in Bumpers (91) but We Came away, When they
began these, It being about 6 a Clock, Everyone slip off,
When they had a Mind, but they that Stay'd till the last,
Which was about 12 a Clock, were really well In for
it. (92)

Sunday 21th: Next day We Went to Chh and din'd
with the Minister Mr Emerson (? -ed.), he having
Invited us the day before. They have only prayers
in the afternoon, after Which we Went and Walkt

---

(89) Saluted is an unusual term for Belcher, he used it
with the Freemason Henry Sherburne (1674-1757).
(90) The treasurer indicates that this was some kind of
fraternity.
(91) Toasting at table Lodges remains a tradition of
Freemasons.
(92) If this "thanksgiving" included an English group of
Freemasons, it is the earliest record in Germany.

about the town with Mr ffoster and went to his house
and took a glass of Wine, a little after Came in
his wife and then the three Eldest daughters, Who are
very pretty women, the youngest of 'Em is a perfect
beauty.

Monday 22nd: This morning I went out a hunting early with
Mr. Stratford & the Rest of the gentlemen of the Compa.,
Mr. Watkinson had provided me a horse. He Invited us
that day to the ordinary room, Where all the Batchelours
of the Compa. are oblige'd to Eat. We had a Very
good dinner and wine abundance. Mr Willett one of
the Compa. a Very Civil man Carry'd us in his Coach to
the Residents, but he was gone out, from thence We went
to Mr. Willet's Stables Where he had his horses and
dogs, after this to the bowling green, Where we drink a
bottle of Cyder, he would have had us gone to the Wine
Cellar, but we wd. not, having drank Enough that day
before.

Tuesday 23d: Next day We went to drink Tea at Mr.
Dangerfield's and to see his house, Which Is the finest
in Hamburg, the 2 or 3 rooms below, are very Rich & fine,
and a fine bed; at the head of Which hang his son &
daughters picture, Which I Mention only because of his
particular fancy, In having his daughters drawn, When she
was but 7 years old, to be like her at 17. But It Seems
ye painter Could not hit her face 10 years older, for
It's Nothing like, she Is Much handsomer than her
picture. We were serv'd all in Silver, and after tea &
Coffee a glass of Rich Cherry brandy and some sweet Meats
there Were 14 at Table and Everyone had a Silver Salver.
He Is a Very Vain Man and Is Mightily pleas'd, When
people Come to see his house; his father Was buried by
the English Compa. (being there porter) (93) but
he has got a great deal of Money, Is Worth they Say 80
Pound or 90000 Pounds str. offers 20000 pounds down
with his daughter, he lives very genteely, Marry'd a
German and Is turned Lutheran. Mr. Strickland, his
Governer & We Supt at home this night and Sent to the
English cooks for Victuals.

---

(93) Porter would be some kind of doorkeeper. In
    Freemasonry the title "Tyler," an important Masonic
    office, was first used on June 8, 1732 (AQC 90/195).

Wednesday   24th: Next Morning We are waited again on the
Resident,   and   found   him   at   home.   in   the evening we
went with   Mr.   Watkinson   to   See   an   oPera   being   the
first day,   they had obtain'd leave to Act Again.   having
been suppress'd for some time,   The occasion of Which was
That   a   troop of dutch Comedians,   from Holland Came and
acted at Hamburg, at which the actors there Complain'd as
being an injury to them and made a party in the Senate &
got them turn'd out but the opposite party,   who were for
the Comedians prevail'd so far as to get the opera forbit
too.   It's   a Very good house,   large Theatre,   Very fine
Scenes & very rich Clothes,   but indifferent actors,   the
Musick Is tolerably good,   from the opera We Went to   the
Wine Sellar; and drank some old hock;

Thursday: 25th: Next day we dine at Mr ffoster's Where we
were   14 at table and very good Compa.   We had the honour
of 2 of the daughters Compa. that Night to ye opera,   the
Eldest would by no means be perswaded to go,   so We   left
her Cover & Mr.   Stratford with her,   Where we found them
at   our   Return,   they   play'd at whist pretty late,   and
then took our leaves tho' unwillingly,   We   Call'd   at   a
Coffeehouse, drank some Tea & Coffee & so home.

ffriday 26th: The morning following We went to Drink Tea
with Mr.   Stratford,   and   in   the   afternoon to See his
garden Where Mr.   Willis Carry'd us,   It   lies   a   little
beyond   Althenau.   He   bought it from one Taxcia the Jew,
and has built stables to it,   Where he keeps 7 horses and
fence dogs. It's on the banks of the River Elbe, and   has
a pleasant prospect,   from it you Can at one View See   7
Kingdoms & Princedoms,   as Denmark,   Hamburg,   Holstein,
Luxenburg,   Lubeck & 2 more,   the Danish   admiral   has   a
garden   Close   by.   On   our   Return We   went to take our
leaves of the Resident about 6 a Clock,   at Which time he
has generally finisht his Lttrs.,   and Is glad of   Compa.
he   kept   us   much   later than We intended having Several
other Visits to Make and was very kind.   He Said We   Must
not   go out of town without Eating with him,   and desir'd
we would Come next day and dine with   him,   and   that   he
should   order   dinner   to   be ready an hour sooner on our
accott. Which we Could not well refuse, tho' Inconvenient
to us.   When we Came from his   house,   It   was   too   late
to   go any Where,   so that We were disappointed ourselves
and baulk'd others,   for Mr. ffoster's daughters   set   up
Expecting us 'till near 10 a Clock."

[** Ed. Comment Follows]
After Jonathan's "disappointment" at missing his visit with Mr. Foster's daughters (there is ample evidence that Belcher was cavalier with the ladies and his letters to women were lavishly embellished), Belcher and Cockburn prepared for their long wagon ride homeward. Before leaving he summarizes Hamburg, providing an insight into this unusual European shipping port, on the Elbe River. Hamburg is located sixty miles from the sea and it was virtually destroyed in the Second World War. The "English Company," in Hamburg, apparently lost their "Charter" in recent memory. The word Charter, or Warrant, is significant to Freemasonry. Prior to 1717, "the test of a Lodge's regularity was probably the possession of a copy of one of the old Charges." (Pick & Knight, 1983 Pg. 353). Belcher's use of the term could also refer to a Charter to an English Envoy in Hamburg.

"Saturday 27th: This Morning early Mr. Cockburn   (94) went to the posthouse to Secure our places, and know ye hour of going. After that We Went to Mr. ffoster's, Where We past an hour on 2 very pleasantly, and then bid ym. adieu, from hence We went with Mr. Colt to See ye famous organ in St. Katharine's Chh, Which indeed Is very fine and very large, has 56 steps 5000 odd hundred pipes the largest of Which I Could not make my arms meet about. The organist Is an old gentleman, and takes it kindly, When Strangers Come to See it. There are 16 pair of bellows belong to it. In the Chh are Several old pieces of painting very good, and I think this Is the only Chh has anything remarkable in it.

They pay no great Respect to their Chhs. here, for there are booksellers shops generally in the porch and in some in the body of the Chh all the week round, from the Chh we Went to the Resident's, Where dinner Stay'd for us, It being half an hour past 12 'ere we Came there. The Sweedish Resident was there (he was Sick, When the publick entertainment was) The Residents Lady Seems to be a Mighty good natur'd Woman, she has an Estate in England and lead mines upon it. They have a son abt. 9 years old, a Wonderful pretty

----

(94) D. E. Cockburn, son of the minister at the Hague, has been Belcher's travel companion since August 11, 1704. Belcher settled the account on October 6.

boy, Speaks french, English and high dutch to perfection,
talks like a man, dances well, and playes on the Spinnet
like a Master. In discourse Mr. Wytch fell a railing
against the King Sweeden, for his affecting to be
Slovenly & Course in his habit and way of living, as if
being neat & genteel was Inconsistent wth: bravery &
Courage;   Which I thought was not very civil before his
Resident, especially seeing he understood English. But
he Is a man that Speaks his mind very freely. We had much
a doe to get away in time, & more to shun drinking too
Much. We had Scarce time to put up our things, and go to
the boat Which was Just going off, Mr. ffoster waited
there to take his leave of us.

Hamburg Is a pretty large town very strongly fortify'd
the walls rather too high are kept in very good repair.
They have a little fort near the town Call'd _____
Very strong, which the King of Denmark laid siege to in
the year____, but was forc'd to raise it with great loss,
It has a Communication with the town undr. ground by
which it Can be daily Supply'd with Men & provisions.
But their greatest security Is in being near so many
Princes for they will Never Suffer anyone to make himself
Master of it, tho' all of 'em wd. be glad to have it. As
soon as one Sends to take it, the Rest Send to Relieve
it.   The streets are much too Narrow, and the Coaches are
oblig'd to Stop and often times put back one for another.
They have a great many Coaches here, and the hacks hardly
to be known from a gentleman's Coach. The better sort
dress very well and live high, they are very Curious in
gardens of which they have a great many about town, the
Way to'Em Is Extremely bad & dirty, as are also ye
Streets in town. They have a Considerable trade, tho'
neither to East or West Indias as yet. But they have
Nothing Near the number of ships, which are Constantly
at Amstr. The town Is very populous, they Reckon near
300000 in it. The government of the town Is very Ill
lodg'd & will prove the Ruine of it at last, If
not Remedied. It's divided between the Senate and the
Burghers, Which one may Call the Mob, They are Still
quarelling and Can never agree to anything, That Is for
the publick good, and ye Senatt have not power Enough of
themselves, Besides they are Manag'd by factious Men for
their own Ends & Interest. The Several Companies of
Trades Men too are Constantly at Warr, and about a Week
before We Came there, two of the Companies Met and
fought, and two or 3 were kill'd out Right, besides

broken heads, arms & ca. and there passes few weeks, that
the mob Is not up, as It was the day we Came away. They
have here a bank Which Is a great ease to the merchts, in
the payment of Money. The Exchange Is not near so big as
that of Amstr. but Is throug'd at the time, It Stands
just on a Canal, and Is Square, Trees before it, a
building over it. The English live here very great and
as other people get money by a great deal of labor &
Constant attendance so one would think they get their's
by drinking & hunting. They have about 3 busy days in
the weeks, the post dayes and their show=day, which is
Wednesday When they stay at home to show What they have
to sell. Mondays & Saturdays they go a hunting & Thursday
Is also an Idle day. Most of 'Em keep horses and dogs,
and they have a hunt's man belongs to the Compa., They
Spend A great deal of money and yet are many of 'Em Rich,
But they drink a great deal too much, and we were told
they did much more formerly, and some of the Batchelours
are otherwise debauch'd. They are Very generous, Civil &
obliging to Strangers, and have Nothing of that Stingy
Mean Narrow hearted humour, which the English in Holld.
have. The English Compa. here keeps up the Cr. of the
English Nation abroad, by their Magnificence, they are
very Much Respected, and with Submission (I believe)
'twas a Wrong Step the taking away their Charter, (**)
they might indeed have Rectify'd the abuses of the
Company (? ed.), but Might have kept it up for the
honour of the Nation. The English Women here have
the Worst of it, they live almost like nuns, and the men
are more given to their bottle, than their Conversation.
Mr. Stratford & Willis went to see the English army, and
were present at the battle of Hochstet, while I was one
day a hunting with Mr. Stratford, he gave me a pleasant
description of the battle; my Ld. Marlborough gave him
leave to furnish the French prisn'ers with money, which
he did and gave them Cr. where ever they went, gave one
of the generals (I think) Tallard) Crs. for 400000 Marks
is about 32000 Pounds St. The English Compa. have great
priviledges from the town & pay no taxes, which the town
gave 'em to incourage 'em to settle their at first, there
being then little trade at Hamburg, but the transporting

(**) Apparently this Hamburg company of Englishmen had
some kind of a Charter, indicating a formalized
Envoy or organized representation from England. No
further information at present.

of beer brew'd there, and the brewers have still best
seats in Chh, as having been formerly the best families
there, tho' of late they have condescended to give one or
2 of 'em to ye Burgomaster and now the town is so much
increased in trade they would gladly be rid of the
English Compa. which indeed is very much lessen'd since
the taking away of the Charter, and will do so more &
more. The resident is a very hearty, jolly man, drinks
his bottle as well as any of 'em, is very well belov'd by
'em, & keeps a good table enough, but never dresses
anything extraordinary. One thing ye English are to be
commended for, they live very friendly and kind one with
another, and you shall never hear ym. speak ill of one
another, neither does one envy another's trade, than
which nothing is more common among the English in Holld.
Hamburg yields a most pleasant prospect, when you'r on
the Elbe, and looks very fine, as you sail from it.
Althenau lies also on the river and is not above half an
English mile from Hamburg which is the reason of it's
name, it was built by the King of Denmark to draw the
trade from Ham: but it's a scoundrel place, none but Jews
live in it. The Elbe is very broad there, and is a deep
slow running river, several little islands in it, some
with houses & gardens. About 3 in the afternoon we went
by water to Harburg, in an open boat, We first run
aground and then had a plentiful Rain, and a Strong
gust of wind, which made us take down our sail, we made
Harburg in an hour & 1/2,

Sunday   28th: We went to the posthouse, Where all the
Waggons go of,

Monday   29th: We paid for our passage only to Nuburg, a
fortify'd town belonging to the Duke of Tell, there was
in the Waggon besides us, a Guelderlander (?-ed.), a
Leipzicher, and a young gentlwoman.

Tuesday 30th: At Nuburg We took another Waggon & paid to
Osnabrug.

Wednesday Oct 1st: Here we got more Compa. a gentleman &
his Servant, and a woman Either mad or a whore or both,
for first she told us, she was to go to Minden, and
When We Came, Where the Waggon goes of to Minden, then
she would not go thither but to Hannover, and as we were
going away, Chang'd her Mind again & would go to

Osnaburg, but she was not 1/4 of an hour in ye Waggon When she would not go to Osnaburg, but only as far as Diepenau Where we left her 'till the Waggon should Return, by Which she was to go back again. We Came late to the gates of Osnaburg, and were forc'd to Call for above half an hour, before we Could wake the Centinel. There we pd. to Nalrder; at Deventeer or guelderlander left us, He was a Roman Catholick, no bigot, and very good Compa.

Thurs. Oct 2. We Came to Naerder on this day a little after three, We dress'd our Selves and took the Skoot at five for Amstr. in which were about 20 boors & 600 remetties of North Holland, drunk, hugging & kissing, singing & dancing like mad, they were all olie (? -ed.) on board their yactch that night, Where I Suppose there would be fine work. The boat Came too late to get in at the boom, & so we were forc'd to let our trunks & things be in the boat all Night, and get the fellow to Watch 'Em and bring 'Em home next morning. The road was much worse by the Rains, than When we travell'd it before, and We had like to have been overturn'd 2 or 3 times & we had a lacrt (?-ed.) horn with us the night we came from deventeer else We had never got Safe over that Heath. About 9 a Clock we Came into the City of Amstr. I went immediately to Mr. Schaick's, Where I again took my lodging, after due Salutations, and a little talk of my travels, I went to bed being much fatigu'd;

Friday 3rd: Next day I advis'd my friends in Londn. of my Safe Return hither and then went wth Mr Schaick to 'Change, Which When over, We went to dinner, & spent the afternoon In Visiting my friends;

Saturday 4th: Next day We went about 10 a Clock and had a good opportunity to See the Synagogues of the Jews wc. as I have before sd., are very noble buildings, they were at their worship, Which Is the Most hoggish & indecent That Can be Invented, They ware their hats while praying to the almighty, & generally in Clokes, and White Silk Scarves ty'd over their hats and faces, they are Continually talking of Secular affairs, asking you What News, the price of Stocks & ca. in their Synagogue, and then to their devotion the Next Minute, Which Is all read out of books in their mother tongue, they have a great Stock of plate belonging to the Synagogues, they have

that which they Call the law of Moses, writ on parchment,
and roll'd round two Sticks of Silver, which are Join'd
together, over them are a parcel of Small Silver bells,
this Is wrapt up in red Velvet, and Carry'd by the Priest
all round the Synagogue, and kiss'd by all the people, or
Else some lay ye hands on it and then kiss their hand,
they Continue in this Confus'd Way of Worship for about 2
hours and then break up, When Stay'd long Enough to have
a full View of this matter, we went home to dinner, this
day Mr. Schaick had invited Collt. Hobby, D. E. Cockburn
&'s son to dine with him, in the Evening I took a glass
of wine wth. Mr. Spranger & Van Rincom, and din'd with
'Em the

Sunday 5th: next day, both parts of the day I went to
hear D. E. Cockburn.

Monday 6th: Monday Mr. Schaick & I walkt about the City
to buy the remainder of What I had occasion for, and
Spent the Rest of the day in drawing out my Invoices &
Setling accott. betwixt him & me.

Tuesday 7th: Next day I din'd again wth Mr. Spranger &
Van Rincom, and after that they did me the favour to
get an ordr. from the Lds. of the Admiralty of Amstr.
to go to See their Storehouse for Men of warr, which
indeed Is very fine & Extraordinary, Is hem'd all round
with Canals & no passing to it but by bridges or boats,
all things there are in the best order, Every particular
ship having a Room for it's Stores by itself, on the top
of the house Is Constantly kept 1600 tuns of Water, and
pipes go from it, which in Case of fire are open'd, and
the house Is presently overflown, here I Saw the largest
load stone, being as big as the Crown of My hat; the
Chief Streets in Amstr. are the halry graaf, the Kisar
graf, & the Prince's graaf, all which are Extremely
pleasant, and have as fine buildings as man would desire
to see, the halry graaf Is the best, there lives
Burgomaster Witsen, who Is a Very Rich Man, one of the
greatest men of the City. This Evening at 6 or 7 a Clock
I went about and took leave of all my friends and at
8 got into the Skoot for Tergow, we had a boat wth. a
roof (as they call it) which we bespoke purposely. The
Roof Is where you have Conveniences Made for lodging and
good beds, much as the great cabbin of a ship,

Wednesday 8th: at 5 the Next Morning we Came to Tergow,
We Rose about 7 & went to their Chh which Is at this
day the most famous in the world for the fine painting on
the glass, Where you have painted the whole history of
the gospel, as our Savior's Eating with his disciples,
his Condemnation, Crucifixion & ca. all done Much to the
life, and will indure many 1000 years, most of it being
now 500 years old, and as fresh as If done but yesterday,
the world has lost this art, and Cannot Come near it,
some have offer'd 50000 Guilders for one window piece.
After this we walkt about 2 hours to view the town, which
Is but Small but Clean & neat as the Rest of the towns of
Holland and It's pretty well fortify'd, from hence we
proceeded in the post Waggon for Moozt a little Country
Village and then to Rotterdam, Where we arriv'd at 11 a
Clock. We went to 'Change, then din'd, and at three
took a small yatch to go down to the Brill, where I put
my things on board the Katharine yatch who had lain a Mo.
Windbound, I Went this Same Night again to Rotterdam, but
Coming about 10 a Clock Could not get within the boom, so
Was forc'd to lye in the yatch, but got into the City at

Thursday, 9th: break a'day, and at one took Skoot for
the Hague, We went to an English ordinary there and took
our lodgings, It was by this time 5 a Clock, We then
walkt to Ryswick which Is a little Village about a mile
from the Hague; Just without the town Stands a palace of
the late King William's which has been famous throughout
the world, Since the treaty of Ryswick, the peace being
Negotiated & Concluded in that house, It's an old house,
but Regularly built looks Noble Enough in the front, It's
only one length of building, not a Square or an N as
they build palaces Now a'dayes, It Stands Sweetly
Surrounded with trees which are Set Very artfully, and
afford an Extream pleasant prospect, look which way you
will upon 'Em and you find 'Em Exact ordr. (even Rank and
file) there are none but Servants live there, kept by the
King of Prussia, who takes this house; as the next heir
of the house of Orange, the house Is without furniture,
a Servant shews it you, and tells you as you pass thro'
the galleries & Rooms, That such a gallery was the place
where the ffrench Ambassadour had his Walks at the
Negotiating of the peace, & that such a one was the
gallery of the allies, and so of the Council Chambers &
anti Chambers, The Room Where the peace Was Concluded
Is a good handsome square Room, not large, the

Ceiling is something arching, Is painted blew & grain'd
with anothr. color, over the Mantle=tree Is the picture
of the late King Wm.'s Grandfather & Grandmother;
(95)
the gardens are but Small; after this We return'd to the
Hague, it being near 8 a Clock, I Sent for my Cozen
Willis   (96)   & agret'd upon going the next day to
Hounslaerdike. We drank a glass of Wine and went to bed;

Friday 10th: Next Morning Early, We walkt to a house of
the late King William's (Call'd the house in the woods)
Which Is another short Mile from the Hague, the Way (as
that to Ryswick) Is Extraordinary pleast. It's Called
the house in the wood from it's being very well Environ'd
with groves, It's but A Small house, hardly worth the
name of a palace, less than the house of Ryswick, It has
but one good Room, that Is Really Noble and Prince=like,
Which Is the hall or dinning room, It is indeed Very fine
full of the painting done by the best Masters, there Is
the whole house of Orange & Nassaw drawn in their
lengths, It's an old house Which King Wm's. great
grandfather bought of an Amstr. mercht., the garden Is
very pretty, but I don't Remember It had any Waterworks,
there Is a Labyrinth done very Nicely with bushes, so
well that When you are in the middle, you Can't find the
way out again, tho' It be but small, the trees are all
the Way as you go to the house are set in Very good
ordr., as soon as We had View'd this house We took
-ssastned (?-ed) to town, and about 12 my Cozen Willis
and Mrs Wedon (whom I had Seen at Hannover) Mr. Cockburn
& I proceeded for Hounslaerdike, another of King Wms.
houses, which is about 12 English miles from ye Hague,
we drove hither in 2 1/2 hours; Went to a publick
house bespoke a mouthful of Victuals, and then Went to
View the King' palace, Which Is a Very Noble building,
It's a Square of House wth. a Court in the Middle;   It
Stands Surrounded with water, by Canals dug quite Round,

---

(95) King William III's grandfather, on his mother's side
     was King Charles I (1600-1649), who was beheaded in
     Oliver Cromwell's time. Charles I married the French
     Princess Henrietta Maria.
(96) Jonathan's Great Grandfather, Thomas Belcher
     (?-1618), had two son's, Andrew (Jonathan's
     Grandfather); and John (1615-1672), the father of
     Jonathan's cousin, Elizabeth, who married Willis.

so that you must pass a bridge to go to it on any Side,
Which Makes it look pleast. & well, It's an old building
and yet Very Stately it looks great & Noble, We walkt
into Every Room, they are all well furnisht & adorn'd
with painting, in this as well as the rest of King Wms.
houses which I saw— there are Small oratorys Which were
made for the late Queen Mary, (97) after she Marry'd
the Prince of Orange, there she us'd to keep her books of
devotion on a little Table, Where there lay a Cushion by,
on the floor, and No Chair in the Closet, Every Morning
before she spoke with any one, she us'd to be Near 2
hours in that oratory, as one of the Servants of the
house told me, who had liv'd with her, This Is one (among
many other) Instance of the great piety of that glorious
Princess; This house as well as that of the wood falls to
the King of Prussia, and Is now lookt after by his
Servants, We Walkt about an hour in the gardens, Which
are Very large, not fine or Extraordinary, Considering
what princes have in these days, the orangery Is Very
large, and deserts very pleasant, here Is a good show
of Strange beasts and fowl, In short It's a fine, Noble
Seat, fit for the Prince it belong'd to, We went from
hence & took our dinner, View'd the Small Village of
Hounslaerdike Which has not above 20 or 30 houses (I
believe) & yet I think one Chh, from hence We Went to
the Hague & in our Way thither went by a Chh, Where was a
bason out of Which was baptiz'd a Woman's Children, who
had as many at one birth as there was dayes in the year
and It's ingraven on the bason as a miracle, that 365
Children were baptiz'd out of that bason, all born of
this woman at one time, but some say this Is only a
delusion of the Roman Catholic priests in former times,
and that the Woman was deliver'd on the 5th of January
and had five children, and from thence they wd. delude
the world by Saying she had as many Children as days in
the year; We got to the Hague about sun=down, & being a

---

(97) Queen Mary II (1662-1694), eldest daughter of
     James II, was fifteen years old when she married her
     cousin, William, Prince of Orange (1650-1702), the
     President of the Dutch Republic. James II lost his
     throne in 1688 attempting to return the Catholic
     religion to England in the glorious revolution.
     William III and Mary II arrived to rule England in
     1689.

Very bright Moon=light Evening, We walkt about the town,
to View the Chhs. buildings, streets & ca. all Which are
Very fine, indeed the whole town Is a near garden of
pleasure and without It are abundance of fine Countrey
Seats and fine walks, here are a great number of Coaches
more than In Amstr. or Rotterdm., I don't Remember I have
Ever Seen any place to Compare with it for delightful
Walks, Regular buildings, and anything you Can Imagine,
adds to the beauty & pleasure of a Sweet, pleasant town,
I lodg'd here this night and

Saturday 11th: next day about 9 took Skoot for Rotterdm.
Where We Came about 12 a Clock, I took my leave of my
friends there, and about 4 took yatch, and Mr. Cockburn
& I went Down to the Brill to the Katharine Yatch Gabiel
Milleson Commander. the Same wth: whom I came over, and
had been in Holland all the time I had been Traveling
into Germany, 6 weeks of the time being wind=bound, Here
I took my leave of Mr. Cockburn wo had been my fellow=
Traveller, I lay on board this Night, and the

Sunday 12th: Next Morning having a fair wind ye Capt
Came to Sail, and from Maeseling=Slags (unsure of
spelling -ed.) My Ld. Portland &'s family Came on board,
who were Returning with us for England, the wind was so
small & the tide so Strong and Seas so high by reason of
a late Storm, that the pilot wd. not Venture out It being
dangerous to go over the pits, a place Just without the
brill harbour, Where the water Is Very shallow, and many
times when there Is a high sea, ships have been stove to
pieces, so We return'd to the Brill Whalfe, & I went
ashore to View the Brill, which Is a small town, about 2
leagues from your Entring the Maese, It's fortify'd Very
Regularly, It's Sweet & Clean like the Rest of Holland,
and the buildings & Streets in good order, but the houses
are Small, the Streets of a good breadth, I Went & view'd
that Which Is Call'd the great Chh, Which Is indeed Very
large, from thence I Went to the house Where the States
of the town treat upon any publick Occasion, there I Saw
pictures of all those of yt town, who declared themselves
& appear'd in arms for the protestant Religion, When the

dutch first broke from the Spanish Monarchy, (98)   they are Noble pieces of antiquity, and done with a great deal of life, I Walkt about the town, view'd the Ramparts & ca. It's but little different from the other towns of Holland, being full of handsome bridges & Canals; I lay there this Night and

Monday 13th: Early Next Morning having a fresh gale of Wind We took our leaves of Holland; we were Convoy'd by 2 small privateers of 8 guns Each who are in the pay of the States general, they went with us from the Brill as far as goree harbour, Where a Dutch man of warr (wo was order'd by the State, to Wait on my Ld. Portland) met us, she had 54 guns, then the privateers Each fir'd 5 guns, gave three huzzas Come up along side & Wish'd us a good Voya., as soon as they had finisht their salutes, our Convoy Comlimented My Lord wth. 15 guns, and Meeting a Dutch East India man bound from Goree to Amstr. he gave us 11 guns this Convoy 7 more, the Pendenvis man of war bound for Hull Saluted My Lord with 15 more; after all Which we gave 5 guns, and then made the best of our way- We kept on our Course with a good Steddy gale all night being as Clear a Moonlight Night as ever was seen and

Tuesday 3re O.S. (note: change back to old style calender- ed.) Early the Next Morning we made the north fore land, as soon as we Came to Margret Road the Man of Warr Came to an anchor & Saluted the yatch wth: 15 guns, We return'd 5, here We Rencounter'd Sr. Clowdesly Shovel (99) with a squadron of 10 line of battle ships return'd from the Aseights (unsure spelling- ed.), from

---

(98) Holland forced Spain out of the Netherlands in the 1630 period, following Spanish opposition to Protestants and heavy taxation. As an aside, the great Dutch painter, Rembrandt (1606-1669) was living during the lifetime of Belcher's cousin, Elizabeth (Belcher) Willis (est 1640-1720 period). Rembrandt had died in poverty thirty-five years before Jonathan was in Holland.

(99) Sir Clowdisley Shovell (1650-1707) was an English Admiral during the 1704 battle over Gibraltar in the midst of the war of Spanish succession during Queen Anne's Reign (1702-1714).

their late Engagement with Count Tholoeye, the ships were
badly (?-ed) maul'd, many lost, their topmast's & top-
sails shed to pieces, about 7 in the evening we came to
anchor a little above Graves End;

Wednesday 4th: the next morning at 8 I hir'd a boat &
came up to London, We got up at 11 a Clock; But I cannot
leave Holland & Germany without giving some general
notion of those places; as for those parts of Germany
which I have seen, the soil is of a yellow sand and
barren, yielding little else but flax, buck wheat & oats,
and yet in some parts you find the countrey very well
wooded with oakes, firrs & willows, about Berlin you
may see good vinyards which are planted hillocks, for ye
better benefit of the sun & they produce pretty good red
wine; the town of Berlin and for some space round it, you
can see nothing but a loose sand, where every step you
take is over shoes, wc I could not but admire at finding
so pleasant a city as that is, most of the towns which I
saw in this countrey are of a very ancient date, and the
houses no wayes magnificent or noble tho' large,
excepting in some of their chief towns as Hamburg,
Magdeburg, Berlin, Osnabrug & ca. In Westphalia you see a
countrey everyway despicable & miserable, the men are all
out at warr, and the women are feign't to plough, sow &
ca. for their maintenance, you shall see there 10 women
to one man, their houses are built for men, horses, hogs
& ca. to enter in at one door, & generally the largest
room in the house is for the entertainment of their
cattle & hogs and you shall see, the people eating on
their table at one end of the room and the hogs at
to'ther, most towns of note are pretty well fortify'd,
the warr being so much in Germany, makes all the people
poor & watched, I travell'd thro' part of the dominions
of 13 Kings, Princes & States as Denmark, Sweedland,
Brandenburg, Brunswick, Lunenburg, Macklenburg, Tack-
lenburg, Bentheny, Osnabrug, Hamburg; Heldesheim,
Wernigoroda, Goslar & Lambspring, all which countryes
that I saw were sterile & almost fruitless- But having
been particular in giving an exact accott: as I could of
the towns by themselves I need not be so very particular
here, only tell you that their Princes are all very
absolute, and their people not much better than slaves.
In Holland you find a low land, the soil muddy and of a
pretty good colour, & yet produces nothing, you shall
hardly see a tree in the countrey, but what are planted
for pleasure and ornament, they have of late in the

Province of Guelderland set up the planting of tobacco,
and have lately built in the town of Amersfort soone
hundreds of large houses for curing tobacco, all the
towns of Holland, are kept very neat & clean and look
very pleasant, very well contriv'd for trade, they being
a people of indefatigable diligence; they have nothing
of breeding, or good manners, a little of which you may
fine in Germany, but the Hollander is boorish to ye last
degree, no air in conversation, nor indeed will they talk
with you, unless about getting of money; most of the
towns have fortifications, some of which are very noble
as particularly Naasden, done by the late King William,
the Towns have generally very high dikes built up with
mud (almost like the ramparts of a fortified towns)
which are to prevent any incursion of the sea, the
towns lie so low, that if you go but about a league from
the great city of Amstr. you can't distinguish anything
of the town only by the steeples of the Chhs, when you
are at a little distance it seems as if the whole
countrey were sea, it lies so very level with the water,
which makes Holld. a dangerous coast, besides the dikes
which are artifially built, nature has provided to
admiration, for the safety of that countrey, by very high
sandbanks which reach near the length of Holland, these
are indeed their greatest safety from the tyranny of the
merciless ocean, they are 2 or 3 leagues distant from the
mainland, standing like a fence or wall in the water; as
for the houses of Holland they are built generally with a
good uniformity and those of the Hague are as fine
edifices as you shall perhaps see in the world, those of
Rotterdm. are built pyramidal for the most part; The
Dutch have the advantage of Engld. in their drink, for
they drink Clarret, Champain & Burgundy in perfection,
having a constant trade wth: France they have it at a
cheap lay & can afford to drink without brewing or
debauching, as we do in Engld. their eating is what an
Englishman can hardly conform to, they eat more fish than
flesh, and the flesh they eat is all spoil'd in dressing
& saucing; This I have in brief hinted as general &
particular an accott. of the towns & countreys (Note:
over the previous word "towns" Belcher wrote a "3"; over
the subsequent "&" he wrote a "2"; and over the last word
"countreys" he wrote a "1" -ed.) I have seen, and other
observations of my travels as I can recollect:

[** Ed Comment Follows]
Jonathan's next comment is almost prophetic. Indeed, he

would attribute his becoming Royal Governor of
Massachusetts and New Hampshire in 1730, to the success
of this journey (see Letter to Benjamin Colman, Feb. 7,
1729/30, in Governor section, Pg. 154-5). This is the
last editorial comment in the Journal. The remaining
Journal illustrates Belcher's systematic, 1699, Harvard
education: (1) a summary of the journal, (2) advantages
and disadvantages of traveling, and (3) his numerical
summary of expenses and milage between towns in this
three month 1704 tour of Europe. Regarding Belcher's
expenses, it is a bit difficult to follow some of his
exchange rates, but it is clear that he was positive of
the value of duckets, guilders, strivers, drittles,
and all the variations in English Pounds. The extensive
financial account at the end of the Journal adds to the
evidence of a well organized, rather considerate twenty-
two year old Jonathan Belcher. Because of the close
relationship between Jonathan and his father (see Pg.
11, 12, 137, 144), the certainty of Jonathan's father
providing the funds for this 1704 European tour, in my
opinion, is obvious. Capt. Andrew Belcher had sufficient
confidence in his associates in Europe, and in his
twenty-two year old son, to take a sizable risk in
Jonathan's growth... Was Capt. Andrew or Lloyd associated
with Freemasonry before 1704? The Journal continues:

"To God almighty who preserv'd me from many hazards in my
travels & return'd me in safety, I desire for ever to
render thanksgiving & praise; & may he grant that I may
hereby be made the more capable of serving my generation,
whenever opportunities offer, then will my desires herein
& the end of this my enterprise be entirely gain'd.

Thursday, 5th: SOME USEFUL OBSERVATIONS FOR ONE DESIGN"T
TO TRAVEL INTO GERMANY

He must inform himself well of what money papers in the
places he goes to, of which he may be fully informed in
Amstr. and furnish'd with all sorts of coin; if he does
not well acquaint himself, he will be a considerable
looser on all the species, he takes wth him and 'twill be
best he takes as much as may return him unless he makes
some long stay there; He may take the greatest part in
gold duckets, upon which he looses nothing in changing
into silver, but rather gains 2 or 3 stivers, provided he
never change them, but at the great towns at Hannover,

Magdeburg & Berlin– they give 4 drittles for 'em, which
reckoning them at 27 Str. a ps. tho' they may be had
sometimes cheaper 2 dyts at Amstr. makes 5 guilders 8
Str., and you may buy them for 5 " 5:– (note: over the
previous number "5" Belcher wrote "gt." meaning two gold
duckets are worth five guilders and 8 strivers, as over
the second 5 is "Str."– ed.) and let him be sure, what
money he takes from the mercht. at Amstr., to take it in
the currtt money, and afterwards change it himself with
the jews, for he'll buy either gold or drittles cheaper
from them, than the mercht. makes him pay for 'em,
Notwithstanding gold is the best money to carry, either
pistoles or ducats (but rather the last for the further
you go up into Germany, the more you get for 'em) yet you
must have silver besides for at the small towns and
places on the road, you cannot change gold, but with
considerable loss, the only silver money you can take
with you is drittles or mark Stuckers as they are call'd
in Amstr. the Germans call 'em florins, one of 'em is 2/3
of a Crown, of those there are several sorts, the best
are those which have a horse on one side, and are coin'd
by the house of Brunswick, Luneburg, then those of Saxony
& Brandenburg, which have the faces of their several
Princes on them, These three sorts pass as all the places
we were at tho' at Hamburg they give but 14 grosch for
them, which is 2 less than at other places, they
pretending their money is so much better, but at Harburg
again they give 16 grisch. The drittles or Florins of
Frankfort will go no where for the value, but at the
place, neither those of Embden, Tryers & those other
little princes or states but in their own dominions, only
those of Embden will go at Osnabrug as well as any, but
those of Frankfort not. No doubt in the hereditary
counties the Emperor's coin passes, but if any other I
know not. Dutch money will go as farr as Osnabrug and you
gain something by changing it there, and in returning
German money as far as Bentheim; Let him inquire always
before hand, what money passes at the place he designs
for, that he mayn't carry more of another species with
him, than serves to bring him there especially of the
small money as groschs, pennings & ca. ye for them he
won't be a great looser any where.

2) The next thing to be known is the voitures or way of
travelling in Germany. Which is altogether in waggon and
in open ones all the way we went except from Naarden to
Osnabrug. The best way certainly is to buy a calash or

chaiese that is to be sure strong enough, and to take
post horses where ever you came for then you are master
of your own time, you travel much easier and with far
greater conveniency. The next to this is to take an
extra=post all the way, for then you may travel at what
hours you please, but are not cover'd from the rain. Both
these are indeed something more chargeable, but by far
the best way of traveling, and if there happen to be four
in company, it will lessen the charge of an extra waggon
very much and bring it all=most to the price of the
common post; you pay as much when you have a coach of
your own, as when you take an extra waggon, That is a
Crown a mile for four horses. One great conveniency of
this is you need not travel at nights, and yet be as
short a time on the road, as the common post that
goes night & day. The third way is by the common
post, that goes by night & day (note: repetition
of similar phrases is exact -ed.) and is very fatieging
especially at first, and very inconvenient for they
generally carry merchandize & ca. besides, and you
are often streightn't for room, besides the trouble of
changing waggons so often, as in some places you do, as
often as you do horses, and so are in danger of loosing
or changing your baggage. If you go by the common post,
be sure to inquire yourself at the post=house, and not
trust to other people's telling you. And if you are out
of the post road (as we were in the Hertz) take an extra
post, to bring you to the first post town, where it
regularly goes off. And by no ,means depend upon their
telling you, the time of the post's moving, for they know
nothing of the post's moving in ye regular towns, the
best way is to make all the hast there you can.

3) Be sure to provide yourself well against rain & cold
and think no clothes too bad to travel in. The Germans
have boots lin'd with furr, & coats lin'd with it also,
and for their head a thick cap with a neck to it, that
comes down to their shoulders, and covers most of their
face before, all these are very necessary & comfortable,
as also a good long cloak, that if you travel a nights
you may pull over your head, for the wind is so sharp
that your face can't bear it, for which reason some
travel with masques, with glass eyes to 'em, be sure to
keep your head and neck warm, and your chaps for you'll
find your teeth so numm'd with the cold that they seem to
be loose in your head, and your gums are so sore, that
you can't bear to put your teeth together but as the fun

& heat increase, they recover. Let your trunks be very
strong and such as will keep out the rain, and if you
have either a fine sword or cane, never lay 'em in the
bottom of a waggon, for they'll be quite spoil'd, and
if you hold 'em in your hand, let not the point of your
sword be uppermost, for either in falling asleep, or if
you should chance to be overturn'd you'd do yourself a
mischief, as some in our waggon experienc'd. And be
sure, whither you travel by the common post or by an
extra to take a couple of good soft cushions with you,
one to sit on and the other to lean your back to, for
you'll find 'em very comfortable as you provide against
cold, so you must against hunger too, for on most of the
roads you can get nothing to eat, or at least, such as
you can't eat. Besides you will find it much cheaper to
carry your own provisions with you, and wine also, some
cherry brandy, knives, forks, napkins & 2 or 3 plates,
tho' generally at the houses you bait at, they'll give
you plates, napkins & ca. and you give 'em some small
matter for the use of 'em. Within the States Provinces
you have victuals where ever you come at dinner=time, and
you can't well use your own provisions 'till past
Deventeer. Let what you take be well season'd and well
put up, and proportion it according to the time, you
shall be on ye road for 2 meals a day, be sure to take a
good parcel of lemmons with you and if in the summer some
loaf sugar, both with mixt with water makes pretty drink.

4) Inquire always before you come to a place, where is
the best ordinary, and go straight thither as soon as you
come out of the waggon, tho' if you stay a week at a
place, 'twere better to take private lodgings, yet the
lodging in an ordinary has this convenience (tho' dearer)
you can have a bit of meat dress'd & a glass of wine,
when you want it. If you lodge in an ordinary be sure to
tell in the morning if you are to dine abroad that day,
otherwise you must pay as if you had eat there. Pay the
landlord every 2 or 3 dayes,– while you have the
particulars in memory, if you think they are too high in
their charge, stand hard for abatemt. some will allow you
to cut of half yr bill, especially at the Keyser's hopf
(note: this was spelled Keyser's hoof on Pg. 89 of the
Journal -ed.) at Hamburg, where the man always sets down
more than he expects or gets. At private lodgings you are
better lodg'd and can eat where you please, if you can
find good company, you had better eat with strangers,
than ye own nation, for then you improve in the languages

you see their customs and manners and you hear the news
of the place. But both on the road, and at towns be very
cautious of ingaging with strangers be well inform'd what
compa. you keep, be civil to all, but let it go no
further than a general acquaintance. If you carry no
footman with you, you can have 'em in every town of note
you come to, let 'em be well recommended; and if you have
to do with any tradesman bargain beforehand, or you must
pay double, and rather provide yourself so well before
you set out, That you ne'd not want to buy anything in
your journey, which else you must do at a dear rate;-

5) When you come to any Court & ca. where are any of ye
Queen's minister's, first pay your respects to them,
unless postday, when they are not to be visited, if there
be any English in town, if of your quality they come to
visit you first. If you can, get Lttes of recommendation
all along to some chief persons, you will find 'em of
great service, especially where you are not known or the
Queen has no ministers and if you are but well
recommended at first to any Envoy you can get from one to
another all along, where it is necessary. And at
Hamburg it may not be amiss to be recommended to some of
the chief merchts. there. Let your first care after the
necessary compliments paid, where due, be, to inquire
after whatever is curious or worthy to be seen in the
place, which dispatch at your first coming, and get up to
the top of a steeple or other eminent place, where you
can have a full view of the town, That you may have a
just idea of it, after this lookout for the best compa.,
& men of learning & ca. by whom you can inform yourself
of what you desire to know, and by whose conversation
you can improve. Be sure to be able to express yourself
in some foreign langue either that of the place,
French or Latine or you will loose a great deal of the
satisfaction you might otherwise have.- Carry some few
books along with you, whereby to spend the leisure
hours you have or else in writing your=remarks of the
place you are at.-

Let your baggage in general be as little & as compact as
you can, for you'll find much baggage very troublesome on
a journey: Thus I have noted some few observations for
travellers, there are many more which might be usefull,
but are too tedious to recite, these if well follow'd are
what may make a man more easy & pleast. in traveling,
than he could otherwise be -

SOME FEW ADVANTAGES & DISADVANTAGES OF TRAVELING

A man without traveling is not altogether unlike a rough
diamond, which is unpolisht and without beauty a man that
has   never been from home must be in some things
unaccomplish'd, & ignorant of many points of   good
breeding, has something more or less of selfishness &
sowerness, and is generally at a loss in strange compa.
especially if above him, neither has he that freedome of
mind necessary to behave himself well in coma., but finds
something,   as it were, that overaws him, and is a
restraint upon him. All this travelling remedies, it
forms him into a civil, courteous behaviour, & by using
him daily to new faces, takes of all manner of bluntness
and   by being with all manner of compa. gives him
confidence & assurance enough to talk with those of the
greatest quality, and takes of (in short) all manner of
restraint that lay upon his mind. It changes his humour
from sower, peevish & fretfull, to pleasant, affable &
most agreeable, his frequent conversing with the ladies
molds him into a flexible & complaisant temper, and his
being often oblig'd to others, makes him ready to oblige
all in his turn.-

Traveling acquaints a man with mankind, he sees the
various tempers & dispositions of men, as well as
different faces. It takes of those prejudices against
countries & religions, and rectifies a great many false
notions he had taken up. For he sees that generally
speaking mankind is much the same, the same tempers,-
inclinations, passions, vices, most pursuing the same
end, that is their gain & profit or pleasure, as their
abilities will allow them, and tho' he sees peoples of
very different religions, yet he can see no difference
in their living and conversation, we are apt to fancy one
another religion, that we are prejudic'd at, has
something in him, that makes him monstrous or odious,
or that we should know him by his face as we do the Jews.
But we find (in traveling) no such thing, we see one as
civil as another, as obliging to those of a different
opinion, his behaviour ye same, in short by nothing can
you distinguish one from another 'till you come to their
Chhs; and indeed in those- countries, where so many
different religions are tolerated, the people live as
friendly as if all of the same.- One more this traveling
gives man is a better history, and a clearer knowledge &
idea of countries and things, than a 12 mos. reading

and study. If a man intends to live by trading and
merchandize, traveling gives him the best opportunity
to settle a correspondency in those parts of the world,
where he may come.

Now altho' travelling be attended with many advantages
profits and pleasures, yet it may not be deny'd that it
has it's disadvantages; Hereby a man is very apt to be
workt into an idle, careless, lazy life, and mind nothing
but spending an estate & pursuing his eye and pleasure,
and often times it brings a man to such an unsteady,
unfixed mind, that he is always rathing from post to
pillar & never consented, for the eye is not satisfy'd
with seeing & ca. and without a very watchful regard to
the divine laws, men are often by traveling expos'd to
the hazard of making shipwreck of a good conscience, by
living too laxly in the duties of religion, and this
happens by mens being strangers to, languages or by
different opinions in religion, which make 'em too nice,
stingy & streight lac'd, some would frequent religious
services but can't understand the tongue, others wd.,
were it not Roman Catholick, Lutheran, Calvinist or the
like, I think the latter are not excusable, but justify
to be censured as men void of charity and a good free,
Christian Temper, for indeed I can't see why they prayn't
take what is good & refuse what they think is bad, even
in the Roman Catholick worship and I doubt not but a good
number of Christians will be added by that Chh, to the
Chh trumphant-hereafter; but I say by living a careless
life & never attending divine service, they by degrees
come to be right void of religion as a thing out of
fashion & so become meek atheist, this is indeed the
condition of many that I met in my travels, but this
is wholly owing to yr. imprudence, & too flexible
disposition to every thing that gives them their liberty
& swing in all manner of pleasures; as I was not very
particular in the advantages of traveling so I shall
forbear in adding up the disadvantages, partly because it
would be tedious, & partly because I would not discourage
any, who for good ends are inclin'd to travel; for after
all is said, yet I must grant that travelling is a great
accomplishment when well improv'd, and the disadvantages
accrewing thereby oftner happen for want of a steddy,
well ballanc'd mind than anything else, and people so
ill inclin'd, can improve everything to their ruin &
misfortune if they please.-.-.- (Belcher next begins his
financial account -ed.).

"An acctt: of the distances of the places thro' wo: I Travelld beginning from the Brill July 24th N.S. 1704-

	Dutch miles	English
1-From ye Brill to Rotterdm	4	12
sail'd in ye yatch		
2-From Rotterdam to Overskye	1	3
3-To Delf	1	3
4-Hague	1	3
5-Leiden	3	9
6-Haaslem	3	9
7-Amsterdam.	2	6
8-Muyden	2	6
9-Naasden	1	3
	18	54

So far by the trackskoot
Now begins the postwaggon

10-Amersfort	3	9
11-Deventeer	6	18
	27	81

German miles

12 Holdesen	2	10
Delden	2	10
13 Benthem	4	20
14-Rheinen	2	10
15-Ipenbury	2	10
16-Osnabrug	3	15
17-Diepenau	7	35
18-Laisey	3	15
19 Hannover	5	25
Carry'd over-	30	231

	German miles	English
Brought over	30	231
20 From Hannover to Heldesheim	3	15
21 To Lambspring	3	15
22- Sasin	2	10
23- Clausthal	2	10
24- Goslar	2	10
25- Wernigoroda	4	20
26- Halberstat	2	10
27- Wonsleben	4	20
28- Magdeburg	2	10
29- Brandenburg	9	45

```
30-   Berlin  .   .   .   .   .   .   .   .   .   9  .   .   .   .   .   45
31-   Febilin .   .   .   .   .   .   .   .   .   7  .   .   .   .   .   35
32-   Kertiz  .   .   .   .   .   .   .   .   .   4  .   .   .   .   .   20
33-   Perlberg  .   .   .   .   .   .   .   .   5  .   .   .   .   .   25
34-   Lentzin  .   .   .   .   .   .   .   .   .  3  .   .   .   .   .   15
35-   Britzin .   .   .   .   .   .   .   .   .   7  .   .   .   .   .   35
36-   Hamburg .   .   .   .   .   .   .   .   .   7  .   .   .   .   .   35
37-   Althenau (A town in Denmark) .   .   .   .   .   .   .    1
38-   Harburg by Water .   .   .   .   .   . 1 1/2  .   .   .    7
39-   FFeseleven (A Town in Sweedland)7 .   .   .   .   .   35
40-   Raten  .   .   .   .   .   .   .   .   .   3  .   .   .   .   15
41-   Nuenburg  .   .   .   .   .   .   .   .   2  .   .   .   .   10
  -   Laisey (which comes into the
              road to Osnabrug
              homeward).   .   .   .   .    2  .   .   .   .    10
                    Carry'd over. 120 1/2 .   .   684
```

```
                          German Miles   English
Brought over  .   .   .   .   .   .   . 120 1/2 . .   684
   From Laisey to the Brill again which you may
      see on the other side is.  .   .   .   .   250
                          All is... .   934
                          English Miles
```

An accott: of my Expenses in my Voya. & Journey to
Holland, Hannover & ca. beginning at Londn. July 8th 1704

```
                          Pounds   Shillings  Pc.
July 8th:
     To money given the Servts. where
     I Lodge'd at my departure .   .   .   3 "    1 "     6
     To a case for knife, fork & ca.   1 "   10 "     0
     To a port mantue  .   .   .   .   .   - "   14 "     -
     To drink wth friends .   .   .   .   1 "    1 "     6
Holld.
July 24th
   N.S.   To my passage in the yatch pd  3 "    4 "     6
     To the gunner for my cabbin .   .   1 "    1 "     6
     To given the ships crew to drink.   - "   10 "     -
     To the cook given .   .   .   .   .   - "    7 "     6
     To the Docter for his civility .   1 "   10 "     -
     To the Cabbin Boyes .   .   .   .   - "    7 "     6
                          13 "     8 "
```

```
                          Holland Money
                  Guildres    Ftrs drs
25. To my lodging one week at
```

Rotterdam	12 "	12 "	–
To drink with friends when I left that city.	12 "	–	–
To my charges on the way while going to Amstr. & seeing the curiosities of the Hague, Leiden & ca.	30 "	– "	–
To packet expence while at Rotterdm. & seeing the curiosites of that place.	30 "	– "	–
Carried Over	84 "	12 "	–

Guilders

Brought over	84 "	12 "	"
August 11th: To my pocket expense at Amstra.	35 "	8 "	"
To pd. part of the waggon at Amstr. for Osnabrug	10 "	8 "	"
To 4 cushions	3 "	13 "	"
To fresh provisions to eat on ye road	19 "	12 "	"
To portidge of our things to the skoot.	– "	9 "	9
To passage to Muyden	– "	12 "	–
To carriage of our coffers . .	– "	12 "	–
To passage from Myden to Naarden	– "	6 "	8
To freight & portidge of our coffers and hampers from Naarden to Muydn.	– "	15 "	–
To seeing the magazines at Naarden	– "	16 "	8
To pd. the remaining part of the waggon to Osnabrug.	26 "	16 "	–
To our dinner at Naarden . .	3 "	7 "	–
To expense at Amersfort . . .	– "	7 "	–
To the postilion at Amersfort .	– "	5 "	8
12th: To expense at Loo	– "	3 "	17
To passage Gelt	– "	1 "	–
To ditto Gelt at Deventeer. . .	– "	14 "	–
To expense at Holden	– "	16 "	–
To ditto at Delden	1 "	6 "	–
Carry'd over	191 "	1 "	2

	Grs	Ftrs	Drs
Brought forward	191 "	1 "	2

13th	" at Bentheine for coffee & to ye postilion.	– "	10 "	–	
	" at Rhein	– "	12 "	–	
	" passage gelt at Rheyn	– "	4 "	–	
	" to the postilion	– "	4 "	–	
	" to another postilion to osnabrug	– "	8 "	–	
	" to a servant at the posthouse	– "	5 "	8	
		193 "	4 "	10	

German money
Drittles Groish

			Drittles	Groish
	" At Osnabrug for passage to Hannover.	" .	. 8 "	– ""
	" For supper & wine at Osnabrug.	" .	. 2 "	– ""
14	" at Diepenau	" .	. – "	5 ""
	" To the postilion	" .	. – "	2 ""
	" At Laisey.	" .	. – "	1 ""
	" For wine & ca. there	" .	. – "	8 ""
	" To the postilion	" .	. – "	4 ""
15	" Postilion at Hannover.	" .	. – "	4 ""
	" pd. at the posthouse for use of a room	" .	. – "	8 ""
	" Carrying our things, to Chapazeau's	" .	. – "	6 ""
	" Coffee & Tea at Chapazeau's.	" .	. – "	6 ""
	" a bag for my wigg	" .	. 1 "	– ""
	" Dinner & wine at Chapazeau's	" .	. 1 "	8 ""
	" at night for burgundy & supper.	" .	. 1 "	3 ""
	" postage for a Lttr to Amstr.	" .	. – "	4 ""
16	" Coach hire to Hazen housen	" .	. 1 "	9 ""
	" a Pair Buckles	" .	. 1 "	4 ""
	" at night for wine & Bread	" .	. – "	7 ""
	Carry'd over	"	19 "	15 ""

			Drit	gros –"
	Brought Over	" .	.19 "	15 ""
17th	" For washing linnen	" .	. – "	15 ""
	" Coach=hire	" .	. 1 "	– ""
	" Supper & Burgundy	" .	. 1 "	12 ""
	" at Church given	" .	. – "	2 ""
18	" Coffee	" .	. – "	2 ""
	" Dinner, supper & wine	" .	. 3 "	– ""
19	" To the barbor	" .	. – "	4 ""
	" Pd for Ltts & ca.	" .	. 1 "	10 ""
	" Dinner, Super & wine	" .	. 3 "	– ""
	" Coach hire	" .	. 1 "	9 ""
20	" Seeing the Chambers of the Court	" .	. 1 "	– ""
	" pd. for milk	" .	. – "	2 ""

	" Dinner & wine	"	. 1	"	1	" "
	" Tea & Coffee	"	. -	"	10	" "
21	" Pd. for a comb & puff for					
	our wiggs	"	. -	"	6	" "
	" pd. for 10 times powdering our					
	wiggs, the lent of one 4 days, &					
	buckling 2 wiggs	"	. 3	"	-	" "
	" Dinner supper & shampain	"	. 3	"	15	" "
	" Coach=hire	"	. 1	"	-	" "
22d	" Mending my sword	"	. -	"	8	" "
	" My L. B.'s man	"	. -	"	6	" "
	" a pair of shoes.	"	. 2	"	-	" "
	" Snuff	"	. -	"	3	" "
	" Dinner supper & wine	"	. 2	"	10	" "
	" The barbour	"	. -	"	7	" "
	Carry'd forward	"	51	"	8	" "

			Dritt	Grosch		
	Brought Forward	"	. 51	"	8	" "
23d	" Washing linnen	"	. 1	"	2	" "
	" Coach=hire.	"	. -	"	8	" "
	" pd. my footman	"	. 2	"	-	" "
	" Lost at cards with ye Princess					
	Sophia	"	. 15	"	-	" "
24:	Given at the Chh	"	. -	"	4	" "
	" Seeing Count de Plat's house	"	. 2	"	6	" "
	" Coach hire	"	. 1	"	8	" "
	" Supper & wine for us & dinner,					
	wine & Coffee for 9 persons.	"	. 20	"	8	" "
	" Coarch hire	"	. 1	"	8	" "
26	" the day we left Hannover					
	" The barbor	"	. -	"	6	" "
	" washing linnen	"	. 1	"	10	" "
	" pd. a footman for 3 dayes service	"	. 1	"	8	" "
	" pd. our land lord for 2 weeks					
	lodging.	"	. 6	"	-	" "
	" The servants of the house	"	. -	"	8	" "
	" mending my sword	"	. -	"	4	" "
	" paper & pack thread	"	. -	"	6	" "
	" Dinner & wine	"	. 1	"	8	" "
	" pd. postage	"	. -	"	10	" "
	" portridge of our things to					
	posthouse	"	. -	"	3	" "
	" pd posthorses to Heldesheim	"	. 4	"	8	" "
	" Postilion	"	. -	"	3	" "
	" given a boy that carry'd us to					
	the dutch convent there.	"	. -	"	2	" "

```
    " To my Ld. Abbot's servant that
      lighted us from hence home  .    .   "  .   . -  "   4  " "
                        Carry'd over   "    114 "  12  " "

                                               Dritt Gro:
      Brought over                     "    114 "  12  " "
27    " Lodging at Heldesheim    .     .    "  .   . -  "  12  " "
      " The poor on the road     .     .    "  .   . -  "   3  " "
      " Posthorses to Lambspring (3 miles)" .  . 4 "   8  " "
      " postilion .    .    .    .    .    "  .   . -  "   8  " "
28th  " Our footman's lodging & ca.   .     "  .   . -  "  10  " "
      " given a servant in the convent .    "  .   . 1 "   -  " "
      " posthorses to Sasin (2 males)       "  .   . 3 "   -  " "
      " postilion   .    .    .    .    .    "  .   . -  "   2  " "
      " at a publick house at Sasin.   .     "  .   . -  "  12  " "
      " posthorses to Clausthat (3 miles)   "  .   . 4 "   8  " "
      " postilion   .    .    .    .    .    "  .   . -  "   3  " "
29    " Seeing the works about the mines
        & to the poor  .    .    .    .    "  .   . 3 "  10  " "
30    " Suppers Dinners & Lodgings & ca.
        (three letter word illegible-ed.)
        this morning.  .    .    .    .    "  .   . 8 "   6  " "
      " the barbour   .    .    .    .    "  .   . -  "   9  " "
      " My going down to the mines & the
        use of a miner's habit .    .    "  .   . 2 "   8  " "
      " To one footman  .    .    .    .    "  .   . 1 "   -  " "
31    " given the gentleman's footman wo
        waited on us about the mines   .    "  .   . -  "   4  " "
Sept 1st  pd. lodging, eating wine & ca.
        to a thig this morning .    .    "  .   . 6 "   -  " "
      " To the maid   .    .    .    .    "  .   . -  "   4  " "
      " post horses to Goslar    .    .    "  .   . 2 "   4  " "
      " postilion   .    .    .    .    .    "  .   . -  "   8  " "
      " Wine & seeing the dome Chh    .    "  .   . -  "  13  " "
                        Carried Over   "  .  156 "  11  " "

                                               Ditt: Grosch"
      Brought Forward   .    .    .    "    156 "  11  " "
2     " fruit .    .    .    .    .    .    "  .   . -  "   1  " "
      " Lodging & eating .    .    .    "  .   . 3 "   -  " "
      " pd. the footman the remaining
        part of his wages & to carry him
        back to Hannover  .    .    .    "  .   . 7 "   -  " "
      " To the maid   .    .    .    .    "  .   . -  "   2  " "
3     " at Wernigoroda .    .    .    .    "  .   . -  "   6  " "
      " Postilion   .    .    .    .    .    "  .   . -  "   2  " "
      " Posthorses from Goslar to
        Halberstat .    .    .    .    .    "  .   . 2 "   4  " "
```

" postilion	"	— "	2 " "
" at Halberstat	"	1 "	2 " "
" at the gate of the town & at Church	"	— "	4 " "
" posthorses to Magdeburg	"	5 "	1 " "
" at the gate of the town pd	"	— "	5 " "
4 " Seeing the Dome	"	— "	4 " "
" Seeing the Kings houses	"	— "	6 " "
" Lodging & diet for a nights & a day	"	3 "	— " "
" To the maid	"	— "	5 " "
5 " at the posthouse for bread & milk	"	— "	2 " "
" pd a porter	"	— "	3 " "
" at Siesa for supper & Lodging	"	— "	12 " "
6 " at Magdeburg for a miserable dinner	"	— "	14 " "
" at Worstermart supper & lodging	"	— "	9 " "
7 " pd the waggoner to Berlin	"	6 "	— " "
" postilion	"	— "	5 " "
" to a porter	"	— "	3 " "
" to a barbor	"	— "	6 " "
Carry'd Over	"	189 "	13 " "

			Dritt grosch–"
Brought Over		189 "	13 " "
8 " grapes	"	— "	5 " "
" Coffeehouse	"	— "	4 " "
" Seeing the Arsenal	"	— "	10 " "
9 " fruit	"	— "	5 " "
" Seeing the King's house	"	2 "	— " "
" washing linnen	"	1 "	7 " "
" at the gate of the city	"	— "	2 " "
10 " Powder	"	— "	6 " "
" To a poor English man	"	1 "	— " "
" Pd lodging, eating & ca to this morn'	"	11 "	3 " "
" Seeing the King's amphitheatre	"	— "	3 " "
" grapes	"	— "	2 " "
11 " Oil for our wiggs	"	— "	6 " "
" grapes	"	— "	2 " "
" putting 3 wiggs into buckle	"	1 "	— " "
12 " Seeing the King's meddals & antiquities	"	2 "	— " "
" Seeing his Rust Kamer	"	1 "	2 " "
" Seeing his Kunst Kamer	"	2 "	— " "
" pd our footman	"	3 "	— " "
" at the gate of the city	"	— "	1 " "

13 " Seeing the King's house at
       Orangeburg . . . . . .   " . . 1 " 8 " " "
    " Seeing the garden there . . " . . — " 8 " " "
    " at the Inn there . . . . " . . — " 6 " " "
    " To the barbor . . . . . " . . — " 6 " " "
    " at the gate of the city . . " . . — " 2 " " "
14 " pd to this morna (?-ed.) diet,
       coachise & ca. . . . . " . .20 " — " " "
    " at Church . . . . . . " . . — " 1 " " "
    " at Lutzemburg given a porter . " . . — " 3 " " "
                    Carry'd Forward   240 " 12 " " "

                                    Dritt groschs
       Brought forward . . . . " . 240 " 12 " " "
15 " at the Queens stables . . . " . . — " 2 " " "
    " at the Academy for limning . . " . . — " 6 " " "
    " for grapes . . . . . . " . . — " 2 " " "
    " Coach=hire . . . . . . " . . 1 " 10 " " "
Prussia
16 " Seeing the King's Crown & his
       other jewels . . . . . " . . 2 " — " " "
    " pd our washerwoman . . . . " . . 1 " 6 " " "
    " putting our wigs into buckle . . " . . 1 " — " " "
    " To my Ld. Raby's porter . . " . . 1 " — " " "
    " pd postadge for 7 miles . . " . . 2 " 10 " " "
    " postilion . . . . . . " . . — " 12 " " "
    " postadge for 4 miles . . " . . 1 " 8 " " "
    " postilion . . . . . . " . . — " 12 " " "
    " Ditto . . . . " . . — " 12 " " "
    " pd. for 5 miles . . . . " . . 1 " 14 " " "
    " postilion . . . . . . " . . — " 12 " " "
    " pd. for 3 miles . . . . " . . 1 " 2 " " "
    " given to beggars on the road . " . . — " 3 " " "
    " postilion . . . . . . " . . — " 12 " " "
    " pd. for 7 miles . . . . " . . 2 " 10 " " "
    " postilion . . . . . . " . . 1 " 8 " " "
    " pd for 7 miles . . . . " . . 2 " 10 " " "
    " 2 postilions . . . . . " . . 1 " 8 " " "
    " Spent on the Road . . . " . . — " 4 " " "
    " Lodging without ye gates of
       Hamburg . . . . . " . . — " 9 " " "
                    Carry'd Over   " . 268 " 8 " " "

       Brought Over . . . . . " . 268 " 8 " " "
19 " portage of our things from
       posthouse in Hamburg to our
       lodgings . . . . . . " . . — " 4 " " "
    " pd. a barbor . . . . . " . . — " 4 " " "

" powder	"	–	"	6
" Coach=hire	"	1	"	–
" for Lttrs	"	–	"	12
" fruit	"	–	"	2
20 " at Church	"	–	"	4
" oil for our wigs	"	–	"	3
" fruit	"	–	"	2
" coffee	"	–	"	2
" sheath to my Lord	"	–	"	6
" paper	"	–	"	3
21 " at Church	"	–	"	5
22 " pd our footman	"	1	"	10
" given the huntsman when I hunted	"	–	"	7
" given the porter of the English housen	"	–	"	9
" paper	"	–	"	1
23 " washer=woman	"	–	"	7
" powdring wiggs	"	–	"	4
" at Billiards lost	"	–	"	5
" porter	"	–	"	8
" Dinner, supper & wine	"	1	"	7
24 " washing	"	–	"	6
" a porter	"	–	"	2
" coach=hire	"	–	"	12
Carry'd forward	"	278	"	15

	Dritt:	grosch		
Brought forward	"	278	"	15
" wine at dinner	"	–	"	6
" Billiards	"	–	"	10
" nuts	"	–	"	2
" Chocolatt	"	–	"	4
" Coach=hire	"	1	"	–
25 " fruit	"	–	"	6
" tea	"	–	"	9
" at Foster's lost at cards	"	1	"	8
" att–	"	3	"	–
" lost with Mr Willis	"	1	"	8
" Coach=hire	"	1	"	–
26 " wine at dinner	"	–	"	6
" a porter	"	–	"	6
" washing	"	–	"	4
" mending my wig box	"	–	"	3
" given at Mr Stratford's garden	"	–	"	6
" powdering wigs for 4 dayes	"	1	"	–
" shaving twice	"	–	"	8
27 " pd lodging & diet from ye 9th to this day	"	14	"	–

" To the Servants of the house	"	.	– "	6 ""
" fresh provisions to eat on ye road	.	. 8 "		8 ""
" pd an English woman for her service	.	. 1 "		8 ""
" Coach 2 dayes	"	.	3 "	2 ""
" portridge of our things to				
Harburg boat	"	.	– "	6 ""
" given to see ye great organ				
at Hamburg	"	.	– "	8 ""
" powdering wigs 2 days	"	.	– "	8 ""
Carry'd Over	"	320 "		15 ""

	"	Ditts.	gro.	
Brought Over	"	320 "		15 ""
" washing	"	.	– "	2 ""
" a pr. of oil skin	"	.	– "	10 ""
" given Mr Watkinson's man	"	. 1 "		– ""
" pd. the boat to Harburg	"	.	– "	4 ""
" portridge of our things to				
ye posthouse	"	.	– "	15 ""
" pd the post waggon as far				
as Nuburg	"	. 5 "		8 ""
" on the road for a fire	"	.	– "	3 ""
28 " at Nieuburg pd ye post				
waggon to Osnabrug	"	. 6 "		– ""
" at the posthouse	"	.	– "	4 ""
29 " at Diepenau	"	.	– "	3 ""
" at Osnabrug pd the post				
waggon to Naasden	"	.21 "		– ""
" at the posthouse spent	"	.	– "	5 ""
" pd. 9 postilions to Osnabrug	"	. 1 "		2 ""
30 " at Rheyn passage gelt	"	.	– "	4 ""
" spent at Rheyn	"	.	– "	4 ""
" at Bentheym for milk, fruit & ca.	"	.	– "	5 ""
	"	358 "		10 ""

		Dutch Money		
		Guilder	Frs	Drs
Oct 1st at Delden	"	– "	3 ""	
" at Holderen for dinner	"	. 1 "	16 ""	
" at Deventeer for wine & Bisket	"	. – "	11 ""	
" passage gelt at the bridge &				
anothr pd	"	. – "	15 ""	
2d " at Amersfort	"	. – "	5 "8	
" passage gelt hoice	"	. – "	4 "–	
" at Naasden for wine	"	. 1 "	4 ""	
Carry'd forward	"	. 4 "	18 "8	

		guildre	frs	Drs
Brought Over	"	. 4 "	18	"8
" To a barbour	"	- "	11	"-
" passage in ye Trackskoot to Amstr	"	- "	19	""
" for our baggage	"	1 "	10	""
" at Muyden Bridge	"	- "	1	""
" at Amstr gate	"	- "	2	""
" for watching the baggage all night		1 "	16	""
" pd 7 postilions to Naarden	"	1 "	9	"8
" carrying my things to my Lodging	"	- "	4	"-
" for a book	"	4 "	-	""
" for a Ryesach lost in ye journey	"	4 "	10	""
" for a cane	"	5 "	-	""
" pd a Saxon that travelled with us some charges he pd for us on ye road	"	2 "	10	""

Spent nothing at Amstr. for 4 or 5
ds. being mostly busy at home wth
Mr. Schaick

7	" given the maids where I lodg'd	"	3 "	2 " "
	" pd the skoot to Tergow	"	4 "	2 ""
8	" Seeing the Church at Tergow	"	1 "	2 ""
	" pd the waggon to Rotterdm.	"	1 "	4 ""
	" Dinner at Penington'd an English Inn	"	3 "	7 ""
	" hire of a yatch to the Brill	"	4 "	10 ""
	" pd. portidge	"	1 "	- ""
	" given the yatch's men	"	1 "	8 ""
9	" a dinner at Brim's an English house	"	1 "	15 ""
	Carry'd Over	"	.48 "	1 ""

		Guilder	frs	drs
Brought Over	"	.48 "	1	""
" a hamper for Clothes	"	1 "	4	""
" fruit	"	- "	4	""
" a skoot to Hague	"	1 "	5	""
" Seeing King Wms. house at Ryswick	"	1 "	-	""
10 " Seeing his house (Call'd the house) in ye wood	"	2 "	-	""
" pd 2 barbors shaving, powdring & ca.	"	1 "	2	""
" Seeing King Wms. house at Hounslacidike	"	3 "	6	""
" Treating the Compa. I Carry'd wth wine there	"	8 "	14	""
" Coach=hire thither	"	1 "	10	""

		gs.	"		"		"	
" Lodging at the Hague diet & ca.	"	.	.	8	"	–	"	"
" Chape for my sword	"	.	.	–	"	5	"	"
" portage	"	.	.	–	"	7	"	"

11 " skoot to Rotterdm.   " . . – " 15 " "

" Dinner for us at Pennington's . " . . 3 " 12 " "

" pd hire of a yatch to the Brill " . . 4 " – " "

" given my fellow Traveller
besides bearing his expenses . " . .48 " – " "

" pd portridge   . " . . – " 6 " "

" pd at the gate of the brill . " . . – " 6 " "

            gs. 133 " 17 " "

" spent at the Brill . . . .   . 4 " – " "

              137 " 17 " "

    Arriv'd at Londn
    Octr. 4th O.S. <u>1704</u>
   given the Capt for my passage " . . 3 " 4 "6
   The gunner for his Cabin . . " . . 1 " 1 "6
       Carry'd forward " 5 " 6 " "

               Pds. Shl Pc.

   Brought forward . . . . " 5 " 6 " "

" given men to drink . . . . " 1 " 1 "6

" the cabbin boyes & ships barbor " – " 5 "–

" pd a graves End boat to
bring me to Londn. . . . " – " 2 " "

" pd the waiter for searching
my trunk . . . . . . " – " 5 " "

" portridge of my trunks . . . " – " – "6

         Pounds " 7 " – " "

That any stranger may come to a right knowledge of the expenses of my journey, he must observe, That as money in England is divided into pounds shill: & pence, so in Germany it's dibvided into Florins or drittles, grosches & pennings: and the money in Holland into Guilders, stivers, dyts, & half dyts: a drittle is worth Sterling 2/5 d (nearest) & 16 good grosches make a drittle for it may also be noted yt these are good grosches & marien, as they call 'em 24 of which make a drittle, they being of courser allay than the good, tho' have the same stamp and bigness; & 12 pennings make a good grosch; so the reader by computation, may easily see the Sterling value of a grosch & penning, I having before given the value of a drittle, & how many grosches make a drittle & how many pennings a grosch; as for the value of dutch money it's more commonly known, they being our so near neighbours, however it may not be Amiss just to hint of it it's value, The intrinsick value of a guilder is generally judg'd to be 22 d frs., and 20 Stivers go to make a guilder & 16 half dyts to make a stiver so underneath you have in short the charge of my travels-

	Vizt	Pounds	Shil	Pence
In Germany 258 drittles (or florins) & 10 grosches which valu'd at 2/5 d ftr is		43	" 6"	7 5/8
In Holland 331 Guilders 1 stiver, 10 half dtr which valu'd at 22 d ftr a guilder is		30	6 11	4/8
In English Money Spent		20	8	-
Total Sterling		94	1	7 1/8

Any that are desirous to make the same tour which I have, may observe, that 30 Pounds might have been sav'd in this accott:, 20 Pounds of which it cost me extraordinary, in bearing the expences of my fellow traveller, & 10 Pounds in several other articles it cost me extraord: by reason of my ignorance in several things, as the coin of the several Princedoms thro' which I went & my passage in the yatch, wc were I to go again, wd. not cost me half so much; yet as to the expence of a fellow Traveller it's almost necessary unless you can meet wth any bound that way, which you very seldom miss of at Amsterdm., indeed I being so absolute a stranger as to the Customs, Countrey, & Languages That were I to go again, rather than be want Compa. I wd glandly be at the Charge I was now.-

London Friday October 5th: 1704

Jonathn: Belcher

(This is the end of the complete 1704 Journal-ed).

Before exploring Jonathan Belcher's activities and associates as Governor of Massachusetts and New Hampshire, Jonathan's 1704-1715 correspondence with John White (1669-1721) is noteworthy.

John White was Jonathan's close friend in America. White also graduated from Harvard, albeit, fourteen years earlier than Belcher, in 1685. Although the Belcher to White correspondence of December 27, 1704, has lost the signature, The Massachusetts Historical Society has two later letters (1708 and 1715), addressed to White from Jonathan. The September 6, 1715, letter opens with significant evidence regarding the trust between the thirty-three year old Jonathan and the forty-six year old White (Belcher's age interests Freemasons, because traditionally, they must be twenty-one years old to become a Freemason). His age is confusing because of the calender change. He was born Jan. 8, 1681/2, thus, he was age twenty-two after January 8, during the year 1704.

"Sir-my affairs calling me to Great Britain, whither I shall be going in a few days, I have taken the freedom to make you, a power of attorney; for the direction and management of all my affairs, in Connecticut Colony... and if they should want any money, or anything else (which I think they will not) you may please, to apply to my honored father Andrew Belcher Esq. or Mr. William Foye, who will supply you with anything wanting in my business. From time to time please give Mr Pitkim, your advice & opinion in the management of Meriden farm & the copper mines...That you would please to take my family under your care, & kind regards during my absence, and take my house for your home. Which I shall esteem a great obligation and in your leisure hours, that you would instruct & instill into my son Andrew the rudiments & foundation of his learning, as he goes along... From time to time, I desire you to advise & consult with my honored father Andrew Belcher Esq. in my affairs." signed, "Your very affectionate friend & humble servant Jona Belcher." (Sept. 6, 1715, letter to John White).

From the White correspondence, it is self-evident that from 1704 to at least 1715, John White was an important friend, and adviser, of Jonathan Belcher. White began his

career as a minister, serving as chaplain to Sir William
Phipps (Governor of Massachusetts from 1692-1699).   Later
he became a Representative to Boston, twenty years as
Clerk of the House of Representatives, and in 1697 Fellow
of Harvard University. White is described: "a gentleman
of unspotted character... His peculiar modesty made him
industriously shun places of Profit and Honor, which the
Government would once and again have conferred upon him."
("History of the Colony and Province of Massachusetts
Bay," Thomas Hutchinson, 1765 Vol. II, Pg. 250, 273).

Regarding Jonathan's son, Andrew, mentioned in above 1715
letter (Deputy Grand Master of New England in 1733), he
would be only eight years old in 1715.

Since Jonathan's father was a merchant that imported
goods from Europe, and was a member of the Council of the
Royal Governor, Joseph Dudley (1702-1717), we might
conclude that he knew many business associates in Europe.
There is other evidence that Jonathan's 1704 trip to
Europe was arranged by someone who knew the affairs of
England: Through   courtesy   of The Massachusetts
Historical Society, Jonathan Belcher, on December 27,
1704, wrote to John White: (I have transcribed the
letter).

                                              "London"
"December 27th 1704"

"Mr. John White"

    "Sir-Since my last of July 7th; I reflect with regret
on my Negligence, That I have not 'ere now done you of
Justice and my self the honour and Satisfaction of
writing you very particularly, for my long silence and
remissness I humbly ask yl pardon, I do assure, it has
not been from any want of a due respect, but in Lond'n a
man hardly knows when to set down to write, so many
pleasing objects Continually prest. themselves to your
View, and every day affords you something new and
diverting, I doubt not but my father has hinted to you my
design of going into Holl'd and Germany, Since my last I
have made a tour of about 1000 miles in those Countries
and its too tedious to relate here, what variety I saw in
those places, so shall omit particulars, 'till I have the
pleasure to set down with you for a mo. or so, only to
relate my travels- I will just tell you that Holland is a

fine, pleasant Countrey a place of vast trade, and a
people neat to ye last degree Germany has many pleasant
towns, at Hannover I was entertained by the Princess
Sophia (who is next heir to the Crown of Engld) as if she
had been my mother, she has done our Countrey the honour
of her picture, which I shall bring with me- Indeed
all parts of Europe, where I have been seem to be
gardens of pleasure and delight, I take a great deal of
satisfaction, in the Revolution of my thoughts on my
travels- I have wrote my father by this Conveyance and
sent him all public news, which doubt not he will
Communicate to you, as I have opportunity shall write
you again, hoping you will pardoning impertinency; pray
remember ye Charge most particularly for shall make
particular inquiry of that matter on my return when ye
leisure will allow, the favor of a line I shall be a
great obligation...health and happiness being with... Sr
a Ess... (The ending of this letter is torn and missing a
signature). The Massachusetts Historical Society has this
Jonathan Belcher document.

For those who have difficulty with the missing signature,
I refer the reader to the correlation with the documented
1704 Journal to the evidence in the letter: the trip
into Holland and Germany, meeting Princess Sophia,
bringing her picture with me, and the verification of
Belcher's association with White in previous
correspondence. I do not want to over-dramatize one
aspect of the letter, however, I was fascinated with the
phrase: "hoping you will pardoning impertinency; pray
remember ye Charge most particularly for shall make
particular inquiry of that matter on my return when ye
leisure will allow..." I believe that statement verifies
Belcher as a Freemason in 1704.

For those not familiar with the "Old Charges" in Freemasonry, the respected and concise Masonic reference
book, published by scholars in the Quatuor Coronati
Lodge states:

"The Name popularly given to over a hundred old
manuscripts written in England or, occasionally, Scotland
during the past six centuries...They generally contain
three parts: an invocation "The Might of the Father in
Heaven, etc."; a traditional history differing widely
from that to which we are today accustomed, commencing
for instance with Lamech and going as far as the time of
King Athelsan; and thirdly, charges general and

particular...The old charges contain many phrases and expressions which have parallels in today's ritual." (Pick & Knight, 1983).

There is one other relevant point to Belcher's December 27, 1704, letter: "from time immemorial St. John the Baptist, whose Festival is celebrated on 24, June, and St. John the Evangelist, whose Festival is celebrated on 27, December, have been the Patron Saints of Free- masonry." (Pick and Knight, 1983).

This is how I interpret the letter: first of all, from previously known evidence Belcher calculated he was a Freemason in 1704 (see September 25, 1741, letter on page 197-198). Second, I believe that on the day of St. John the Evangelist's Festival, in 1704, the twenty-two year old Belcher, who graduated from Harvard fourteen years after the thirty-five year old John White, was using a little college humor in a gentle way with his old friend in the December 27, letter: "hoping you will pardening impertinency," he slyly begins, then Jonathan continues to pursue teasing his old friend, the Clerk of the Massachusetts Assembly: "pray remember ye Charge most particularly," then to emphasize the credibility of his challenge as a new Freemason from London: "for shall make particular inquiry into that matter when ye leisure will allow." The frisky Jonathan Belcher, unmarried and two years out of graduate school, had been accepted as a Freemason 3000 miles away. He was also coming from England with a fond Masonic tradition, to test White's memory of one of the "Old Charges."

In my opinion it was apparently meant as an entertaining off hand remark about Belcher testing White's knowledge of Freemasonry. Because of the date, and because of Belcher's 1741 calculation that he was a Freemason in 1704, it is also an important new document which seems to verify Jonathan Belcher's word: he was a Freemason in 1704. One of six known in the world today, who directly claimed to be a pre-Grand Lodge era English Freemason. It will be most interesting to hear the opinions of Masonic scholars regarding this new discovery: a December 27, 1704, Belcher letter from London.

Having established Belcher's very close association with John White, it is productive at this time to leave 1704

in London, and briefly skip ahead in time to examine
Jonathan's association with another White twenty-eight
years later. Belcher was Governor on Oct. 3, 1732, and
he wrote a letter to George Bunker, senior Judge of the
Court of Common Pleas for the County of Nantucket, for
the benefit of Timothy White (1700-1765). Timothy was a
minister on Nantucket for seven years and his funds were
exhausted. Belcher showed an uncommon interest in
Timothy White:

"Sir-As I am one of the Commissrs for the Indian
Corporation in England, I have had the opportunity of
knowing from time to time the difficulties that several
ministers who are preachers to the Indians met with, and
among the rest those of the worthy Mr. White at your
Island, and of whose circumstances I have also been
inform'd once & again by some of the rev'd ministers of
this town...Upon the representation of these things I
sent for him, and have had a long talk with him...he
bears an extraordinary character...I therefore think that
the whole island, and particularly those that attend him
at the publick worship have a great blessing in him, and
I hope you will all think so and as it has pleased God in
his Providence to set me in the station of a father to my
country... I shall not doubt your inclination & care to
justify my conduct...Wou'd it not be greatly to the
advantage of all that attend on Mr White to have a church
gather'd & to have him ordain'd for your paster... Pray,
consider seriously of all I have said...I am sure neither
you nor I shall repent of what I have thus written. I
wish you the blessing of this & a better world, and am
Sr, Your assured friend. Jona Belcher."

Some might criticize the letter. By today's standard, for
a Governor to request a Judge to become involved in an
individual's religious success is not perceived as being
benign. But this is the eighteenth century. Here was a
Governor of a Province searching for a way to help a
friend in a delicate matter. His opening statement, "I am
one of the Commissrs for the Indian Corporation in
England," is almost amusing. There is evidence that
Belcher was careful in dealing with Indians in colonial
America, but one might be skeptical of Belcher's motive
toward the American Indian in this matter. The fact that
Governor Belcher controlled the wages of judges in 1732
adds to the raw boldness of the whole episode. It is a
trivial incident, but it helps to explain the extreme

complexity of Jonathan Belcher: a polished social style, boldness, courage, deviousness, loyalty, scheming, sympathy and manipulation of others. It will take another correspondence to David Dunbar to reveal another characteristic of Belcher, his theatrical temper toward those he did not respect. Belcher wrote no other letters to anyone named White in the Belcher Papers. His old friend, John White (1669-1721), born in Roxbury, Massachusetts, twenty year clerk of the Massachusetts House of Representatives, had died of small pox. In fact there is an interesting footnote to history regarding his death:

"When the small-pox broke out in 1721, of 5889 persons who took it, 844 died." Inoculation was introduced, "contrary to the minds of the inhabitants in general, and not without hazard, to the lives of those who promoted it, from the rage of the people." Of 286 who were inoculated, chiefly by Doctor Boylston, only six died, one of whom was (John) White, who according to Boylston, "thro' splentic Delusions, died rather from abstinence than the Small-Pox." He was "a weak and infirm Man, and had been so near 30 years, sometimes consumptive and very spenetic,...through very cautious and timorous, yet wou'd be inoculated." ("Sibley's Harvard Graduates," Vol. III, Pg. 345-6).

John White was buried in "Mr Belcher's Tomb, ye upermost of the wall in ye South buryiny place. Gloves and Rings." ("Samuel Sewall's Diary," Dec. 13, 1721 entry. (M.H.S., Vol. 47, Pg. 296/297). I assume, Reverend Timothy, who graduated from Harvard in 1720, was a relative of John White. Because of the December 27, 1704, letter to John White, and the above mention of "gloves" at his funeral, it is not unlikely that John White was at least a Freemason, and very possibly an earlier Freemason than Jonathan Belcher.

After the adventure in Europe, Jonathan married Mary Partridge, in Portsmouth, New Hampshire, daughter of William Partridge. They married on January 4, 1705/6, after a sixty mile ride from Boston, on the "motion of the gentlemen that accompanyed him, they were Marryed the same night as he came off his journey in his boots. The Wedding was celebrated on the Tuesday following (Belcher's birthday), where there was a Noble and Splendid Entertainment for the guests, and honoured with a Discharge of the Great Guns of the Forts." ("Boston News-letter," Jan. 7-14, 1705/6). Captain Andrew had a "thanksgiving" for his son's save arrival and attended the wedding with his thinning hair shaved, wearing his first wig ("Sewall Diary," Pg. 538, 540).

Mary (Partridge) Belcher (1685-1736), is believed to be a Quaker (B. P., Vol. VI, Pg. 37, 94, 164). Jonathan and Mary raised the following children:

Andrew (1707-71), Harvard 1724, Registrar of the Court of Admiralty, member of the Council, Deputy-Grand Master of New England in 1733. He married on April 5, 1754, Elizabeth Teal (daughter of Governor Belcher's second wife by a previous marriage). There is evidence that Andrew was in London with his father in the 1729 period (see Benjamin Colman letter on Pg. 155). This is interesting to Freemasons, since Andrew was of age (twenty-one years old) to become a Freemason on November 7, 1728. Probably he was made a Freemason in 1729, in England, four years before it was organized in Boston. Andrew was selected as the first Deputy-Grand Master of New England in 1733. Andrew died in Milton, Mass.

Sarah (1709-1768), married Byfield Lyde Esq. in 1727. Later in the research a connection between The Duke of Wharton and one David Dunbar will arise. Byfield Lyde's sister married a close friend of Dunbar's, a man named George Craddock (1684-1771). Craddock, from England, lived in Massachusetts, and wanted to be Governor. The importance of the bitter relationship between Belcher and David Dunbar cannot be overstated. Thus, Craddock, friend of Dunbar, and relative by marriage to Belcher, was opposed to Governor Belcher (see Nov. 28, 1733, letter to Richard Partridge, Pg. 174).

Jonathan (1710-1776), Harvard 1728, Chief Justice, Provincial Grand Master and Lt. Governor of Nova Scotia. Jonathan's correspondence from Governor Belcher provides significant insight into the Governor's close associates in England. Jonathan studied law at Cambridge, (England) and Oxford, being supported (and well criticized for excessive spending), for ten years by his father. The cost was substantial: letter dated January 24, 1739, from the Governor: "13,369.1.3 Pounds, accounted here a very good estate, and is (I assure you) a large proportion of mine, and after allowing for a proper fortune for your sister and a double portion for your elder brother (according to my present view of things), the above

sum will be too large a share of my estate for you..."
Jonathan Jr. was also in England on his twenty-first
birthday (see Nov. 1, 1731, letter from Governor Belcher
to Jonathan Jr. Pg. 183-5). In view of the fact that
Jonathan Jr. was a leader in Freemasonry (Provincial
Grand Master of Nova-Scotia), it appears that being made
a Freemason in London, on or about their twenty-first
birthday, was a tradition of the Belcher family.

William (1712-?) apparently died young;

Thomas (1713-?) apparently also died young.

After his first child was born, Jonathan returned to
Europe in March, 1708. Queen Anne, of England (1666-
1714), had lost the last of her eighteen children in
July 1700, succession would pass to Sophia, who Belcher
met in 1704. The future Governor Belcher arrived in
Hanover a second time in 1708 and informed the heir to
the English throne as follows:

"having now made a journey purposely to throw myself at
your Royal Highness's feet...I herewith, offer you the
thanks of Her Majesty's Governour in New England for your
Respect to that Countrey, and have brought with me the
Candles of which I formerly spoke, and an Indian slave, A
native of my Country, of which I humbly ask your Royal
Highness's Acceptance" ("Colonial Society Massachusetts"
Vol. 20, Pg. 100).

Jonathan also wrote to John White from London November
16, 1708:

                                        "London November
                                          16th: 1708"
"Mr. John White"

"Sir It's with no small blushing & regret, That I'm'e
(I am ye-ed.) forc'd to own This my first Since my
arrival a'this Side the Water, But I have been So
Continually hurry'd With one little Affair or other, That
indeed have hardly had time to pay Common Civility, to
many relations & good friends. With you, yet should I be
silent Any longer It would be unpardonable Where I must
tell you, yours of the 5th: July P (Post-ed) Capt. Sill
which I rec'd 29th Sept. N.S. at Amster (Amsterdam ed.)
Was (I think) one of the Most Welcome favours Ever Came
to my hands, in That It hapn'd to give me the first

FIRST AMERICAN BORN

accott of the Welfare of my dear Spouse & Mrs Sarah for
God's goodness to them both I desire With all Sincerity
to offer all blessing & phraise Dr. Sir Yer ffriendship &
favour in Visiting my Wife and family (in my absence) Is
infinitely beyond any personal respect you Could shew me,
To retailiate Such yer Respect, I would always Most
fondly beg an Occasion, My Ever honoroured & Dear Father
Writes me Constantly yet the obliging accott you gave me
of the state of his health is most gratefull & pleasant;
I rejoice in the favour of Heaven our poor distressed
Province, by guarding & protecting our Coastal ffrontiers,
am heartily sorry for the great devastation made by
the numerous flocks of Worms ("flocks of Worms" is an
accurate transcript-ed). I see there is an altercation
in the Council, Whither for the better you are best able
to Judge."

The Governor of Massachusetts at this time was Joseph
Dudley (1702-1716). Dudley wanted his son, Col. William
Dudley (Harvard 1704), to be elected Treasurer of Harvard
in the 1713 period. After John White was chosen as the
Treasurer, Dudley wrote to the overseers: "His Excy was
pleased to manifest his dissatisfaction,...thot it wd. be
Mr. White's prudc. not to accept." It my speculation that
the 1708 dispute in the Governor's Council, mentioned in
the above letter to White, was associated with this
later issue (i.e. Governor Joseph Dudley's bias for his
son taking White's job). The 1708 Belcher letter to John
White continues:

"My Brothr Noyes (this would be Oliver Noyes, who married
Belcher's sister, Anna-ed) Writes me in Augtt That the
ffrence Indn's had form'd a design, On our frontiers, But
that it had Miscarry'd by a disagreemt Among themselves,
God be phraised. I see in mercy to our poor Province, he
is still Willing in the wise and best Manner to defeat
their bloody designs. I have once & again lookt over your
Memorial Relating to N Engld & have shown it to Some
others, I have indeed So many affairs of my own, That
would the Countrey have allow'd Me gratuity of 500 Pounds
I Could not have been faithful to' Em, But It's my
opinion There Will Never be any thing done for the good
of the Country, Unless Some diligent ingenious Son
be Sent from us, or one Chosen here & a handsome
Maintenance, With the Charge of Sollicting allow'd him,
Barbadoes, Jamaica, Antigua, New York & little Carolina
Constantly maintain agents here & feel the benefit...

there's no settling one foot before to'ther here without
money...If the gentlm of our Assembly (John White was
Clerk of the Mass. Assembly-ed) wou'd happen to reason
& be at the Charge of a good Agent to Reside here,
they'd soon find ye accott ballanc'd by the benefits the
Queen wd. grant in assisting us to destroy all the
ffrench Settlements..."

The above letter illuminates a few of the struggles in
the colonies: political favoritism, French and Indian
War, natural disasters in the form of "flocks of worms,"
and it is apparent that political favoritism was
also well established in London and the formation of
Colonial agents were well underway. It is also apparent
that Jonathan was seeking a role in that struggle.

Belcher's brother-in-law, Richard Partridge (1681-1759),
was an agent in London for the Colonies. Partridge
is believed to have first gone to London for his father,
Lt. Gov. William Partridge, in the 1701 period. His
father was involved with shipping in the Portsmouth, New
Hampshire area. The son, Richard, was a Quaker and a
respected colonial agent for roughly forty-two years
in London: he represented Rhode Island in 1715, New
York in 1731, New Hampshire 1731-1741, New Jersey in
1733, Massachusetts in 1737, Pennsylvania in 1740 and
Connecticut from 1750-1759.

Partridge intervened in solving boundary disputes,
battling oppressive legislation, such as the Molasses Act
(which he eventually lost); he hired attorneys (the
respected Ferdinando J. Paris), drafted petitions,
published pamphlets (perhaps "The Case of the Northern
Colonies" located in the John Carter Brown Library), he
hired engravers to prepare presentations of maps before
the Lords of Trade (Senex was the best map engraver of
the day), he gave "20 Guineas as a gratuity for service,"
and "presents of wine to a gentleman for service," he
would prepare dinner invitations to the coffee houses to
make valuable friends... such as "1 Pound 3 Shillings
and 4 Pence for a treat to a person who was serviceable
in giving information in Parliamentary affairs," and he
spoke before the House of Lords in opposition to
legislation that would "seriously menace colonial trade
in molasses, rum, and sugar..." In a word Richard
Partridge was the eyes and ears of many Colonies in
London. (Reverence to the above quotes, "The New England

Quarterly," <u>Richard   Partridge: Colonial   Agent</u> by
Marguerite Appleton, Vol. 5, April 1932, Pg. 293-309).

While Partridge was agent, Jonathan made five trips to
England/Europe as follows:

First voyage to London: Spring 1704 to ? estimated one
     year.
2nd: March 1708 to spring 1709 (ship "Dragon," man-of-
     war, one year.
3rd: September 1715 to ? estimated one year plus. During
     this trip to London Belcher stayed at Whitehall, met
     and solicited for Samuel Shute's Commission as Gov.
     of Massachusetts (B. P., Vol. VII, Pg. 264-268,
     letter to Horace Walpole, brother to Sir Robert).
4th: January 1728 to August 8, 1730. (ship "Blandford,"
     man-of-war, one year eight months. Belcher became
     Governor in 1730.
5th: March 10, 1743/4 (ship "Polly," Capt. Goad)-Aug. 8,
     1747- 3 yrs. Belcher was reappointed Governor of
     New Jersey in 1747 (Note: Jonathan's wife, Mary,
     died Oct. 6, 1736).

Before becoming Governor of Massachusetts, Belcher began
his political life as a tithingman of Boston in 1714,
an early form of policeman who observed drunkenness
and disorderly activities, town accountant, and
Governor's Council from 1718-1720; 1722-1723; and
1726-1727. Meanwhile, the mercantile house of Andrew and
Jonathan Belcher prospered, by importing articles of
choice, good Madeira Wines, furnished supplies for the
colonial armies, participated in provincial loans,
invested in Simbury copper mines, and speculated in
Maine lands. Captain Andrew Belcher shipped grain
to Curacao, against the Selectmen of Boston's wishes
during times of grain shortages ("If they stopped his
vessel, he would hinder the coming in of three times as
much." ("Sewall Diary" Vol. II, Pg. 384/5). Jonathan's
warehouse was robbed, in 1720, of: "a White Hair Camlet
Cloak lined with Blue, a Suit of Cinnamon Coloured Broad
Cloth lined with silk, a Drab Riding Coat, a Book
Entituled, Magnalia Christi Americana, A New England Law
Book, and several other printed Books... of a value of
near seventy or eighty Pounds." ("Boston News Letter,"
Feb. 1-8, 1720; above also compiled from "Sibley's
Harvard Graduates," Vol. IV, Pg. 437, and "Dictionary of
American Biography," Johnson, Vol. 2, Pg. 145).

We might reasonably hazard a guess that Captain Andrew Belcher was involved in the golden triangle: Rum to Africa, slaves to Jamaica or one of the nearby Caribbean Islands, and sugar, molasses, or Spanish dollars back to Boston. They shipped flour, fish, meat and lumber to the Caribbean, tobacco, furs, Indigo and Naval stores for manufactured goods in England;   and primarily the intercolonial trade which was growing yearly. The 1700 period was a spectacular period to be involved in the profits of trade...and England wanted part of the profit.

The aristocratic young Jonathan Belcher's relationship with Massachusetts politics was also growing. It is doubtful that the following would have occurred without the support of Governor Joseph Dudley or his father, Andrew, who was on the Governor's Council: In 1712, Jonathan, age thirty, according to Judge Samuel Sewall's diary, "comes to me and speaks very freely for passing the Act about Bills of Credit; said I should do well to be out of the way rather than hinder so great a good." ("Samuel Sewall Diary," II, Pg. 65). As a further insight into Belcher's personality, Judge Samuel Sewall (1652-1730) was the presiding judge who condemned nineteen people to death at the Salem, Massachusetts Witch trials in 1692. Sewall repented that action in 1697. Jonathan was apparently not intimidated by the sixty year old Sewall in 1712. In fact there is significant evidence Jonathan Belcher was not easily intimidated by anyone.

The Bill's of Credit were designed because of the inflationary period to accept depreciated currency. It is estimated that the 1730s value of money between England and America, favored England by a rate ranging from five to roughly ten to one. Jonathan's view of inflation favored the merchants in 1716. One year before his father, the irascible Capt. Andrew died, Jonathan, an English nobleman (Sir William Ashurst), and Jonathan's Harvard Classmate, Jeremiah Dummer, bribed Colonel Elizeus Burgess (a favorite of the inflation party), not to accept a Commission from the King as Governor of the Province of Massachusetts. More about that issue later. (see "Boston Commissioner Records 1700-1728," Vol. 8, Pg. 155).

The public opposed Belcher's support of the merchants and after being dropped from the Governor's Council in 1728,

Belcher   changed inflationary views for a brief time.   He
regained popularity.

Before exploring Jonathan's activities and associates   as
Governor   of   Massachusetts,   it   might be worth while to
submit   the   following   extract   from   his   contemporary,
Thomas Hutchinson (1711-1780), the last Royal Governor of
Massachusetts Bay Colony.   Hutchinson was a member of the
Massachusetts Assembly during the later part of Belcher's
administration.   He also   wrote   a   1765 History of the
Massachusetts Bay Colony. The following   lengthy   extract
describes Belcher from "Hutchinson's History":

"Being   the   only   son   of a wealthy father,   he had high
views from the   beginning   of   life.   After   an   academic
education in his own country,   he traveled to Europe, was
twice at Hannover, and was introduced to the court there,
at   the time when the princess Sophia was the presumptive
heiress to the British Crown.   The novelty of   a   British
American, added to the gracefulness of his person, caused
distinguishing notice to be taken of him, which tended to
increase   that   aspiring   turn   of   mind   which   was very
natural to him.   Some years after, he made another voyage
to England,   being then   engaged   in   mercantile   affairs
(this   would   probably   be his 1715 voyage to London-ed),
which,   after his return home,   proved,   in   the   general
course   of   them,   rather unsuccessful,   and seem to have
suppressed or   adbated   the   ruling   passion,   but   being
chosen   agent   for   the   House   of   Representative, (this
would be his trip to London in 1728-ed)   it   revived   and
was   gratified   to   the   utmost,   by his   appointment to
the government of Massachusetts-bay   and   New   Hampshire,
and   before   itself   in every part of his administration.
Before he was governor,   except in one instance,   he   had
always   been   a   favorite   of   the perogative (opposed to
inflationary   issuance   of   currency-ed),   and   afterwards
he   did   not   fail   of   acting   up   to his principles.   A
man of high principles cannot be too jealous of   himself,
upon   a   sudden   advancement   to   a   place of power.   The
Council never enjoyed less freedom than in his   time.   He
proposed   matters   for   the   sake   of their sanction than
advice,   rarely failing   of   a   majority   to   approve   of
his   sentiments.   He   lived elegantly in his family,   was
hospitable,   made   a   great   shew   in   dress,   equipage,
&   c.   and   although   by the depreciation of the currency
he was curtailed   of   his   salary,   yet   he   detained   any
unwarrantable   or mean ways of obtaining money   to supply

his expenses. By great freedom in conversation and an
unreserved censure of person whose principles or conduct
he disapproved, he made himself many enemies. In a
private person, this may often pass with little notice,
but from a governor it is very hardly forgot, and some
never ceased pursuing revenge until they saw him
displaced." ("History of Massachusetts Bay," Thomas
Hutchinson, 1765, Mayo Edition, Pg. 281).

From Hutchinson, we begin to see into the tug of war
between the Governor and the elected members of the
Assembly. What could Boston do against an English King,
who appointed their governor? Could a governor merely
"propose matters to his Council," rather than take their
advice? The solution, of the elected members of the
Massachusetts Assembly, was to resist paying the Royal
Governor his salary! That precise strategy had been
working just fine in Boston, thank you, against Governor
Shute (1716-1723). Hence, Hutchinson, as an elected
Assemblyman, in 1737, rubbed shoulders with those who
expressed frustration with England's Colonial Government.

Ironically, Hutchinson was a victim of Boston politics
himself. Six years after Jonathan Belcher was dead, a
mob in Boston virtually destroyed Hutchinson's mansion,
one of the finest houses in Boston. They broke down
his door with axes, tore away the wainscot, beat
down the petitions, knocked off the cupola, and by the
morning of August 27, 1765, his house was laid flat. His
money was stolen, his library thrown into the muddy
streets of Boston and his trees were "broke down to the
ground." This was four years before he was acting
Governor, and six years before George III appointed him
as Governor in 1771!

"Hutchinson's History," was easier to write than it was
to be the Royal Governor of Massachusetts before 1775.

So much for Hutchinson. For a further insight into
Jonathan Belcher, we must examine our colonial
government and Jonathan's rise to power.

The commonly mentioned Stamp tax, battles for land with the French and Indian War, stationing of British troops, and closing frontiers to settlement are often listed as contributing causes of the American Revoltion in 1775. Another problem in colonial government was the restriction of trade. The so-called Acts of Trade were passed by Parliament in England between 1651 and 1761. These laws began encroaching into colonial profit, and controlling profit spelled trouble. As early as 1645 a law was passed which prevented whale oil being shipped to England in any ships except English vessels or ships manned by English seaman. By 1651 the problem with Dutch and colonial shipping was addressed by attempting to prevent any foreign product being shipped into England except on English ships, or manned by 75% English seaman. Smuggling was rampant, and I expect that the mariner, Captain Andrew Belcher (1646-1717), was one of the many smugglers. The Acts of Navigation became ridiculous in 1672 when products shipped between the colonies were required to go first to England.

A second problem was the organization of colonial government. The King reserved the right to "discontinue the representation of the people, whenever he should find it inconvenient, and after he had solemnly engaged this privilege." (Belknap, 1831 edition, Pg. 90). Because the King appointed the Governor and the Governor's Council, (with the ministers to the King giving a nod of approval), the government of the people was effectively in the hands of key ministers to the King. The Governor appointed many State officials (Judges, Sheriffs, Naval Office, Attorney General, Register's of Deeds and Probate etc.), but often was advised from England.

A third problem was the struggle of the land owners:

"The yeomanry were the proprietors of the soil and the natural defenders of their own rights and property; and they knew no superior but the King." (Belknap, Pg. 90, 1831 edition). The land grants were often not surveyed: where were the property lines in conflicting grants of land? What was a settler to do if ownership was uncertain? Who would help with their problems: Indian wars...epidemic disease...isolation, and

problems with shelter and food. Even the best trees
could not be sawed into lumber without breaking
the "King's Mast Trees" law. Who would enforce the
people's interest among the Governor's appointed friends?
How would property disputes be resolved when one was
dealing with a struggling farmer with a musket in the
wilderness? Yet as early as 1690, Massachusetts paid
taxes of about 20,000 pounds sterling.

Because of these problems, Boston began to develop an
inimitable political identity which was subtly opposed
to controls from England. As early as 1718, Elisha
Cook (?-1737) was elected to the Council and Governor
Shute rejected him. The citizens of Boston began to
elect Elisha Cook as Selectmen (1719) and for most of
the 1719-1737 period, as Representative to the General
Court. The hard drinking, Harvard educated, Elisha Cook,
is believed to have created the back slapping organized
elections ("caucuses") of pre-Revolutionary Boston. The
Royal Governor of Massachusetts, Samuel Shute (1716-23),
and acting Governor, William Drummer (1723-1728), began
to feel the heat of opposition.

Meanwhile, Jonathan Belcher's sister's husband, George
Vaughan (1676-1725), of Portsmouth, New Hampshire, had
been commissioned Lieutenant Governor of New Hampshire on
the recommendation of General Stanhope in 1716. (see
Belknap, Pg. 183). Jonathan's father was on Governor
Dudley (1702-16) and Shute's Council, in Massachusetts
between 1702-17. Jonathan's father-in-Law, Wm. Partridge,
had been acting Governor of New Hampshire in the 1697
period. Jonathan's close friend, John White, had been
the Clerk of the Massachusetts House between 1701-1721.
Jonathan was a member of Governor Joseph Dudley's Council
for four years between 1718-1727. In a word, Jonathan
Belcher, who was born in a tavern in Cambridge, had not
only visited with George I and his mother, in 1704, he
was closely aligned with the government that Elisha Cook
opposed. As we proceed into the appointment of Jonathan
Belcher as Governor, the fascinating struggle between
the colonies and English power is often revealed. The
American Revolution began quietly.

One key problem that consumed Massachusetts and New
England, in the 1720-1740 period, was the scarcity of
money. Scarcity was followed by a flood of worthless
paper currency. Inflation followed. As the economy

slipped there were two opposing philosophies: the
"Populists," led by Elisha Cook, physician, lawyer, and
land owner, who favored increasing the supply of paper
money; and the "Prerogatives," led by Governor Shute and
supporters like Jonathan Belcher. Wealthy merchants of
Boston were logically opposed to weakened profits created
by credit and later inflationary payment.

Elisha Cook's role as a Representative in the Assembly
began to take shape as one who would strengthen the
rights of the people. Control of tax revenues was his
first target. Before 1720 the governor with concent
of his Council drew funds from the treasury for
various projects. After 1720 "the house not only
destined the money, when put into the treasury, but
provided that none of it, except some trifling sums for
expenses and the like, should be issued without a vote of
the whole court ..." (Hutchinson, 1765, Pg. 287).

There were other methods of controlling the Governor: in
1716 it was feared if the "populist," Colonel Elizeus
Burgess, accepted a commission as Governor then he would
force inflationary times. Thus, Sir William Ashurst
(Richard Partridge's father was an old friend of the
Ashurst family; "N.E.Q.," Vol. V, Pg. 294), Jonathan, and
his Harvard classmate, Jeremiah Dummer (brother to Lt.
Governor, William Drummer), all three then in London,
revitalized a practice that was not unusual in the
eighteenth century. To quote a respected eighteenth
century historian Jeremia Belknap (1744-1798):

"Ashurst, with Jeremy Dummer, the Massachusetts agent,
and Jonathan Belcher, then in London, apprehending that
he (Burgess-ed) would not be acceptable...Dummer and
Belcher generously advanced, (1000 Pounds to Burgess
ed) to resign his commission;" and Colonel Samuel Shute
was appointed in his stead..." (Belknap, 1831 edition,
Pg. 183). In effect, it was a bribe to stop the King
from appointing an undesirable Governor to Massachusetts
Bay Colony.

The reader might be rather disgruntled that even the
respected historical scholar, and founder of the
Massachusetts Historical Society, Reverend Jeremy
Belknap, would define the open bribe of 1000 Pounds as
"generously advanced." The modern reader might be mildly
appeased by recalling Clifford Shipton's wise words
describing the eighteenth century:

"Governor Belcher does not deserve the abuse which has been heaped upon him by historians, his fawning for favors and his petty political schemes were those of the time employed by English courtiers and statesman such as Bolingbroke, Marlborough, Harley, and Walpole."
("Sibley's Harvard Graduates," Vol. 4, Pg. 448).

Thus, the King could appoint a Governor, but the King had to deal with Boston. After Colonel Burges declined the governor's office for 1000 Pounds, another Colonel, Samuel Shute was commissioned Governor of the two unruly Provinces in October, 1716. Shute delt with the Indian raids, petitions for plantations which upset the surveyor of the King's woods, poor wages from the Provinces, and his enemies, led by Elisha Cook, who charged Shute with attacks on Boston in a petition to the King from a town meeting. Finally, the military man's frustration with colonial politics was enough, Governor Shute departed for England rather hastily, in June of 1723 (Belknap, Pg. 197). Cook also headed for London in his role of representing the people of Boston. He encountered a disappointing two year effort to battle England's right to control government in the colony. Massachusetts and New Hampshire unhappily continued struggling with Indians and inflation for the next five years.

In November of 1727, on his way to Hanover, Germany, age sixty-seven, George I died. Jonathan had met his more socially oriented son, George II, at Hanover in 1704. It was an appropriate time to be in London.

By 1728 the estate of Jonathan Belcher had reached its zenith. The next adventure leading to the Governor's chair related to Belcher being appointed by the Connecticut Assembly (approximately Oct. 1728): "to attempt to secure a reversal in England of the decision in the important case of Winthrop vs. Lechmere, which was threatening the validity of all land titles in the Colony" (Connecticut Historical Society Collections). Having this reason to go to England, The Massachusetts House joined in the frolic and on December 20, 1728 voted that "Whereas Jonathan Belcher Esq. is intended on a voyage shortly to Great Britian...he be desired and impowered upon his arrival there to be aiding and assisting Francis Wilks." ("Journals of the House;" Mass. Hist. Soc., Vol. VIII, Pg. 391). Wilks role was to represent the Province of Massachusetts Assembly in the matter of a wages dispute against the Governor of Massachusetts.

While Jonathan was in London serving Connecticut and the agent for Massachusetts, the missing Governor of Massachusetts and New Hampshire was about to be replaced by George II. The retired Colonel Shute was briefly considered for a reappointment as Governor, but he recalled an unpaid 500 Pound debt that Belcher had used to enhance his previous commission as Governor (see "Sibley's Harvard Graduates," Vol. IV, Pg. 438). Ex-Governor Shute declined the office.

Enter into Boston, on July 22, 1728, Governor William Burnet, son of Bishop Burnet, who when complaining of the length of grace before meals as he traveled from Rhode Island to New Hampshire, was told by Col. Taylor:

> "The graces will increase in length, till you come to Boston; after that they will shorten till you come to your Government in New Hampshire, where your excellency will find no grace at all." ("History of New Hampshire," Jeremy Belknap, 1831 John Farmer edition, Pg. 223).

Forty-seven days after he first set foot into Boston as Governor, William Burnet died, probably as a result of his carriage tipping over on the Cambridge Causeway at high tide. ("Provincial Papers," Vol. IV, Pg. 555).

Belcher, explains in his own words what happened next in a letter to Benjamin Colman:

"...In a few hours after Mr. Wilks & I rec'd the Accott of his death We Wait'd on the King's Ministers & gave them the first News of it, & immediately Apply'd for Gover Shute, and that Very day dispatcht an Express to him (70 Miles in the Countrey) had his Answ In 24 hours, and he made the best of his Way to Town yet after a Calm Consideration of his being so far advanc'd in life & Easy in the Circumstances of it he made his Complimts of Gratitude to the King & his Ministers & desir'd to be Excusd from Accepting the Governmt- Would he A'gone No one Else Coud- After this I fixt my Eye Upon the Matter & pursud it in such A manner As brott the desird success, When it Was first Mentiond to the King by a great

Minister (this minister, according to Jonathan's later
correspondence was Charles Townshend, Secretary of State
in 1729 -ed.) the King Askt if it Was the same Mr Belcher
Who Was twice at Hannover, It Was Answered Yess and the
King remembd Me in a Very kind Manner and the same
Minister told me If I Valud the being Gover of My own
Countrey My having been at Hannover now provd one of the
happiest Articles of My Whole life...Since my Appointmt
to the Governmt I have my lodgings Within 5 or 6 doors of
the Royal Palace & am almost Everyday I live at the King
& Queen's Levee..." Belcher also notes his son, Andrew,
being in London, age twenty-two: "Andrew comes over in
handsome business; he has had many opportunities to Marry
to his advanta. & I coud' a'been pleas'd he had embracd.
but he seems indifferent, he is young, & I am content. If
he lives he thinks to See England again in another time."
("Colman Mss," Mass. Hist. Soc., Feb. 7, 1729/30).

"Belcher was appointed Governor on November 27, 1729, and
two days later kissed The King's hand, "After which his
Excellency and the Gentlemen trading to New-England,
(probably Richard Partridge, Francis Wilkes, and others)
dined elegantly at Pontack's." All brackets mine.
"Belcher's Commission (as Governor of Massachusetts and
New Hampshire) was dated January 8, 1729/30." ("Sibley's
Harvard Graduates," Vol. IV, Pg. 439). As one example of
Belcher's association with London, and his accommodations
at Whitehall, he did not return to America as Governor
until nine months after being commissioned as Governor.
He arrived in Boston aboard the English war ship,
"Blandford," on August 9, 1730. Boston was 100 years old.

Belcher arrived amid processions, "gun's which were
bursting in every part of town... His Excellency was
conducted by his Civil and Military Attendants to a
splendid Entertainment at the Bunch of Grapes..."("Boston
News Letter," Aug. 6-13, 1730). The "Bunch of Grapes," in
1733, was the meeting place of St. John's Lodge of
Boston. Both political parties greeted Belcher in Boston
as their own, but after the September 9, 1730, meeting of
the General Court, Belcher was only paid 1500 Pounds for
his services as agent, and was refused His Majesty's
wishes to pay a salary to the Governor. This last,
Jonathan half-heartedly challenged, and according to
Sibley: "In effect Belcher had betrayed the British
Government into one of the most serious political defeats
it had ever sustained in the Colonies." ("Sibley's
Harvard Graduates," Vol. VI, Pg. 441).

In fact the Governor's wages were a yearly battle long before Belcher. It was a technique of Boston's Representatives controlling the Royal Governor, as led by Elisha Cook's cronies. Jonathan may have been cautious about rocking the boat, more than necessary, at the beginning of his administration in Boston.

Events turned out differently in New Hampshire. Belcher supervised two Lt. Governors at this time, William Tailer (1677-March 1731/2), of Massachusetts, and John Wentworth (1672-Dec. 1730), of New Hampshire.

John Wentworth was involved in the first incident in Belcher's administration: being a cautious New Englander, and unaware who would become governor in those days, he wrote letters of congratulations to both candidates! Belcher and Samuel Shute. Belcher was unaware of Wentworth's bold attempt at diplomacy, until his first trip to New Hampshire to Wentworth's home, in the fall of 1730. Jonathan felt Wentworth was a hypocrite, and promptly refused to share his salary from New Hampshire (as had been previously done), with Wentworth. Belcher allowed only minor fees amounting to 50 Pounds a year to Wentworth, from such items as licenses and certificates. From that time forward, the Wentworth family and their close friends in New Hampshire were prominent individuals who opposed Jonathan Belcher: they were led by Theodore Atkinson (1691-1779), member of Belcher's Council in 1732, and later Secretary of State in N. H. in 1741; Benning Wentworth (1695-1770), who was also on Jonathan's Council, in 1732, and later became Governor of N. H. (1741-1767), Benning is believed to be a Freemason; and a serious problem, David Dunbar (Lt. Governor, 1731-41).

The fact that Lt. Gov. John Wentworth (Benning's father), died within five months after his argument with Jonathan, did not solve the problem. The Benning Wentworth alliance had friends in London. Enter, David Dunbar, the new Lt. Governor of New Hampshire.

David Dunbar was a very time consuming problem for the administration of Jonathan Belcher. Dunbar, commissioned by the King and arriving in New Hampshire in June of 1731 was a thorn in Belcher side. The date is interesting because Jonathan's English patron, Secretary of State, Townshend, had an argument with his brother-in-law and Prime Minister of England, Sir Robert Walpole, in 1730. Townshend resigned as Secretary of State in 1730.

Whoever recommended Dunbar, as Lt. Governor in 1731, was not a favorite of Jonathan's. Dunbar didn't like to take orders from Belcher from the beginning. One example is that Dunbar thought he could appoint the Captain of the fort William and Mary. Belcher explains the situation (after Dunbar complained to London), to the Secretary of State in England, The Duke of New Castle, Thomas Pelham, on October 29, 1731:

"But when the Capt of the Fort William & Mary wrote me in these words, -"As to the fort your excellency has been pleas'd to favour me with, the Leiut. Govr sayes he shall never accept your commission for it, for that, he sayes, he looks upon with contempt, but swears no body shall command there but by commission from himself." With submission to your Grace, I then thought it high time to assert the King's honour and to let the Leiut. Govr (and all the world) know such insults were intolerable, and certainly such behavior cannot be consistent with the duty of a Leiut. Govr to his Capt General & Govr in Chief, but must produce anarchy & confusion in a government." ("Belcher Papers," Vol. VI, Pg. 12).

There is another interesting angle to David Dunbar. He was supported from England by one of the Lords of Trade, Martin Bladen. As an aside, Martin Bladen was a Freemason (AQC, 40/33), and there is significant evidence that Martin Bladen was supporting David Dunbar to make life difficult for Jonathan Belcher's government ("Belcher Papers," Vol. VII, Pg. 100-106). At any rate, the Lords of Trade were one of Jonathan's immediate superiors, regarding orders from the King, financial Trade control, reports from the Royal Governor, and general trade intermediary between the colonial government and the King of England. In brief, when the government of the colonies did not submit to the orders from the King, Jonathan Belcher was answerable to the eight members of the Lords of Trade and others. The plot would thicken between Belcher, David Dunbar, and the financially powerful Lords of Trade.

In the midst of these political struggles, the spirit of many colonists was tempered by overwhelming problems. Twenty families buried all their children because of a disastrous throat distemper in Hampton Falls, N. H., in 1735. There were other problems: the distasteful taxes, control of resources, and periodic Indian attacks did not ease the burden of the working class. There was, moreover, blatant corruption among office seekers from two camps: friends of friends in England, and friends of friends in America. Belcher, for example, had given his son-in-law, Byfield Lyde, one half the salary of the Naval Office, and the other half to his own son, Andrew Belcher. By Act seven and eight of King William III (1650-1702), the Governor was supposed to be the Naval Officer, yet George II's order was for Benjamin Pemberton to replace Belcher's choice. Jonathan was advised to attempt and save the position, but Belcher is reported to have replied, "Although the King could not make a naval officer he could make a governor, and he was forced to give up his son-in-law." (See Lawrence Shaw Mayo's edition of "The History of the Colony and Province of Massachusetts Bay," by Thomas Hutchinson, Pg. 285).

In view of some of the above activities: (1) encroaching into colonial profit, (2) control of land use, (3) the King's domination in spite of agreements, (4) Judicial dependence, (5) political unfairness, and all of this in the face of, (6) a struggle to survive 3000 miles from England; it was predicable that colonial government would eventually be summarized by the likes of Patrick Henry: the delegate to the first Continental Congress proclaimed to the Virginia Provincial Convention in 1775: "Give me liberty or give me death."

Indeed, other Freemasons, such as Benjamin Franklin, George Washington, and John Hancock, would not accept the growing unfairness of English control in another generation. But Jonathan Belcher would be still be walking the tightrope of colonial government, holding the reins of New Jersey, 120 years after his grandfather settled in the new world. It is productive, even today, to examine the struggles of Jonathan Belcher's administration, in order to better understand the United States Constitution.

Before we explore Jonathan's later activities and associates as Governor, let us now explore Freemasonry as it relates to Jonathan Belcher.

There are limits to the known information about Belcher as a colonial Freemason, much less in England. The Quatuor Coronati Lodge in London, consisting of no more than forty Masonic scholars, at one time, from around the world, has published 103 volumes of Masonic research since 1886 which will fill a ten foot bookshelf. Yet, even the immensely regarded "Quatuor Coronati Transactions" only devote a few paragraphs to the first known, American born, Freemason. Indeed, even in America, very little has been published about Jonathan's Masonic activities. The reason is clear: Masonic evidence about Belcher is meager. It is my belief, after this brief chapter, that the most productive approach toward understanding Belcher's association with Freemasonry is to explore his life in a broader context... for this chapter, I will attempt to provide an overview of the known information about Belcher and Freemasonry.

For those who wish further information on early American Freemasonry, I would suggest "Colonial Freemasonry," L. C. Wes Cook-editor, 1973. Other valuable references include the "American Lodge of Research," in New York City, The "Philalethes Society," in Highland Springs, Va., the "Missouri Lodge of Research" in Fulton, Missouri, and the library at the Museum of Our National Heritage in Lexington, Massachusetts.

For a start, it is appropriate to mention the difference between Boston and London in the early 1700s. Boston Freemasonry was derived from a population of 15,000, compared to 500,000 in London. Traditions in colonial America were barely 100 years old, London had recorded traditions for centuries. In 1733, Belcher was a fifty-one year old Governor of the Massachusetts Province when the tailor, Henry Price, became the first Grand Master of Freemasons in New England. Furthermore, in 1733, Belcher had been a Freemason for twenty-nine years. Henry Price was only eight years old when Belcher became a Freemason.

Thus, we must begin with England. Many scholars believe that Freemasonry grew out of "convivial English Taverns" in the 1600s. In that time of civil wars, "there was an obvious need for secret societies in which opinions could be expressed" (Batham, AQC 103, 35). But Freemasons kept no known official records before 1723. Thus, 1704 Masonry

was a very different Fraternity, in the city of London,
when Jonathan was initiated, (Pg. 198) than the newly
created Freemasonry in Boston in 1733. London Masons had
written a Masonic Constitution and added nobility to
their leaders in 1723. Belcher's home lodge was from the
"old days," and based on the new evidence in this
research, confirming that he was indeed in London in
1704, it was undoubtedly in England. My opinion is that
further research may reveal that his later brother-in-
law, Richard Partridge, may tie in with Belcher becoming
a Freemason. Partridge was a colonial agent, in London,
as early as 1701 (see Pg. 189-195).

In an effort to explain the limited Masonic information
about Belcher, it is worthy of emphasis that Belcher was
very cautious about his activities as Governor. He often
used coded words when referring to his opponents, and
the early activities of the pre-Grand Lodge era
Freemasons, included biased opposition, which did not add
to a pre-Grand Lodge era Freemason's inclination for
publicity... particularly if he was a Royal Governor with
the usual opponents in Boston and London (see "anti-
Masonic Leaflet of 1698" in "Early Masonic Pamphlets,"
by Knoop, Jones, and Hamer, 1978 edition, Pg. 34).

Today, there is little of this so-called "secrecy" among
Freemasons, but during various times in history,
Freemasons were virtually threatened if they belonged
to this old fraternity of fellowship and harmony. Hence,
it is my speculation that Freemasons before 1717 were
much more cautious of protecting their traditions than
the open discussions and publication of books that are
more typical today.

One of the fascinating aspects of Freemasonry to me,
however, is not only the similarity of the language and
traditions today, to that of the early eighteenth
century, but it provides an insight into the activities
of historically significant individuals. In fact, no one
really knows how old the Fraternity is. The theory of
scholars today, that it originated in England, and
was separate from the organized stone masons, suggests
that Belcher was carrying on a tradition of his family's
ancestors from England. Other scholars believe Freemasonry evolved from stone masonry, this theory is
particularly evident in Scotland. We have no proof of
where he became a Mason. For now, we return to Boston.

It is July 30, 1733. We are in Boston at the corner of King and Mackrell Lane (now State and Kilby Streets). Over the door of a tavern is an oak, carved sign of a bunch of grapes. Inside, a thirty-six year old tailor, Henry Price, had not only organized a "Provincial Grand Lodge of New England and Dominions and Territories thereunto belonging," he also granted a petition to the First Lodge of Massachusetts, St. John's Lodge of Boston.

After Jonathan Belcher's son, Andrew, was selected as the first Deputy Grand Master of New England, by Henry Price, the Governor reciprocated by appointing Price, "Coronet," with the rank of Major in 1733 ("St. John's Lodge of Boston," 1917, Pg. 202).

On March 29, 1734, the "Boston Gazette" published: "On Friday last at Mr. Lutwytche's long room in King Street, was held a Grand-Lodge of the Ancient and Honorable Society of Free and Accepted Masons where his Excellency Governor Belcher and a considerable Number of the Fraternity were present."

September 23, 1741, St. John's Lodge, of Boston, "Voted that next after the G.M. (Grand Master of Masons in Mass. at this time was Henry Price-ed) the Late Governor (Note: Belcher was replaced as Governor by April 30, 1741-ed) of this Province, is to be toasted in the following manner, viz: To our R. W. Bro. the Honble Mr. Belcher, Late Governor of N.E. with 3/3/3=9..." (this is a traditional toast of respect still in existence at Masonic Lodges).

Next was the famous September 25, 1741, gesture by St. John's Lodge of Boston, in which Belcher was thanked for his work as a Freemason and in which he responded in a letter, calculating that he was accepted as a Freemason in 1704 (See Pg. 197-198).

The only other known records of Jonathan as a Freemason are: Feb. 8/9, 1743/4, concerning the entertainment of Governor Belcher; September 26, 1744, when Governor Belcher was in London (Jonathan began his attempt to be reappointed Governor in 1744, succeeding in 1747-ed) and he visited the Grand Lodge at London with a letter from the First Lodge in Boston; Summer of 1747, when the Lodge sent a letter of congratulations to the Governor on his appointment as Governor of New Jersey; September 3, 1747, when the Lodge sent a letter of congratulations that the Governor had arrived safely in New Jersey; and October 6, 1747, when Governor Belcher from Kingswood House in Burlington, New Jersey, wrote a letter in acknowledgement of thanks for the letter of September 3, 1747, (Johnson, "Freemasonry in America prior to 1750").

To summarize, there are very few indications of Belcher's activities as a Freemason in America. The Charter members of St. John's Lodge of Boston, in 1733, included the Governor's son, Andrew, age twenty-six, who was also the first Deputy Grand Master. Andrew, according to Charles Smith, of the 1894 Belcher Papers Committee, which were published by the Massachusetts Historical Society, "was without ambition, and had none of his father's restless ambition". (Preface "Belcher Papers," Vol. VI, Pg. xvi). The other seventeen Charter members of St. John's Lodge of Boston had virtually no correspondence with Governor Belcher, and were mainly of a younger generation. Benjamin Pemberton, a 1734 member of St. John's Lodge in Boston, and came from London in 1733 (B. P., Vol. VII, Pg. 167), was described (Nov. 8, 1734) as an "insolent jackanapes" by Belcher. The Governor's close nephew, Andrew Oliver, who benefited from several Belcher letters in 1733, was thirty-four when he joined St. John's Lodge in Boston, in 1740. Jonathan Belcher, with political friends as well as opponents in American Freemasonry may not have been active with the younger Boston Freemasons of 1733.

Those Freemasons that have been identified in records that exist, in Portsmouth and Boston, who received letters from Belcher include: (in Portsmouth) Henry Sherburne (1674-1757), and George Mitchell (1693?-1755) (John Tufton Mason, Benning Wentworth, and Joseph Sherburne are only mentioned in other letters). In Boston, Belcher wrote to, or mentioned, only his nephew, Andrew Oliver (1706-1774); James Crawford (young son of Governor Belcher's old friend); his son Andrew; and the previously mentioned Benjamin Pemberton.

Retired attorney Gerald Foss, Grand Lodge Historian Emeritus of New Hampshire, has studied the St. John's Lodge No. 1, of Portsmouth, N. H., for many years. His findings verify Sherburne, Mason, and Mitchell as Free-masons, and B. Wentworth, and J. Sherburne are believed to be Freemasons. ("Three Centuries of Freemasonry in

New Hampshire." Foss). Among the 1000 pages of indexed, transcribed and printed Belcher correspondence (1731-43), neither Henry Price, nor any of the eighteen <u>original</u> members of St. John's Lodge, in Boston, (except Andrew Belcher) is mentioned in a single letter. Further, from the hand of Francis Beteilhe, Secretary of St. John's Lodge of Boston, comes the Beteilhe manuscript, with a list of fifty-seven names including "His Excelly Jona Belcher Esqr." That manuscript includes the identity of members of the Lodge addressed to the Grand Master of England, the Earl of Loudoun, on June 23, 1736 ("American Lodge of Research," Vol. VII, No. 2, Pg. 159). Comparing that list of members, to Belcher's correspondence as Governor, only a young man from England, John Smith, who is trying to settle an estate, and the four previously mentioned members are noted in Belcher's exhaustive correspondence. On the other hand, Henry Sherbourne (1664-1757), whose house was used for the first meeting of St. John's Lodge No. 1, in Portsmouth, N. H., and who Belcher wanted for his Lt. Governor, received over 50 letters.

It is certainly possible that Belcher was active as a Freemason in Portsmouth, or Boston, and those records are lost or were not recorded. In Portsmouth, for example, "an extensive research was conducted throughout the town of Portsmouth of descendants about 1820-21 for old minutes believed to have been made...no minutes exist for 1736, 1737, or 1738." (Foss letter).

Although the early records of Portsmouth cannot be located, Belcher was compulsive in writing letters to individuals who could be of use to his work. Other than Henry Sherburne, there is very little evidence in his letters to Americans. Although Belcher is given credit for supporting Boston Freemasonry in the 1741 period, it is not unlikely that his motives were more oriented towards the sophistication of nobility in the Grand Lodge of England, than to the "raw production of the wilds of America" (Jonathan Jr.'s introduction to Lord Townshend from his father (B. P., Vol. VI, Pg. 92; Dec. 30, 1731).

The additional Masonic insights about Belcher, in this research, will be recaped in the conclusion. Meanwhile, keep in mind that documentation of pre-1717 Freemasons is extremely rare (Belcher is only one of six <u>that claimed</u> to be a member, conceded to be in England). We know that the following were Freemasons in Boston as early as 1736:

BOSTON FREEMASONS: 1736, FROM BETEILHE MANUSCRIPT

Mr. Henry Price, G.M.
His Excelly Jona. Belcher Esqr.
Andrew Belcher Esqr.
Benja. Pemberton Esqr.
Henry Hope Esqr.
Capn. James Cerke
Capn. Roger Willington
Mr. John McNeal
Brethren made in Boston (**)
Mr. James Gordon D:G.M.
Mr. Benja. Barons S.G.W.
Mr. Robert Thomlinson J.G.W.
Capn. Robert Maclean M.
Mr. Hugh Mc.Daniel S.W.
Mr. John Osborne Jun. J.W.
Francis Beteilhe Secy.
Charles Bladwell Esqr.
Doc. Thos. Moffatt
John Overing Esqr.
Mr. Thoms. Phillips
Mr. Andrew Hallyburton
Mr. Thos. Oxnard
Capn. Willm Hinton
Capn. Robt McKnight
Capn. Webber Gofton
Capn. Robert Smith
Capn. Willm Frost
Capn. Robert Boydd
Capn. Benja. Hallowell
Doc. Robert Gardiner

Mr. Chars. Gordon
Mr. Alexa. Trann
Mr. Sam. Pemberton
Mr. Willm Wesson
Mr. Robt. Kenton
Mr. Robt. Peasely
Mr. Peter Prescott
Mr. John Baker
Mr. Sam: Curwin
Mr. Anto. Davis
Mr. John Smith
Mr. Sam: Wethered
Mr. Hugh Scott
Mr. John Gordon
Mr. Richd. Pateshall
Mr. Frans Johonot
Collo. Jona. Morris
Capn. John Fraizier
Capn. Jas. Farrell
Capn. Giles Vandellure
Capn. John Huggott
Mr. Fredk. Hamilton
Mr. Thos. Molony
Mr. Edmd. Ellis
Mr. Luke Vardy (Master
   of the Royall Exchange
   Tavern
Capn. James Forbes
Mr. Moses Slaitterrey
Mr. Alexa. Gordon

Henry Price (AQC 92/114), Andrew Belcher (Pg. 155), and the Governor (**), were probably made Freemasons in England. Other than the presumed Henry Price of New England, who was number twenty on the list at the Rainbow Coffee House (warranted as Masonic Lodge No. 75 on July, 17, 1730) in London, no hard evidence exists.

Forty years after 1736, we had created a Declaration of Independence and started a war with England. Perhaps we will learn more about the evolution of that struggle, and the elusive early Freemasons, by exploring Jonathan's activities and associates while he was Governor.

CHAPTER EIGHT: PROBLEMS FOR THE GOVERNOR

There were four basic problems in the fall of 1731:

First was the Governor's wages. The Massachusetts Assembly did not have a "just sense of their duty to his Majesty in settling my salary agreeable to his Royal instructions." ("Belcher Papers," Vol. VI. Pg. 14 to Lords of Trade). In addition to the Governor's wages, there was coupled with that problem the inflationary item of issuing money out of the treasury, and the Governor's instruction not to issue any bills of credit: "for a longer term than those were to remain current which had been issued, none of which extended beyond the year 1741." The result: charges were due each year and the adequate taxes delayed. Even today, this sounds familiar. Thus, by 1741, the taxes were more than had been accumulated in the past four or five years altogether. Because of the scarcity of money and bills of credit being issued in other colonies, this led to the irrepressible merchants of Boston issuing their own currency: "110,000 Pounds redeemable in 10 years at 19 Shillings per ounce of silver. As soon as silver rose to twenty-seven shillings per ounce, the notes were hoarded and no longer answered the purposes of money." (Hutchinson, 1765, Pg. 287-9).

Second was David Dunbar, "if we might be quit of that uneasy gentlm Coll Dunbar; and as his being Leiut Govr is no sort of service to him, nor can I (with submission to your Lordships) believe it any to his Majesty or that people, I wou'd still pray that Coll Henry Sherburne might be my Leiut Govr there." ("Belcher Papers," Vol. VI, Pg. 19, to Lords of Trade).

Third was the boundary line between New Hampshire and Massachusetts. This issue eventually went to court in England before the King: "I am sorry that the long depending affair of the disputed lines is not yet brought to any conclusion, altho' I have taken indefatigable pains in both Provinces, and the two Assemblies have past several votes & acts, & have met one another by their Committees, & according to the best Judgement I can make after all their attempts one with another, I think the line never will be settled here by the two governments, but the borderers thereon will still lye open to great

inconveniences & cruel hardships from both governments;
and upon this article I must say, my Lords, in
justice to New Hampshire that they have been very willing
& ready to submit to the decision of this affair in
exact conformity to his Majesty's instruction;   but
the Massachusetts have made too many obstacles &
difficulties, nor do I think they have been so candid &
fair in the matter as N. Hampshire has been." ("Belcher
Papers," to Lords of Trade, Vol. VI, Pg. 16).

Massachusetts was beginning to exercise its muscles
against England long before 1775. But there were
consequences in opposing the King of England: Massachusetts would lose the boundary dispute. The King awarded a
huge tract of land to New Hampshire about the time he
replaced Belcher in 1741. Meanwhile, Dunbar was aligned
with the Wentworth family and other Belcher opponents.
Two weeks after Dunbar arrived in New Hampshire he was
writing letters to the Board of Trade alleging Belcher's
government was oppressive, grievious, and arbitrary.
Fifteen individuals from New Hampshire requested Belcher
be replaced in July 1731. But Belcher's close friend,
Richard Walton (the Governor's Secretary), fought back
with a petition with a hundred names and sent it to
England at the same time.

Forth, was the opposition to Belcher because of his late
Lt. Governor's ill treatment and death. This is the
eighteenth century opinion of Belknap:

"Benning Wentworth (son of the late Lt. Governor John
Wentworth) and Theodore Atkinson, who had married (John
Wenworth's) daughter, were at the head of the opposition.
The latter was removed from his office of Collector of
Customs, to make room for Richard Wibird; the Naval
Office was taken from him and given to Ellis Huske
(Huske's son, also named Ellis, was a Postmaster and is
said to have recommended to the British Government, the
Stamp Act of 1765-ed); and the office of High Sheriff,
which he had held, was divided between him and Eleazar
Russell. Other alterations were made, which greatly
offended the friends of the late Lt. Governor; but
Belcher, was satisfied that his conduct was agreeable
to his commission and instructions, disregarded his
opponents and (he) apprehended no danger from their
resentment." (Belknap, 1791, Pg. 225).

Although Jonathan may not have been accurate in his initial assessment of his opponents, in the mist of these struggles, Governor Belcher began to solve these problems by looking toward England. He quickly build up a correspondence through his agents, his brother-in-law, Richard Partridge, and his son, Jonathan Jr., in England.

Richard Partridge and Jonathan Jr. would be virtually overwhelmed with correspondence from Jonathan. Each ship to England would carry bundles of gifts, letters and seemingly endless orders addressed to Partridge and the college bound Jonathan Jr. The Governor of Massachusetts and New Hampshire ordered Partridge, and Jonathan Jr., to read each letter, reseal it, and then personally deliver the letter all over Great Britain. Beyond that, the Governor wrote scores of letters directly to his son and Partridge with incredible persistence, demanding action on minute details.

Jonathan Jr. was carefully directed how to marry, whether to wear a wig, how to study, who to visit in England, who to write to in America, how to spend his money, what coffee-houses to attend, what people were writing about him from England, what gifts to buy, who to deliver gifts to, and occasionally allowed him to make decisions for himself. But this is not the whole story. Jonathan Jr. was given sincere devotion by his father, and he was also given tremendous opportunities to understand his father's goals in government. The Governor, as previously stated, gave Jonathan Jr. 13,000 Pounds in 10 years for his education and support at Cambridge and Oxford. But the Governor was a tough task master, his son, at one point disappeared into Ireland, for a considerable time, in an apparent effort to escape his father's driving ambition. The Governor wrote to his son: "You may depend, there is no dodging or evading with me. No, you must be punctual in your obedience to what I require; & your delayes in such things justly provoke me, and really, Sir, believe it, if I cannot have the account of the expense of my money, I will stop my hand from letting it go." (B. P. Vol. VII, Pg. 368, dated January 27, 1740/1). Predictably, by February 28, 1740/1, Jonathan Jr. wrote to his father (B. P. Vol. VII, Pg. 384).

Let us explore further. Jonathan was a meticulous man, he kept duplicates of all his correspondence as Governor in a letter book. London would hear from Boston.

CHAPTER NINE: THE BELCHER PAPERS

The "Belcher Papers" (B. P.), consist of Jonathan's letters between September 6, 1731, to July 25, 1743, (except April 21, 1735, to August 24, 1739). The two volumes include notes by scholars and an extensive index. The Massachusetts Historical Society also has manuscripts of Belcher from 1704-1754. Regarding the Craft, I did find letters and references to men in England who were Freemasons, Belcher mentions two coffee-houses in London that are known Masonic Lodges, and there are several clues to Belcher's old friends in London. He also noted the first two noblemen who were Grand Masters of England: The Dukes of Wharton and Montague were mentioned briefly, Wharton in this section, Montague in the appendix. (AQC refers to "Quatuor Coronati Transactions," the reference identifying most Freemasons, see Pg. 159). Governor Belcher focused on six frequent correspondents:

1. Jonathan Belcher Jr. (1710-1770): his youngest son in London, arriving from Boston, on August 1731.
2. Richard Partridge (1681-1759): his brother-in-law and N. H. agent in London. Partridge, as previously noted, (Page 145-6) was a respected colonial agent for Rhode Island, New Jersey, New York, Massachusetts and Connecticut. He had been in London since 1701.
3. The Lords of Trade (and other ministers to the King in appendix: Pg. 219, 231 for Privy Council/Trade).
4. Richard Waldron (1694-1753): the Governor's Secretary in America. Waldron was considered Belcher's closest friend and strongest supporter. He was born in Dover, New Hampshire, graduated from Harvard in 1712, and was the grandson of the famous Major Richard Waldron. The grandfather, a native of Somersetshire, and one of the first settlers of Dover, aside from his courageous military activities in the 1670s against the Indians, he was speaker of the New Hampshire House of Representatives in the 1666-1679 period. Waldron was promtly replaced by Belcher's successor, and opponent, Benning Wentworth in 1741.
5. Francis Wilkes: the Governor's Massachusetts agent in London. Wilkes was also helpful to Jonathan Jr., who recently arrived in London (August 1731).
6. Henry Sherburne(1664-1757): New Hampshire Freemason, one time prospect for Lt. Governor of New Hampshire. Nickname: "old H."

Jonathan's letters were also sent to roughly 250 other
individuals, both in America and England, some of whom
were extremely close friends. Some of the significant
individuals that Belcher wrote to, or mentioned in his
letters, are included in the appendix of this research.

First, are samples of his letters to illustrate his
administration annually. Second, is a selection of
letters to illustrate various points of interest.

First Section:

The Belcher Papers begin a year after he arrived in
Boston with his Commission as Governor. In the autumn of
1731, he traveled to his government in New Hampshire.
The trip into the woods of New Hampshire was classic
Belcher. On Sept 14, 1731, Belcher was greeted at the
border and "usher'd into the Province by Seventy Horse,
besides the blue Troop (and exclusive of the Gentlemen
who waited on him from his other Government)..."   ("The
New England Weekly Journal," Sept. 30, 1731). Belcher
requested Henry Sherburne to meet him at Hampton with
"the troop," and accompany his party on the ten mile ride
into his headquarters in Portsmouth. The family of
Governor Belcher's wife, Mary Partridge, lived in
Portsmouth, and they were probably visited by the
Governor. The Governor would Commission the new
Justices; learn the news of the two vessels seized who
had made a breach of the Acts of Trade; find that the New
Hampshire Assembly had a new act regarding the boundary
dispute between Massachusetts and New Hampshire; and
discover... disapprovingly, that his Massachusetts
Lieutenant Governor, Col. William Tailer (1677-March 1,
1731/2), had mysteriously embarked on a fishing boat for
the Isle of Shoales (seven miles off Portsmouth)... then
took a schooner eastward, at 11 O'Clock the night before
Belcher arrived (B. P. Vol. VI, Pg. 4/5).

"Old H," was one of Belcher's friends in Portsmouth. He
was also one of the wealthiest men of Portsmouth. Henry
was elected to the New Hampshire General Assembly
in 1720, Councilor 1728-1757, Chief Justice of the
Superior Court 1732-1742, Treasurer of New Hampshire in
1732, and several years thereafter ("Three Centuries
of Freemasonry in New Hampshire," Pg. 489). As has
been previously noted, Freemasons of Portsmouth first met

at Sherburne's house in 1736. "Old H" was a Charter
member of St. John's Lodge No. 1, in 1736, and the first
Treasurer of the Lodge from 1736-1741 (Foss, Pg. 488).

It would be reasonable speculation that Freemasonry
existed in Portsmouth before the 1735 Charter request
to Massachusetts.

There is an early example of the close association
between Belcher and Sherburne. On Sept. 6, 1731, Belcher
wrote a letter to his Secretary, Richard Waldron,
regarding his near relative, Colonel Byfield, who was
traveling from Boston to Portsmouth, New Hampshire:

"Take Coll Sherburne, Judge Gambling, and who else you
think proper, to meet him on the road. I have given him a
letter to Sherburne, and you must take care he asks him
to lodge at his house. Mind what I say, & don't let the
other people be before you in their respect. You know he
is my friend & near relation." (B. P. Vol. VI, Pg. 449).

As an example of Belcher's attention to the smallest
detail, he also wrote to "Old H," informed him of
Byfield's proposed journey, and desires that Byfield
should lodge at his house (B. P. Vol. VI, Pg. 449). This
theme of carefully laying the groundwork for various
trivial issues is frequently seen in the Belcher Papers.
It was irrelevant whether, or not, Byfield had anything
earth shattering to accomplish in Portsmouth, the fact
was that the Governor of Massachusetts was personally
going to arrange accommodations for his seventy-eight
year old relative. In a word, when it came to detail,
Governor Jonathan Belcher walked the full mile.

Meanwhile, by the end of 1731 Boston was broke. Consider
Belcher's correspondence to the Lords of Trade on
December 4, 1731.

"I now cover to your Lordships the Journals of the
House of Representatives...your Lordships will see I have
communicated to them his Majesties additional instruction
to me respecting the support of his Govr, and I am
sorry...I have no expectation of their granting my
support...All the ships expected from London this season
being arriv'd I can't hope to hear any thing from your
Lordships on this head 'till March next, and your

Lordships must be sensible how difficult it will be for this government to subsist to that time without one shilling in the treasury." (B. P. Vol. VI, Pg. 68).

We can conclude that Boston was not only unwilling, but unable to pay the Royal Governor his wages. Jonathan paid his expenses out of his pocket. His 70 Horse escorts into the New Hampshire government, his postage sent in all directions, and his rather immodest living standards were a problem. Ships did not sail overseas during the violent December to March weather, and money from England was wanting.

The above letter illuminates another aspect of Jonathan's personality: His driving ambition to solve problems created a variety of emotional reactions. He would exaggerate, criticize, create guilt, and plead with a wide range of correspondents. Jonathan was always throwing the ball to someone...and if they didn't catch it, he would most assuredly, throw it back again.

The plot thickens. The Lords of Trade want Belcher to provide an account of "laws made, manufactures set up, and trade carry'd on which may affect trade, navigation and manufactures of Great Britain." (B. P. Vol. VI, Pg. 69).

Belcher describes laws which encourage the production of hemp ("bounties of twenty-nine shillins for every 112 pounds of water rotted, well cured, and clean dressed hemp"); and a "bounty for the raising of flax; twenty shillings for the duck or canvas (30 shillings to the undertaker for canvas)." Belcher describes manufacturing of "brown holland for women's ware, importation of callicoes, linnen, cotton for sheeting and shirting, a paper mill set up three years ago which makes about 200 Pounds a year, forges for making bar iron (or hollow ware), one slitting mill" (this probably is some form of clapboards or shingles--ed.), as to "the country people who us'd formerly to make most of their own clothing out of their own wool don't now make a third part of what they wear, but are mostly clothed by British Manufactures." (B. P. Vol. VI, Pg. 70).

As to New Hampshire, Belcher mentions, "the British act passed imposing a duty for the supply of powder to the

fort William and Mary (which was stolen by the colonists
before the Revolution-ed), an act prohibiting the export
of Iron ore, wool is much reduced due to British
manufacture, flax is manufactured into linnen due to the
influx from skilled Irish immigrants. Export of masts,
yards, bowspirts, boards, staves, and rafters for
England, but principally to Spain and Portugal, and some
to the Charrible Islands, with Lumber and refuse fish and
the better sort of fish to Spain, Portugal, Italy etc.
Some sloops go in the winter (with English and West India
goods) to Virginia, Maryland and Carolina, etc. and
return with corn and flesh." (B. P. Vol. VI, Pg. 71).

It does not take to much imagination for one to see the
handwriting on the wall. The Knowledge that Belcher
provided to the Lords of Trade was a response to a
request. If a Royal Governor wished to keep England
happy, he had best follow instructions. But such
information formed a strategy for raising taxes. The
colonies produced no gold or silver. The colonists were
only allowed to trade goods for Manufactoring from
Britain. In spite of the 160,000 deer hides sent to
London from Charlestown, South Carolina in one year,
England wanted more of the action. England had her own
problems with debt. The French and Indian War, and the
Seven Years War created over 150,000,000 Pounds of debt
by 1760. The trappers, woodsmen, fishermen and farmers
of New England would pay. But England's diverse colony
had teeth that would bite back at "taxation without
representation" one half century after Belcher wrote to
the Board of Trade.

The Board of Trade would also receive more letters
from Jonathan Belcher. Between the efforts of his
agents in London, and his incessant correspondence,
London would be aware of problems in New England.

January 5, 1732/3, to the Board of Trade:

"...and now cover to your Lordships the remaining
Journals of their House; upon which I think your
Lordships will easily observe that the House of Repr of
this Province are continually running wild...Your
Lordship will find upon the King's Council's not agreeing
to their vote of taking the publick affairs of the
governmt into their hands... they made a vote yesterday

fully impowring a committee of their own house to write
the agent from time to time... This, most certainly,
is assuming a power they have no right to... the
perverseness and obstinacy of the House of Repr...
seem now to be hastening to a crisis... the King's
government can subsist any longer without his Majesties
immediate care... Officers and soldiers will certainly
desert...being naked and unable to do their duty for want
of their just pay... About six months ago I made a tour
into the eastern frontiers, and survey'd all the forts
there... For really my Lords, if things thus continue (or
still grow worse) this government and Province is in a
fair way to fall into all confusion and be lost." (See
B. P. Vol. VI, Pg. 242).

The House of Representatives in Boston, which was
"continually running wild," was headed by Elisha Cook,
popular elected member of the assembly. There was also a
younger Boston opposition developing. Thomas Hutchinson
and Andrew Oliver (The Governor's nephew) were opposed to
the silent acceptance of Cook's prearranged elected
officials in the Boston caucus.

Belcher wrote to Richard Partridge June 30, 1733:

"Mr. Cook made all the opposition in his power to the
bill for my support...I look on him as the author of all
the trouble & contention ...I have dismissed him from his
Judge's place." (B. P. Vol. VI, Pg. 311).

Jonathan was not totally an alarmist, although he did
tend to emphasize problems. He waded into controversy,
controlled his opposition and argued his position with
the powers that be in England.

One might speculate that the Lords of Trade were not
enthusiastic about receiving mail from Belcher: He
had problems, he wanted help, he complained of things
over which he had no control, he needed money, he
wanted to get rid of David Dunbar, he quoted his
Majesties instructions forbidding their instructions and
yet he persistently requests that the Lords of Trade ask
the King to sign his submitted bill regarding increasing
trade credit. (B. P. Jan. 12, 1732/3, Vol. VI, Pg. 249).

In a word, trouble was brewing in Boston and Jonathan
Belcher made a lot of noise. The fact that Boston was

the beginning of the Revolutionary War substantiates
Belcher's alarm. But the question is, was Jonathan part
of the problem or part of the solution? Next year
Jonathan picks up the hammer again:

Nov. 27, 1733, to the Board of Trade:

"Your Lordships say you presume the determinations of
his Majesty in Council and of the House of Commons upon
disputes the Assembly have had here with the Crown have
been sent me by the Agent of the Province... the
Agent... is cautious of even writing me a letter, lest he
should give umbrage to the Assembly, whom he looks upon
as his principles and masters (and not the King's
Govr)..." (B. P. Vol. VI, Pg. 428).

The agent Belcher is speaking about is Francis Wilkes,
who he wrote to twice a month between 1731-1733. The
Governor was exaggerating a bit. Before continuing with
the above letter, consider the following extract from a
letter to Richard Partridge, agent for New Hampshire,
regarding a conspiracy against Belcher:

Nov. 28, 1733, to Partridge:

"I am in the next place, brother, to say to you that I
have all the reason in the world to believe that Coll
Dunbar (being now intirely routed from Pemaquid) is
making all the interest he possibly can at home to be
Governor, not only of N. Hampshire, but of this Province,
and Mr. Cook, who is my mortal enemy, is join's with him
in it, and Mr. Craddock (who went in Sheperdson) will
help all he can... The King knows, and his ministers, and
all the world, how faithfull I have been to his
majesty..." (B. P. Vol. VI, Pg. 434).

After asking Partridge, his brother-in law, for "steady
application" of help from Sir Robert Walpole, the Duke
of Newcastle, and Charles De La Faye against his
enemies Dunbar, Cooke etc., Belcher continues to list
his problems in the above, Board of Trade, letter of Nov.
27, 1733:

"I would pray your Lordships to instruct me in what I
observ'd in my last as to the part former Assemblies here
have acted in presuming to appoint committees to take
care of building & repairing the King's forts... I have

nothing to add to the account I sent your Lordships last
year concerning laws made, manufactures set up, or trade
carry'd on... except it be the private scheme I have
transmitted to your Lordships for circulating a large sum
of bills of credit... it is very extraordinary that his
Majesty can govern & command his Provinces (as publick
bodies), and yet private persons shall presume to run
counter to his royal orders...I must... recommend to your
Lordship that Rhoad Island and the neighboring colonies
to this Province may be strictly forbit issuing any bills
of credit... As to the bill past twice in the Assembly of
this Province for emitting fifty thousand pounds in bills
of credit, on a foundation of gold & silver, I am still
of the opinion that it is the best projection has been
yet hit upon for reducing what are called bills of credit
to some steady standard, and such an emission of bills to
be under the orders & directions of the government wou'd
best of all secure the trade of Gt Britain to & in this
Province... I have no sort of interest in this matter, my
Lords, but what I say is in duty to the King...The people
here, my Lords, find an easier & quicker account in
lumber and fishery than they can do in raising naval
stores... there are but few people & labour consequently
very dear, the raising of new things (as Iron & hemp are
in this country) must be attended with some extraordinary
encouragmt; and as I mention'd had a good bounty been
given by Parliamt of Gt. Britain...twenty or thirty years
ago... Gt. Britain had before this time... have render'd
her independent of all the northern Crowns. But without
such encouragement... As to the revoking my 15
instructions respecting the repealing of laws, your
Lordship will observe my commission from his Majesty
sayes, "Whereas by a Royal Charter under the Great Seal
of England, & ca, and for your better guidance and
direction we do hereby require command you to do and
execute all things in due manner that shall belong unto
the trust we have reposed in you, according to the
several powers and authorities mention'd in the said
Charter," ...no doubt but your Lordships are fond
enough that the King's instructions shou'd agree with &
not contradict the Royal Charter... I shall be going in
about three weeks to my other government of N. Hampshire,
and on my return shall do myself the honour of writing
your Lordships again..." (B. P. Vol. VI, Pg. 432-3).

Here we see a most fascinating side of Jonathan Belcher.
There is a mouthful of information regarding colonial

problems in New England. But the underlying theme is that
Belcher is manipulating the Board of Trade as he
maneuvers his agents into positions of applying pressure
against his opponents, Cooke, Dunbar, and others. I
think it is fair to state that Belcher is using the King
as leverage against the Lords of Trade. His rather bold
response to their revoking his fifteen instructions, can
only be described as a shrewd underpinning of their own
power. In the midst of this development, Martin Bladen,
early Freemason, and supporter of David Dunbar, is a
member of the Board of Trade. Bladen would not be
overjoyed with the letter.

Jonathan Belcher, product of colonial American affluence,
education, and boldness might not be as easy to dispense
with as his primitive colonial background would suggest.
The Board of Trade was well aware that he had known King
George II since 1704, that the former Secretary-of-State,
Charles Townshend, was his patron and on the Privy
Council to the King, that his brother-in-law, Richard
Partridge, was a formidable agent in London, and his
son's management of English trade generated numerous
wealthy and influential associates in England.

Jonathan Belcher was a problem who knew how to fight
in the eighteenth century. In the next year, his battle
with his New Hampshire enemies, Theodore Atkinson,
Benning Wentworth, and David Dunbar, reaches the Board
of Trade. In brief, his opponents had sent letters
to the Board of Trade requesting various relief from
Jonathan's authoritarian methods against them. Belcher's
friend in London, Sir Charles Wagner, had sent copies
of these letters back to Jonathan for an explanation.
Belcher's response rambles on for eight pages. The
following extracts illustrate his methods against his
opponents:

October 2, 1734:

"I am much oblig'd to your Lordships for the justice you
have done me in serving me with copies to make an
answer... It is very extraordinary for Mr. Thomlinson to
say, "It was fully made to appear to your Lordships that
the sd. Mr. Atkinson was not only a fit person to be of
his Majesties Council, but the most fit & proper person

in that Province." This would have been high arrogance
for the man himself to have said, and I think a great
folly... for I am sure he is one of the greatest enemies
to his King & to his country... respecting the Royal
Magnamus for Mr Atkinson & Mr Wentworth... as to my
refusing to swear them (as members of the New Hampshire
Governor's Council-ed) when I did so, I long since told
your Lord ships that I refus'd it because of their
rudeness and insolence in not writing to me or sending me
their mandamuss, nor coming to me 'till I had been
several weeks in the Province, and they had done all the
mischief they cou'd in the Assembly as members of the
House of Representatives, and when I went last winter to
N. Hampshire I sent for Messrs Atkinson & Wentworth &
offer'd them their oaths, which they refus'd to take,
pretending they cou'd not serve in the Council because
they belong'd to the Repr House... As to their being
friends to Coll Dunbar, I think he shou'd be asham'd
to own them... And I wou'd now, my Lords, return
particularly to the affair of my salary, and admire Mr
Dunbar, or anybody for him, shou'd imagine he had the
least shadow of reason to make a claim to an iota of
it... The governmt of N. Hampshire is not this day worth
to me 100 Pounds Sterling a year, that it's almost a
shame to call it a government. The Provinces here, my
Lords, have not been us'd to give any thing to a Ltt
Govr, nor will they, because they say while they have a
Ltt. Govr he is an officer of no service to them... Had I
my Lords, 100,000 Pounds depending on this affair, in the
true & genuine light I have set it on your Lordships, I
cou'd submit it as a point of law to the twelve Judges of
England, or as a point of equity to the nicest Chancellor
in the World... Were I, my Lords, to give bread out of my
own mouth, I believe Mr Dunbar wou'd be the last person I
cou'd bear to feed, his study being nothing else but to
do me all the ill offices in his power... it can't be
suppos'd I will bear any of his insults & not teach him
his duty... I am sorry Mr Dunbar has given me occasion to
give your Lordships the trouble of such a tedious
letter..." (B. P. Vol. VII, Pg. 127).

Your Lordships' most obedient & humble servant. Jonathan
Belcher."

The above letter is an early hint into some of the
simmering problems which later caused a war after being
written in the following document:

(The   King)   "has   dissolved   Representative   Houses
repeatedly,   for   opposing   with   manly   firmness   his
invasions   on   the   rights   of   the   people... He   has   refused
for   a   long   time,   after   such   dissolutions,   to   cause   others
to   be   elected;   whereby   the   Legislative   Powers,   incapable
of   Annihilation,   have   returned   to   the   People   at   large   for
their   exercise.   He   has   forbidden   his   Governors   to   pass
laws   of   immediate   and   pressing   importance..."
(Declaration   of   Independence).

The   tenuous   relationship   between   Belcher   and   his   Lt.
Governor,   David   Dunbar,   would   bubble   away   for   several
years.   The   struggle   between   the   Lords   of   Trade   and
Belcher's   opponents   adds   to   the   confusion   of   who   is
running   the   store.   Dunbar   headed   for   England   in   the
spring   or   early   summer   of   1737.   Belcher   writes   to   Dunbar
April   25,   1737:

"You   say   you   certainly   imbark   this   week,   but   I   am   told
the   gout   has   got   hold   of   your   toe.   I   hope   you   won't   let
it   prevail   to   stop   your   (talk   of)   voyage.   I   say   this,
because   I   found   in   yours   to   me   of   Decr   last,   you   were
willing   I   should   have   hindered   it... but   I   have   had   so
many   letters   from   you   in   six   years   past,   saying   you   was
resolved   to   go   home,   go   home,   that   I   shall   not   believe
it   'till   some   vessel   tells   me,   they   have   met   you   to   the
eastward   of   St.   George's."   (B. P. Vol. VII,   Pg. 202).

Jonathan's   wit   barely   conceals   his   frustration   with
Dunbar,   Surveyor   of   the   King's   Woods.   Dunbar   had   created
problems   with   the   loggers   of   New   Hampshire   due   to   his
determination   to   preserve   the   King's   royal   mast   trees.
Dunbar's   men   were   seizing   logs   and   large   quantities   of
lumber   (3000   logs   in   1733,   B. P. Vol. VI,   Pg. 360).   To
the   colonists   who   hand   sawed   the   trees,   this   was   war.

In   the   Exeter   riot   of   1734,   Dunbar's   men   were   beaten   by
New   Hampshire   colonists   disguised   as   Indians,   the   rigging
and   sails   of   their   boat   were   slashed,   and   a   hole   punched
in   the   boat's   hull   (Belknap,   Pg.   232).

Jefferson   may   have   been   reflecting   on   such   uprisings   when
he   wrote:

"He   (The   King)   has   excited   domestic   insurrections   amongst
us...(Declaration   of   Independence).

The   Belcher   papers   skip   ahead   to   1739.   The   Governor   is still unable to collect his wages from the Massachusetts Assembly. There was the old problem of raising paper money with out "any honest and solid foundation", the inflation has turned a one Pound note into one forth of its value:

"I surpose there had been emitted by this time by the Assemblies of this Province as much paper currency as would have been half a million of nominal pounds, and wou'd have reduc'd their value to less than half a crown in the pound of the good & lawful money of the Province, which is seventeen pennyweight of silver to pass for six shillings. What a fraud & deceit..." (B. P. Vol. VII, Pg. 225). Later in the year, Belcher emphasizes the inflation problem to the Lords of Trade: "will be of more fatal consequence to the Plantations than the South Sea bubble was in the year 1720 to Great Britain." (B. P. Vol. VII, Pg. 360). In the same letter the tax burden: "Massachusetts... paid a tax of above twenty thousand pounds sterling in one year near fifty years agoe, when I suppose they were not one third so large as at this time in people or estate..." (B. P. Vol. VII, Pg. 360-361).

The climax of the first section of the Belcher Papers is a bizarre scheme of subterfuge which resulted in Belcher being replaced as Governor in both Provinces (1741). In this case, Belcher was a victim of colonial politics. The following is compiled from Hutchinson's 1765 history:

Hutchinson made a trip to England, as Belcher's agent in November of 1740. The purpose of the voyage was to lobby Parliament to prevent the colonies from issuing any more paper money without a solid foundation or fixed value (B. P. Vol. VII, Pg. 341). Belcher was frustrated that two private companies were issuing 140,000 Pounds Sterling (equal to 800,000 Pounds in Massachusetts) of worthless paper currency. At that time there was no protection in the law for preventing private corporations creating inflation and issuing paper currency. Hutchinson stated that the private Land Bank (which was issuing the currency) happened to hire Belcher's brother-in-law, Richard Partridge, to represent their interests in England. Partridge "engaged zealously in opposing the petitions to the House of Commons, and gave out bills at the door of the House." In effect, Partridge was unknowingly opposing his brother-in-law, Governor Belcher in 1740. Belcher's response to Partridge (B. P. Vol. VII, Pg. 363): "I take a particular notice of all

you say about what is call'd hear the Land Bank, & am
heartily sorry you appear'd so much in favour of a thing
so full of fraud & of all other mischiefs that the nature
of it will admit of. Surely you never enter'd into
the merits of this vile combination, or it had been
impossible for you to have done the least thing that
should be favouring it. No, you are too honest a man."

Belcher's opponents, took advantage of this conflict
between the Governor and his brother-in-law. Hutchinson
continues:

"It was said that all Mr Belcher's opposition to the
scheme (meaning opposition to worthless paper currency),
in the Province, was mere pretence; had he been in
earnest, his agent in England (meaning Partridge) would
never venture to appear in support of it, and this was
improved to Lord Wilmington to induce him to give up Mr.
Belcher, and it succeeded." (Hutchinson, 1765).

The muddy situation grows darker: an anonymous and
fraudulent letter written by Belcher's Massachusetts
opponents, and disguised in a real cover letter of
Reverend Benjamin Colman, was mailed to the Governor
of the Bank of England, Samuel Holden. Holden was
a close friend of Colman and had contributed 4,847
Pounds to Colman's Brattle Street Church in Boston. The
letter stated that Belcher was secretly attempting to
undermine the Congregational Church in concert with Roger
Price (1696?-1762) of the Kings Chapel in Boston, and
Timothy Cutler (1684-1765) rector of Christ Church in
Boston. This letter was a fraud. Benjamin Colman, of the
Brattle Street Church, had been a close friend of Belcher
for over a half a century. Although it is conceded that
religion and politics intermixed in the colonies (B. P.
Vol. VII, Pg. 175 to Bishop of London).

Step three, according to Hutchinson, was led by two
Massachusetts opponents of Belcher, in England (not
identified) who took advantage of the doubtful election
of Lord Euston in Coventry, England. The Massachusetts
men promised to "secure" Euston's election to the Duke of
Grafton if Belcher was replaced. They achieved their
objective by selecting the wealthy dissenter of the
established Church of England, Brough Maltby. Maltby was
told that unless Lord Euston was elected in England,
Belcher, with the Episcopal Clergy in New England was
conspiring to ruin the Congregational Church. This was
untrue, obviously to remove Belcher. Hutchinson concludes

the bizarre yarn with the following statement: "This
account I received from Mr. Maltby himself, who
lamented that he had suffered himself to be so
easily imposed on. A few weeks longer delay would
have baffled all the schemes. The news of his (Belcher)
...displacing a great number of Officers in the Land
Bank, and his zeal and fortitude were highly applauded
when it was too late. Being in London at this time, I had
the opportunity of fully informing myself of these
facts..." (Hutchinson, 1765, Mayo edition, Pg. 303).

To summarize the first section of the Belcher Papers,
serious problems were created between the ministers to
the King and Jonathan Belcher because of Jonathan's
opponents in the colonies. The most persistent opponents
developed because of Belcher's petty dispute with his
late Lt. Governor of New Hampshire, John Wentworth, and
Belcher's dominant personality in selecting his appointed
favorites. The response from England was to send David
Dunbar, "who had few qualifications, other than poverty
and friendship of men in power." (Belknap 1791).

Subsequently, all of this grows into a royal personality
battle because of: growing problems over lack of money in
the colonies, need for more taxes in England, opposition
to wages for the Governor by the Massachusetts House
of Representatives, competition with neighboring
colonies, political/religious squabbling, fraudulence
between office seekers, riots associated with lumber,
marketing regulations in Boston, and the fascinating
possibility that fortunes could be made in America.
Meanwhile, even after Elisha Cook's death in the 1737
period, his political machine continued to feed the
flames in the Boston centered Assembly. In one word the
colonial government was corrupt. It was corrupt for
several reasons and more than a few wondered if a
revolution was simmering... could Independence from
England reorganize this mess?

There was always some minister to the King who would
oppose a Governor for a member of Parliament. The Prime
Minister, and real ruler of England (1721-1742), Robert
Walpole, for example (B. P. Vol. VII, Pg. 404).

Belcher Papers-Second Section:

Let us now turn to another side of the Belcher papers.
Regarding Belcher's closest associate in England, I would

select Lord Charles Viscount Townsend (1676-1738). The phrase which begins with "I can't help repeating..." is particularly interesting because it identifies the Secretary of State, Townshend, who recommended Becher to be Governor. Townshend resigned in 1730 over an arguement with his brother-in-law, Sir Robert Walpole, but remained on the Privy Council to the King.

Belcher's letter is dated December 30, 1731: "...I pray to God that this may find your Lordship in a confirm'd health at the Parliament house, as well as in the Privy Council, that his Majesty & your country may reap the advantages of such a counsellor and such a patriot. I can't help repeating that the obligations your Lordship has laid me under can never be obliterated, and nothing wou'd be so pleasing to me as an opportunity of giving some convincing proofs of the great sense I retain of your Lordships goodness to me. (note: Belcher starts a new paragraph and explains the resistance of the Massachusetts Assemblies to fix a salary for the Governor, and after explaining that 3000 pounds is inadequate, Massachusetts is in poverty, and he would ask that his Majesty would allow him to take the money. After thirty-seven lines of explanation he continues to relate to Townshend) "...As I am fond of calling your Lordship my patron and the author of the favor & honor I enjoy under his Majesty, I have thought it my duty to give your Lordship this particular account of the situation of the affairs of this government... Yet I must still beg your Lordship's patience while I introduce to your Lordship's presence the bearer, my youngest son...concluded on the study of law in order to practice for his future employment in life, and to that end is now in chambers at the Middle Temple... if your Lordship will according to your wonted condescention & humanity allow him (now & then) to pay his duty & obeisance to you, I shall esteem it a great honour done me, him, & my whole family, as well as a good basis whereupon to build his future fortune..." (B. P. Vol. VI, Pg. 90).

It is noteworthy that Lord Townshend's son, Charles, was a Freemason at The Old Devil at Temple Barr Lodge on the 1723 list (AQC 40, Pg. 237). However, I have not located any correspondence between Belcher and the Freemason, Charles Townshend Esq.(1700-1764). Belcher did write a letter to Lord Townshend's second son, Thomas Townshend, which reinforces the importance of Lord

Townshend's role in Belcher's life.

Thomas was one of the members of Parliament for the University of Cambridge for over forty years, and one of the Tellers of the Exchequer. He died in 1780. The letter from Belcher to Thomas is dated November 2, 1734:

"...My noble patron, the Rt Honble the Lord Viscount Townsend (for what reason I know not), was pleased while I was at Whitehall, (Belcher lived at the Royal Palace in the February-July 1730 period-ed) to treat me on all occasions with the greatest condescension and humanity, and sometimes with an uncommon freedom, and finally did me the great honor of mentioning me to the King to be Govr of my native country. I say, it is to him, and him alone, that I owe this great respect, and favor, and I and my whole family shall acknowledge it to the latest date of time..." (B. P. Vol. VII, Pg. 137).

Further evidence of Belcher's friends in England are included in his correspondence to his favorite son, Jonathan Jr., who had recently arrived in London to begin study in Law at Cambridge and Oxford. The correspondence is dated November, 1, 1731:

"Dear Jonathan, My last was 26 July Post Cary, since which I have rec'd yours of 1, 14, 31 of same month, & August 16 post Foster, N. York... I heartily ascribe blessing & praise to God, your preserver & redeemer, the great author of all mercies, for your safe arrival in London, and can't be thankfull enough for the signal preservations you met with in your passage, nor for the great civility, respect, & honor you find from all orders & ranks of men." (B. P. Vol. VI, Pg. 27).

From the introduction it is apparent that his son wrote every two weeks and that he arrived in London approximately August 1731, two years before Freemasonry was organized in Boston. The date is relevant to Freemasonry because it took about three weeks to sail to London and Jonathan Jr., the later Provincial Grand Master of Nova Scotia, was of age to become a Freemason on his twenty-first birthday, July 23, 1731. The letter continues and mentions several of the Governor's old friends in London:

"I was sorry to hear of the death of my old friends, Mr.

Caswell & Mr. Bull, and that the former had left his
family in such melancholly circumstances. The small
things you desire are (Posted by ship by Captain-ed)
Homans, as in Postcript. I take notice with a great deal
of gratitude of Mr Newman's affectionate regards to you,
and that he had allow'd you to be under his roof 'till
your chambers were ready. This was uncommonly kind."
(B. P. Vol. VI, Pg. 28).

These individuals are worthy of further research as
possible pre-Grand Lodge era Freemasons. Mr. Bull was
John Bull, husband of Hannah. Mr. Caswall was John
Caswall, brother of H. Caswall. Mr. Henry Newman (1670-?)
was born in Massachusetts, a librarian at Harvard and
later agent of New Hampshire in London. He died in
London. The letter continues:

"But I am above all oblig'd to your good uncle that he
seems to have adopted you for a son (This would be
Richard Partridge, the Governor's agent and brother-in
law-ed). My dear Son, you will see by the several letters
now under your cover, unseal'd (which you will read,
seal, & deliver) that my soul is unwearied in it's care
for your wellfare & happiness." (B. P. Vol. VI, Pg. 28).

The enclosed letters were addressed to the Speaker of the
House of Commons (Arthur Onslow (1690-1768), the Duke of
NewCastle (Thomas Pelham 1693-1768), former Governor of
Massachusetts (Samuel Shute 1662-1742), and the Agent in
London for Massachusetts, Francis Wilks (?-1742). All of
the above letters requested "goodness and favour" to
Jonathan Jr. Next the letter mentions "instructions"
that the Governor had provided his son before he left for
London:

"The instructions I gave you at parting with what I left
upon my last voyage to Gt. Britain (and which I think you
took to London) were so full that I hardly know what to
add, but desire you often to peruse & pursue them.
Remember that you was devoted to God in your infancy, and
that those vows have been renewed & ratified by you at
adult years... hold fast your integrity, and let no man
take your crown. ." (B. P. Vol. VI, Pg. 29).

The letter next mentions a Massachusetts Councilman,
"Horseman;" "Dr. Watts" (Rev. Isacc Watts (1674-1748);
"Calamy," (Rev. Edmund Calamy (?-1732); "Mr. Morton."
(John Morton, apparently elderly in 1741; "Jefferies and

Chandler," and "Belcher," (John Belcher, a cabinet-maker in St. Paul's Churchyard, London, who was born in 1664 and a cousin of Governor Belcher). Belcher also mentions Sir Robert Walpole, Edward Cartaret, Henry Bendish, and Thomas Sandford.

Since Governor Belcher is one of six known individuals in the world who directly claimed to be a pre-Grand Lodge era Freemason in England and his two sons were Freemasons who were both in England at the age of twenty-one, before Freemasonry was organized in Boston; I would submit there may be a few pre-1717 Freemasons in the above letter.

Belcher writes to Jonathan on December 6, 1731, about his social selections:

"...Some people have flurted as if you spent too much of your time at the N. England Coffe House. The Temple Coffe House, Dick's, or the Rainbow wou'd be much more to your advantage." (B. P. Vol. VI, Pg. 79).

Dick's Coffee House (AQC 40, Pg. 231), and The Rainbow (AQC 92, Pg. 113), are noted because they were London taverns which have been established as Masonic meeting places. The Rainbow has also been identified as the meeting place of Henry Price, Grand Master of New England in the Grand Lodge of England's minutes of 17 March 1731.

At this point it is timely to introduce the tense relationship between Belcher's Lt. Governor, Col. David Dunbar, and Governor Belcher.

May, 2, 1734: "...I wish you had spar'd yours of the 15, April, and thereby yourself & me the trouble of the reply; and if we do not for the future pursue the King's interest with a better harmony, I will endeavour that it will not be the fault of, Sir, Your Honour's humble servant. Jona Belcher." (B. P. Vol. VII, Pg. 50).

And four months later, the relationship had not improved. September 9, 1734:

"...if you have nothing else to do than to gratify your vanity by showing your talent in a rude way of writing I hope you will think such parts of your letters well answer'd by the silent neglect and contempt of, Sir, Your Honour's humble servant." (B. P. Vol. VII, Pg. 118).

With the above extracts, I trust we have dispensed with
the direct nature of Belcher, and with the bitter
feelings that existed between Governor Belcher and his
Lt. Governor and surveyor of the Kings Woods from 1731 to
1737. It is also interesting to point out that Governor
Belcher made many enemies with such directness. That
trait, combined with his "fawning for favors" from his
friends, created a fascinating struggle for power between
the colonies and England. Belcher had made sufficient
enemies by 1741, for King George II to replace him in
both colonies. However, in defense of Belcher, he went to
England in March 1743/4, and was told by the ministry:
"Mr. Belcher, no charge or imputation lyes against you,
nor need you give yourself or us a trouble of the nature
you mention. It has been the King's pleasure to remove
you, and you must submit, as we all must in such cases,
and when there may be a proper opportunity we shall not
forget to serve you." ("Proceedings Mass. Hist. Society,"
Vol. IX, Pg. 15).

Jonathan Belcher was eventually allowed to kiss the
King's hand and he published his Commission as Royal
Governor of New Jersey on August 10, 1747. The
significance of David Dunbar (Lt. Governor under Belcher
from 1731-1737), with respect to Freemasonry is related
to an offhand remark from Belcher regarding the colorful
second noble Grand Master of England, Philip, Duke of
Wharton (1698-1731). Belcher wrote to Sir Charles Wagner
(1666-1743), a distinguished English Naval Officer, who
became one of the Lords of the Admiralty (1718-1742). The
letter is dated October 28, 1739. In this correspondence,
Belcher is very frustrated with his Lt. Governor, David
Dunbar. Dunbar was a native of Ireland, and a reduced
Colonial in the British Service. Dunbar's "appointment
was made by the recommendation of the Board of Trade; of
which Martin Bladen was an active member and bore no
good will to Governor Belcher." (Belknap, 1831 edition,
Pg. 226). Martin Bladen was an early Freemason (refer to
AQC 40, Pg. 33). In any case, it will later become clear
that Belcher and Bladen were probably unfriendly because
of Belcher's political scheming regarding Dunbar. The
offhand remark from Belcher's October 28, 1739, letter to
Sir Charles Wagner is as follows:

"I don't believe he (David Dunbar) would stick at
anything to extricate himself out of this poverty and

wretched circumstances, and to keep his head above water.
I have often been ashm'd to hear him (David Dunbar) tell
how he made the late imprudent, unhappy Duke of Wharton
drunk in Spain & then betray'd him to the ministry at
home. Nor do I suppose he would scruple to betray his own
father if he might reap an advantage by it." (B. P. Vol.
VII, Pg. 228).

The Duke of Wharton was the Grand Master of England in
1722/3. I have found no evidence, to date, regarding
Dunbar being a Freemason, but the previous letter
exists. My initial speculation was that Belcher may
have known that Wagner was a sympathizer of Wharton's,
and the statement was included to further discredit
Dunbar. The whole affair remains a mystery, but it
certainly opens a door of research into the life of David
Dunbar, and the possibility of Sir Wagner being an early
Freemason. My only information on Wagner is that he
was a distinguished English Naval officer (1666-1743) and
that he was one of the Lords of Admiralty (1718-1742).
(B. P. Vol. VI, Pg. 386).

Regarding Belcher's early trips to Europe, the following
is informative because it elaborates on his early trips
into England in his various travels: 1704/5; 1708/9;
1715; and 1728/30. It is addressed to The Bishop of
Lincoln, Richard Reynolds (Bishop from 1723 to his death
on Jan. 15, 1743/4):

"...I have my Lord, at one time & another spent about
six years in Europe, -twice in Hannover before the happy
Protestant succession took place; once at Berlin, Hambro,
in Denmark, in several principalities of Germany, three
times in Holland, and once I made progress thro the
kingdom of Great Britain (500 miles in length) and I have
my Lord, the satisfaction to think that no country (I
have seen) maintains a greater awe & sense of God &
religion than New England does even at this day." (above
quote exact, includes brackets) dated November 18, 1731
(B. P. Vol. VI, Pg. 54).

To a James Belcher, in Dublin, apparently a distant
relative is confirmation of Governor Belcher's
ancestor. Also mentioned were some of his Belcher (ier)
relatives in London, and his trip to England in 1704.
Correspondence dated August 25, 1732:

"...thanking you for the particular acctt of your
family, which I find lived in the reigns of the two
Charles's at Shipton-Olive in Gloucestershire, which
joins to Wiltshire, in which is the little Village of
Kingswood, where liv'd Robert Belcher, a weaver in the
year 1604, from whom I suppose myself to be decended, and
was as far as I cou'd run up my family when I was in
England in 1704. (*)   As to the family of Belchier
at Gilesborough... I never cou'd find whether we were
really related... There is one Mr. John Belchier,
a cabinet maker in Paul's yard, London, and a William
Belchier, his brother, an apothecary in Covent Garden,
and Jams Belchier, another brother, an inholder at
Kingston upon Thames. All these gentm I know. They
are men of good substance & figure, and I believe
related to us." (B. P. Vol. VI, Pg. 177).

For miscellaneous interest, the following letter details
Belcher's rather exact dress standards. He ordered the
following alterations from Jonathan Jr., on July 1, 1740:

"...In this bundle is a leathern wastecoat & Breeches,
which get lac'd with gold in the handsomest manner, not
open or bone lace, but close lace, something open near
the head of the lace. Let it be substantial, strong lace.
The buttons to be mettle buttons, with eyes of the same,
not buttons with wooden molds & catgut loops, which are
good for nothing. They must be gilt with gold & wrought
in imitation of buttons made with thread or wire. You
must also send me a fine cloth jockey coat... I must
also have two pair of fine worsted hose to match this
suit, a very good hat, lac'd or not, as may be the
fashion, and a set of silver buckles for shoes and knees,
& another sett of pinch-beck... These things may cost 16
or 18 Pounds..."(B. P. Vol. VII, Pg. 307).

(*) This date, 1704, coupled by the previous letter of
    January 15, 1743/4, in which Belcher states "once I
    made progress thro the kingdom of Great Britain (500
    miles in length) is noteworthy. It is reasonable
    speculation, that after a three month, 934 mile tour
    of Germany etc., completed on October 4, 1704, this
    genealogical research was completed before he left
    London on July 8, 1704. An ample time to gain "friends
    in London," do his research (he visited his cousin at
    the Hague on July 30, 1704), and become a Freemason.

In my view, the most interesting insight into colonial
government is derived from Belcher's letters to Richard
Partridge. The following extracts reveal that savvy
colonial agent in London:

Nov. 1, 1731: "I take a very particular notice of every
clause of all your letters, ... As you observe I must
walk very circumspectly lest the King's Ministers shou'd
think I am not zealous enough for the honor of the
Crown and lest the House of Commons shou'd think I
bear too hard upon the priviledges of the people. I'll
endeavour to steer as nicely as I can between both."
(B. P. Vol. VI, Pg. 38).

Partridge obviously reminded Belcher of common knowledge
in London: ministers to the King were clearly aware of
those who are not loyal to the King... and the House of
Commons was well aware of arrogance of power. Thus, in
the very beginning of Belcher's administration, Partridge
reminded his brother-in-law of the key problem of English
colonial government: walking a tight-rope between the
King and the people. Belcher outlines his strategy to
Partridge, who has been in London for over thirty years:

"I take notice you have a great deal of freedom with the
Duke of Newcastle, and that his Grace is very friendly to
me. We must take care to pay him great duty & respect &
not offend him... I see the Lords of Trade have not been
very friendly...we must treat them with good manners, and
if they will be unreasonable we must endeavour to do our
business with the King & his immediate ministers... I
find the Board of Trade now begin to complain that I
write too much; it's hard to please them... I hope the
cheeses I sent (posted by-ed) Shepardson were distributed
as I directed tho' you say nothing abt 'em..." (B. P.
Vol. VI, Pg. 38-9).

His early colonial strategy from Massachusetts and New
Hampshire was simple: do not offend the ministers to the
King, when resistance to our goals occurs deal directly
with the highest ministers to the King. Gifts to
appropriate individuals will not hurt.

The fact was, Belcher had few options. It was a style
of accepting the boss, and hoping he could solicit the
key ministers to the King to help with colonial problems.
Other than a revolution, his approach was as good as any.
But the dilemmas magnify at home: because the King

can dispose of a Royal Governor on a whim, and because the Massachusetts Assembly controlled spending, the first problem was to obey the King's order for the Assembly to pay the Governor. One year before George Washington was born, the Board of Trade was opposed to Belcher accepting a lesser wage than the King declared. Belcher was stuck. The wages to the Governor were usually late, usually a battle, and usually paid grudgingly... the Royal Governor didn't need any more problems from England to collect his check. The following extracts to Partridge illustrate that issue:

December 1, 1731: "I take notice of Jonathan's memorial to the Lords of Trade for leave to take the Assembly's money, but I hear they opposed it to the last (especially Coll Bladen), which seems to me unjust & unreasonable. I take in the kindest manner your hint about the expensiveness of the government, and will retrench as much of it as I possibly can. I know of nothing extra-ordinary, but that I keep four horses, and a private gentm keeps but two. It wou'd make a great murmuring in the province if I liv'd out of town..." (B. P. Vol. VI, Pg. 82).

The last comment is curious... did the Board of Trade want the Royal Governor of Massachusetts to move out of Boston to reduce his spending? Belcher was a large land owner in Massachusetts and Connecticut, he was not about to leave Boston for want of a pay check. Belcher's dry humor regarding the Board of Trade member, Martin Bladen is apparent in the following: "... I admire Coll Bladen shou'd be so attacht to Coll Dunbar. I'm sure he'll never be any honour to him."

As a clarification of Belcher's comment, he might have said: "I'm surprised that Bladen is friends with Dunbar, for Dunbar is a moron." Belcher will be less inhibited in the years ahead, indeed, in the next statement, he uses the term mandamuss (meaning a written order to enforce the performance of a public duty) and rejects with mornfull scorn the latest appointments to the Governor's Council:

"I shall be very glad to have the mandamuss for Messrs Waldron (Belcher's Secretary), Gambling & Dennett to be of the Council at Piscataqua (meaning Portsmouth, New Hampshire); but by all means prevent Peirce, Atkinson & Wentworth and the other tools he has nominated for

Councillors. To have such a sett of his creatures at the Board wou'd be a sad plague to me." (B. P. Vol. VI, Pg. 84).

The Belcher/Partridge relationship is a sharp contrast in personalities. Partridge, the quiet, subtle, Quaker, and Belcher the blunt, flashy, aristocrat. Both were raised by wealthy parents in New England and they were a formidable team to represent the best interests of the colonies. They were both well versed in the political style of English government and they both were survivors determined to make a difference. The taxation policy in the colonies, which went to the Church of England was one of their early achievements. The following letter to Partridge is an excellent example of that unfair taxation policy and Belcher's early reform for Quakers:

"I got a bill past both Houses (& have sign'd it) in favor of your Friends (Quakers-ed)... The copy of the law I enclose to you (this law, "An Act further to exempt Persons commonly called Quakers, within this Province, from being taxed for and towards the support of Ministers" was passed December 24, 1731-ed). But I must observe to you that the people & clergy of the Chh of England here are angry & much offended that I have taken such care of the Quakers. This I am not much concern'd about, since I think I have done right." (B. P. Vol. VI, Pg. 94).

After Belcher's Massachusetts Lt. Governor dies (William Tailer), he writes to Partridge on March 6, 1731/2:

"the sudden death of Leiut Govr Tailer obliges me to trouble you again by this conveyance, to desire you to join with Mr Wilks (Massachusetts agent-ed) in getting Majr Paul Mascarene to succeed him at Leiut Govr of this Province. He came over with me 23 years ago in the Dragon man-of war..." (B. P. Vol. VI, Pg. 104).

Again, we see the technique of appointing officials in colonial America. It was necessary for colonial agents in London to solicit approval from ministers to the King. The several month delay and conflicting interests of friendships, in England, was an obvious obstacle to efficient government. Mascarene was not selected by the King, he chose Spencer Phipps, adopted son of former Governor William Phipps (1651-1695). Belcher rolled with the punch: "Since it's the King's pleasure, I'm perfectly easy abt the Leiut Govr that's appointed, but certainly there's no comparison between the men." (B. P. Vol. VI, Pg. 173). Another problem occurs:

Because Belcher was changing various office holders there were complaints in the form of a petition from fifteen individuals in New Hampshire. Belcher responds to the Duke of New Castle on April 26, 1732: "It is really, my Lord Duke, so trifling that I believe the Lords of Trade barely thought it worth an answer. If every 15 disaffected persons in a Province may give his Majesty, his ministers, & his Govr the trouble of such complaints a Govr may be wholly employ'd in exposing the groudless humours of such unreasonable persons. The address sent to his Majesty the last year, sign'd by 100 persons in my favour I hope may sufficiently balance this foolish affair." (B. P. Vol. VI, Pg. 118-9). Belcher sent the letter to Partridge to read and deliver to the Duke. He mentions to Partridge: "you'll see what I now write to the D.N. Castle & Secry Popple that I hope upon the whole with good council to argue the matter. You'll find sufficient to stop any order from the King for giving him more power... " (April 27, 1732, B. P. Vol. VI, Pg. 121). Thus, Belcher is attempting to organize, as best as possible, his Council and desired appointments. It is a delicate balance and opponents are inevitable. In the midst of the intriguing struggle for power, Sir Robert Walpole is known to have had an international spy network (AQC 99/189), possibly the Bladen/Dunbar alliance was part of that information gathering body. Another problem arises:

April 27, 1732: "I shall not fail of making the Bishop of Lincoln's friendship and interest at Court... I find Coll B___n (Bladen-ed) is my enemy, yet he writes me fair and plausible. It must be on Dunbar's acctt & for no other reason, and no doubt he influences the Board of Trade to my prejudice; we must therefore constantly apply to their superiours that I may be treated with justice and reason... I shall have a full talk with Mr Reynolds, & see if he inclines to be Leiut Govr of N. Hampshire... I have already made him Naval Officer. Pray, how came he to be struck out of the list of Councellors? I fancy it was by Dunbar's means..." (B. P. Vol. VI, Pg. 121).

It appears from Belcher's letter that Richard Partridge

had previously asked Belcher to select Reynolds (The Bishop of Lincoln's son) for Lt. Governor of New Hampshire. My perception is that Belcher is a bit frustrated with London: Who is going to be a suitable Lt. Governor of New Hampshire for the Bishop of Lincoln and the Governor... isn't there some other place for his son to work? Problems grew out of Belcher's strategy of soliciting ministers to the King: if you wanted to be Royal Governor, there were favors expected by nobility in England. Favors might have been expected from a Lord, perhaps the wife of a Lord, or maybe the Bishop! Could one run a government in this mess?

Jefferson had a another strategy forty-three years later: "That to secure these rights, governments are instituted among men, deriving their just powers from the concent of the governed; that, whenever any form of government becomes destructive to these ends, it is the right of the people to alter or abolish it..." (Declaration of Independence). The revolution was premature in 1732.

Belcher writes to Partridge about the very real cost of approving his recommendations to ministers to the King:

"Nov.25, 1732: "You will find by the inclos'd to the Secry of State (William Stanhope) & Lords of Trade that I have nominated Coll Joseph Sherburne, Capt. Ellis Husk, & Capt Richard Wibird to be members of his majesties Council in Nw Hampshire. And you have herewith Coll Sherburne's letter to yrself that he will pay the charge as soon as you let him know it. I don't suppose there will be any opposition to these gentlm, and so the charge will not run as high as upon the last." (B. P. Vol. VI, Pg. 220).

A month later, Belcher was angry at Partridge for his cost of subsidizing office holders from England:

Dec. 19, 1732: "You have offer'd out of all reason in behalf of Mr Reynolds for the Leiutenancy of N. Hampshire. If I might have it for 50 guineas to-morrow I wou'd not give it. If Reynolds shou'd not be able to get the commission & to pay the 150 guineas, I wou'd by no means advise you to advance it for Coll Sherburne, unless you have his particular orders & promise to repay you. If Reynolds gets it, I think he ought to pay you also the 20 guineas advanc'd to Jerry Dunbar. There seems to me no reason that I shou'd bear the burden & charge where

others are to reap the honor & profitt..." (B. P. Vol.
VI, Pg. 224).

This was adding insult to injury. Not only was the
Massachusetts Assembly refusing to pay the Royal Governor
his wages, Belcher had to fight others, to avoid paying
bribes, in England, for office seekers in the colonies.

The theme of applying pressure, in London, to ministers
to the King continues for ten years. Belcher constantly
informs his agents of all his correspondence. Caution
is emphasized because of the unknown outcome of political
office seekers in London. There is absolutely no doubt
of Partridge's integrity or his dedicated work for the
colonies. He died famous and insolvent. He was respected
as agent to Connecticut, Rhode Island, New York, New
Jersey, New Hampshire, Pennsylvania and Massachusetts. He
had but two avenues to solving colonial problems in
London: sway ministers to the King by talk and money.
Money worked best.

As Belcher noted in 1708, to John White, "There's no
setting one foot before to'ther here (in London) without
money..." The Prime minister of England, Sir Robert
Walpole, also admitted his government had bribed members
of Parliament and that it was part of achieving progress
in government. Walpole, one of the great Prime Ministers
of England, and despised by Belcher after 1741, was not
guilty of personally taking bribes. Walpole left public
life three years before he died, poorer than when he
began forty years earlier. Belcher certainly lost money.

However you care to interpret the integrity of English
government in 1730:   because Richard Partridge was a
trusted and close associate to Belcher; and he was born
in America, where many of his close relatives lived; and
he spent most of his adult life in London, lobbying
ministers to the King for several colonies, he is one of
the most interesting associates of Belcher during this
fascinating pre-Revolutionary War era.

Because Belcher's financial strength was derived from
private enterprise, and he was anchored to the colonies,
with ties in England, he was a survivor. His idealism
was tempered by the King's strength, but Belcher's power
existed before the Revolution because of his fortune. He
was pragmatic, but he was also unafraid to stand up to
Dukes and Lords. Belcher was raised in a tavern by an

THE BELCHER PAPERS 195

independent father, who made a fortune as a self-made
mariner in the seventeenth century. With that background, and his ambition, Jonathan offered power from the
colonies that was more difficult to ignore in London.

There is one curious mystery about Partridge: since he
was in London, when Belcher first arrived in 1704, did
Partridge introduce Belcher to Freemasonry? At this time
there is no evidence of Richard Partridge being a Freemason. There is a well known Robert Partridge (1747-
1817), of Norwich, England, who was a Deputy Grand Master
for Norfolk, between 1783 or 4 to 1817, but I do not know
if he was related to Richard Partridge (1681-1759).

I expect that genealogical research in England will be
able to shed light on that possibility. As usual,
when it comes to pre-Grand Lodge era research, new
information is remote. Yet, the connection between
Belcher and Partridge is very close: same age, born sixty
miles apart, their fathers were both mariners and
associated with colonial appointments from England,
Belcher married Partridge's sister within months after he
returned from England in 1705, they had an extensive
correspondence relating to business and social matters,
and Belcher signed his letters "your affectionate
brother." But that, indeed, is inadequate proof of
another pre-Grand Lodge era Freemason.

As a brief diversion to illustrate the mystery of
exploring early Freemasons, Elias Ashmole (1617-1692)
was a Fellow of the Royal Society and founded the famous
Ashmolean Museum at Oxford in 1677. Ashmole listed
several pre-Grand Lodge era Freemasons in his diary when
he joined the Fraternity on October 16, 1646: Penket,
Collier, Sankey, Littler, Ellam and Brewer. Thirty-six
years later, Ashmole noted in his diary (March 10-11,
1682) and identified additional Freemasons: Knight,
Borthwick, Woodman, Grey, Taylour, Wise, Shorthose,
Shadbolt, Wainsford, Young, Hamon, Thompson and
Stanton. Ashmole included first names, for details see
AQC 65/35. Ashmole left 1,860 manuscripts, even at book
size, we are talking about six, 300 page books, but
there are only two other slight references to Freemasonry
(Pick & Knight, 1983). Belcher wrote to no one identified
above in his existing papers. In fact among all of his
correspondence as Governor (over 1000 pages), he never
used the word Freemason.

Regarding letters to Freemasons, or those closely
associated with Freemasons, Martin Bladen was a member of
the Board of Trade. Belcher wrote to the Board of Trade,
as Governor, several times, frequently he criticized
Bladen's friend, David Dunbar (i.e. "if we might quit
of that uneasy gentm Coll. Dunbar; and as his being
Lieut Govr is no sort of service to him, nor can I
(with submission to your Lordship) believe it any to
his majesty..." dated Oct 29, 1731). But Belcher was
undaunted, after being ignored by Martin Bladen for
several years, he wrote to him on December 3, 1739:

"...Altho' I had wrote you 4 or 5 years agoe, to which
I had not receiv'd the favour of an answer, yet I find by
my copy Book that I wrote you again the 19 June, 1736, by
the hands of Capt Durell, & which, he wrote me, he
deliver'd; & upon a review of it I cannot but confirm
everything I then said, & by your continued silence you
might well expect not to be persecuted with any more
unwelcome letters from me, & if this proves so, I will
ask 1000 pardens & 'a' done. Will you allow me, Sir,
to be free & expostulate with you as one gentm might
with another. After I had kist the Kings hand for
my governments & resided at Whitehall, I have said
on all occasions that nobody treated me with more
civility & more gentlemanly than did Collo Bladen. I
should therefore be glade to know what I have done as a
Govr or as Mr. Belcher to give you disgust... My friends
tell me, from a coldness they find in Coll Bladen to my
interest my affairs labour at your Board. I freely ask
pardon if I have unwittingly given you offense, & desire
you to let me hope for your future favour & kind offices,
& I will promise you never to dishonour your friendship."
(B.P. Vol. VII, Pg. 251).

Apparently nothing came of the offer of reconciliation,
as that was the last letter addressed to Bladen which was
published by the M.H.S.

Regarding the Freemason, Dr. Pellet, it appears from the
following Nov. 7, 1734, correspondence, that Belcher only
knew of Pellet through another source, Mr. William
Shirley:

"...Mr Shirley told me he was well acquainted with Mr.
Rider, the Sollicitor General, with Dr. Pellet and Mr.

Spence, the later is Sargent at Arms to The House of Commons, and Pellet is his uncle. They both have the honor of a free access to the D. of N. Castle and a good acquaintance with all the Pelham family, and Mr. Shirley has been so kind as to give me three enclosed letters for the Sollicitor General and for the other two gentln, to each of which you'll see I have ventured to add one of my own, and wish they may together do you some service..." (B. P. Vol. VII, Pg. 154).

To Dr. Pellet and Mr. Spence, Governor Belcher sent solicitations of Jonathan Belcher Jr. Correspondence dated Nov. 9, 1734.

Other correspondence with Freemasons is located in the appendix of this research. Note James Brydges, father of the Grandmaster in 1738.

William Shirley, mentioned above, was born in England in 1693, became Governor of Massachusetts in 1741, and died in Roxbury Mass in 1771. I have previously thought that William Shirley was not a Freemason because of the following quotation, however, I feel it is more accurate to state that it is unknown if Shirley was an English Freemason, and it appears from the following statement that he may have been a loyalist to Freemasonry.

Regarding Shirley's quotation, soon after he became Governor he responded to an invitation from the mother Lodge in New England, St. John's Lodge in Boston:

"I return the Ancient and Honorable Society my thanks for their address, and invitation of me to the Mother Lodge of Free and Accepted Masons in America; And they may rest assured that their loyalty and fidelity to his Majesty will always recommend the Society to my favor and protection." ("Stalwart Builders," 1971, Pg. 15)

Before closing this brief look at the Belcher papers, let us review the following correspondence between St. John's Lodge of Boston and the subsequent letter from the replaced Governor Belcher:

"On Friday Septemr. 25, 1741, the Committee appointed by this Lodge waited upon the Honble. Mr. Belcher & c. and made the following speech.

"Thrice Worthy Brother-

We being a Committee by the Mother Lodge of N. England,
held in Boston to wait on you, to take this opportunity
to acknowledge the many favours you have always shewed
(when in power) to Masonry in general, but in a more
especial manner to the Brethren of this Lodge, of which
we shall ever retain a most grateful Remembrance."

"As we have had your protection when in the most exalted
station here, so we think its incumbent on us to make
this acknowledgement having no other means to testify our
gratitude but this; And, to wish for your future Health
and Prosperity which is the sincere desire of us, and
those in whose behalf we appear and permit us to assure
You we shall ever remain
                    "Honoured Sir
           Your most Affectionate Brethren
                & Humble servants
                Peter Pelham Sect:
            in behalf of the Committee."

"To Which We receiv'd the following Answer,"

"Worthy Brothers-
   I take very kindly this mark of your Respect. It is
now thirty seven years since I was admitted into the
Ancient and Honble: Society of Free and accepted Masons,
to which I have been a faithful Brother, & a well wisher
to the Art of Masonry-

I shall ever maintain a strict friendship for the whole
Fraternity; & always be glad when it may fall in my power
to do them any services.

           J. Belcher"
   ("St. John's Lodge of Boston," 1917 edition, Pg. 33)

That record in the St. John's Lodge is the best evidence
of Jonathan Belcher being a Freemason in 1704.

We might summarize that evidence as a response to a
courtesy visit by St. John's Lodge of Boston, after it
was known that Jonathan Belcher was about to be
replaced as Governor of Massachusetts.

The purpose of this research has been to explore evidence regarding Jonathan Belcher which will enhance the above statement and add to the general knowledge regarding his life. Before turning to our conclusions we might review one letter verifying that Jonathan was well aware he was about to be replaced as Governor in 1741.

June 29, 1741, to Henry Sherbourne, Freemason from Portsmouth, New Hampshire (B. P. Vol. VII, Pg. 400):

"I have letters of 30 April, advising me that Mr. Shirley was appointed Governor of the Massachusetts, and Mr. Wentworth of New Hampshire, and it comes from so good hands that I have no reason to doubt it. As in all other things, so in this great event, I desire patiently to submit to the will of the alwise God... I very kindly salute you and Madam Sherbourne & all your good family."

Jonathan Belcher sailed for England, nearly three years later, aboard Captain Goad's ship, "Polly," on March 10, 1743/4. He returned to America (New York), on August 8, 1747, with the Kings Commission to him as Royal Governor of New Jersey. I would expect, between 1744 and 1747, that Jonathan left a trail in England. For a start, Belcher became engaged in England, to Mary Louisa Emilia Teal, a Quaker. "Her imperial royal Majesty the Empress-Queen of Cesarea" was called from Burlington, New Jersey, and they married on September 9, 1748. This research will not explore Belcher's activities as Governor of New Jersey.

I might mention an extract from Belcher's letter to his son, Jonathan Jr., dated August 7, 1734: "I see you had rec'd my picture from Mr. Caswall. I think it is not much like, tho' a good piece of paint, done by Mr. Philips of Great Queen Street out of Lincoln's Inn Fields. I am surprized & much displeas'd at what your uncle writes me of Mr. Newman & your having my picture done on a copperplate... Such a foolish affair will pull down much envey, and give occasion to your father's enemies to squirt & squib & what not...Burn the plate and all the impressions..." (B. P. Vol. VII, Pg. 97).

The mezzotint engraving was by the Freemason, John Farber, (1695-1756) the younger (AQC 40, Pg. 39).

But John Farber, Jonathan Jr., The Massachusetts

Historical Society, and I will amuse ourselves in the end. The engraving, "from a portrait of uncertain date, painted by Richard Phillips", made copies which still exist. Two copies of this engraving are at the Historical Society, in Boston.

Before beginning my conclusion of this research, I might mention the illustration of Belcher in this book. That particular likeness is rare because the painting was restored by the Massachusetts Historical Society in 1977. Fortunately, the meticulous restoration removed extensive overpainting of another wig and clothes (face unchanged). Our illustration is after the restoration. Note: cheek length curly wig (rather than the overpainted shoulder length wig), a rather sporty red coat (rather than the overpainted dark blue coat with gold frogs), and a detailed green brocade waistcoat (rather than the overpainted yellow waistcoat). As previously noted, Jonathan was rather a dandy, and fussy in his dress (see letter about his clothes, Pg. 188), but in our illustration, based on the cut of the cloth and the way it drapes at the waist, the waistcoat appears to be buttoned incorrectly, probably to show off the white stock with ruffle. This painting makes for interesting speculation.

Belcher was in London, as an agent for Massachusetts and Connecticut, throughout 1729. It is my theory, since Belcher was appointed governor, unexpectedly, on November 27, 1729, that our painting was barely finished before that date. Meanwhile, the exhausted artist, Lippoldt, who had carefully depicted a gentleman's style wig and snappy dress was then asked to revise his work more befitting a governor. The overpainting was signed "F. Liopoldt pinxit Anno 1729" (note, artist name misspelled). No doubt Franz would approve of his carefully restored original brush strokes. Jonathan's reaction might be prudently summed up as justifiably dubious. The short wig, frog-less coat, not to mention the button, may all have annoyed him.

For those curious about the overpainted version, see "Sibley's Harvard Graduates" (Vol. IV). Other paintings of Belcher are at Harvard, Princeton University and the State Capitals in Boston and Trenton. Although not as flattering as the flowing wig versions, I prefer our restoration because it is the original 1729 Jonathan.

SUMMARY AND CONCLUSION

Jonathan Belcher was not unaware of his opportunities in government as early as 1704. His father was on the Massachusetts Governor's Council, and his purpose of traveling to Europe centers around the common continential educational tour practised at that time. It also centers around meeting the heir to the English throne.

Between the 1704 Journal, the Dec. 27, 1704, John White letter, and the previously mentioned letters documenting Belcher's activities in England in 1704 (Pg. 188), it is evident that Jonathan Belcher had the opportunity to become a Freemason in England in 1704.

With respect to the Masonic implications in the 1704 statement: "pray remember ye Charge most particularly for shall make particular inquiry of that matter on my return when ye leisure will allow..." That statement, spoken when Belcher was barely out of graduate school and still under his father's roof, has been discussed in detail in the text. It is my conclusion that the casual remark is new evidence of Belcher, as a Freemason, in London, in 1704. The date of the letter, as noted in the text (Pg. 139), is also relevant because from "time-immemorial," December 27, has been the Festival of St. John The Evangelist, one of the patron saints of Freemasonry.

With respect to Captain Andrew Belcher, again from the John White correspondence, it is evident there was a strong business alliance between Jonathan and his father. In fact, without Captain Andrew Belcher's influence, Jonathan's life would have been very different. I think the offer of financial help from the mysterious Mr. Stone, the English merchant at the Hague in 1704, is a quiet clue to the reputation of Captain Andrew Belcher in Europe.

Regarding the probability of Captain Andrew Belcher encouraging his son to become a Freemason, certainly Freemasonry is indifferent to the wealth of individual Freemasons, but the bond of Jonathan and his father, which is demonstrated in many ways in the 1704 Journal, and other correspondence, adds to the speculation that Captain Andrew was important in suggesting that Jonathan become a Freemason.

The English heritage, the "Blue Anchor Tavern," the mariner background of Captain Andrew Belcher, and even the ninety dozen gloves at his funeral, adds to the possible Masonic affiliation.

Belcher's letters of recommendation from his friends in England, in 1704, to see the Electress of Hanover are interesting. The meeting in Hamburg ("Bumpers") in 1704, is another example of Belcher's participation with various individuals in "convivial coffee-house activities." I would conclude that there is new 1704 evidence, in Germany, that Englishmen were practicing fellowship closed related to Freemasonry.

John White, Lord Townshend, "Lloyds," John Joe, Richard Partridge and "my priceless friend, "Mr. Van Schaick, are interesting Masonic studies in the 1704 period. It seems the English implication of the 1704 Journal is worthy of a more extensive study by Masonic scholars. Wharton has his critics, but there was a time when he had fewer critics. From AQC Volume 31, Pg. 166, is an interesting speculation between one "Lloyd" and the Duke of Wharton for example:

"Wharton was, in 1716 or 1726, created Duke of North-umberland by the Old Pretender (see "King James III" in Index-ed); it is said to have anticipated, or repeated, his exploit in Swaledale by drinking the health of King James the Third at the English Embassy in Paris."

   "A boon companion of the Duke and Musgrave was one Lloyd, who figures in the Duke's ballard celebrating a drinking match at Edenhall:"

   "Then step'd a gallant 'squire forth,
      Of visage thin and pale,
   Lloyd was his name, and of Gang Hall
      Fast by the River Swale."   (AQC 31, Pg. 166).

There are many other areas of exploration that can be derived from this book. In fact, because of the nature of exploratory research, it is true that there are now more areas to pursue than I am able to conclude of early Freemasonry. One general idea that I have thought about is that Belcher did not correspond with the Freemasons who were children of his old English friends. It has occurred to me that Jonathan's old powerful friends,

Stanhope and Lord Townshend, may have been pre-Grand Lodge Masons. I was interested, for example, that Belcher's powerful friend from England, Envoy Stanhope, arranged to have Belcher introduced to the Electress of Hannover in 1704. Yet only the next generation of Stanhopes: Charles, Phillip and William are named on the 1721 and the 1730 list of Freemasons (AQC 40, Pg. 235; and AQC 25, Pg. 227). The same is true of Charles Townshend's support of Belcher. Townshend's son is on the 1723 list (AQC 40, Pg. 237). Again, the same occurred in the case of the first Duke of Chandos, James Brydges (1673-1744), his son was Grand Master in 1738, but Belcher did not correspond with any of the sons of these important men who were known Freemasons. Because the sons of Townshend, Stanhope, and Brydges were significant Freemasons while their fathers were alive, and because the parents of these Freemasons were all close friends with a known pre-Grand Lodge era Freemason, Jonathan Belcher, I would conclude two points: 1. It is not unlikely that either Townshend (1676-1738), Stanhope (1673-1721) or Brydges (1673-1744) was a pre-Grand Lodge era Freemason. 2. Many distinguished pre-Grand Lodge era Freemasons who were active in politics, may not have aligned with the more public style of Freemasonry after it was formalized in 1717.

For example, by the time the 1723 Book of Constitutions was written, Belcher was in London by January 1728. Belcher left London in the July 1730 period. If the Governor did attend a Lodge, such meetings as are attributed to the Duke of Richmond on February 6, 1730, at the Horn Tavern in Westminster are noteworthy (See AQC 37, Pg. 114). Governor Belcher was clearly at Whitehall when the Masonic meeting of February 6, took place in Westminster (Pg. 155). In fact the surnames of Freemasons associated with that meeting are closely related to Belcher: Lord Harrington, Charles Stanhope, and the initiation of the Duke of Grafton (See Belcher correspondence to Charles Fitzroy, Duke of Grafton, for a church request in 1731). But no evidence of Belcher's presence has been located in English Lodges.

Probably the closest this book comes to identifying additional pre-Grand Lodge era Freemasons is in the letter of Nov. 1, 1731, to his son. Jonathan Jr., arrived in London in the August 1731 period. In that letter (Pg. 183-5), which identify several of Belcher's old friends in London, shortly after his son was of age to become a Freemason (he remained in London ten years), he also stated:

"The instructions I gave you at parting with what I left upon my last voyage to Gt. Britain (and which I think you took to London) were so full that I hardly know what to add, but desire you often to peruse & pursue them. Remember that you was devoted to God in your infancy, and that those vows have been renewed & ratified by you at adult years... hold fast your integrity, and let no man take your crown..."

Regarding Freemasonry and Jonathan Jr., perhaps the minutes of the Bear and Harrow Lodge in Butcher's Row, near Temple Bar would be productive. You will recall that Jonathan Jr., mentioned giving a present to the Duke of Montague in 1731. The Duke, of course is mentioned on the 1730 list of the Bear and Harrow (AQC 48, Pg 102). It is pure speculation that Jonathan Jr., may have attended that Lodge. The Devil Tavern near Temple Bar is another Lodge that was attended by the Duke of Lorraine's crowd on December 3, 1731. If Jonathan Jr., was a Freemason in the 1730s, I would expect he would attend such Lodges. To the best of my knowledge, in spite of gifts to Past Grand Master Montague, Jonathan Jr.'s Masonic affiliation in England is virtually unknown. Jonathan Jr. (1710-1776), is listed as the Provincial Grand Master of Nova-Scotia in the subscribers list to the first philosophical book on Masonry ever published: the 1772 Boston edition of Wellins Calcott's, 1769 "A Candid Disquisition etc."

"Pontack's," in London, would make interesting Masonic research. Belcher dined there after he had been commissioned by the King to be Governor.

In an effort to locate other pre-Grand Lodge era Free-masons, who may have associated with Belcher, I believe that the 1728 to approximately late June 1730 period and the 1743-1747 time frame is the most likely time to discover Belcher attending a known English Lodge. Regarding the late June 1730 estimate, he arrived in Boston on August 8, 1730, aboard the ship "Blandford man-of-war".

Regarding the Anderson account "sandwiched in between the records of the meetings of Grand Lodge, held on the 14

May and 24 June, 1731," is the "occasional Lodge at Sir
Robert Walpole's House at Houghton Hall in Norfolk." (See
AQC 37, Pg. 109). I believe that Governor Belcher
was not in England when that meeting occurred. It is
noteworthy, however, that Belcher is associated
with the Stanhope family, The Duke of Newcastle and
Walpole. Regarding James Anderson's critics of his fairy
tales, and his resulting lack of credibility, the 1731
contemporary account is far more credible, as Bro.
Gilbert Daynes elaborated on nearly three generations ago
(AQC 37, Pg. 124).

I think it is fair to state that the Belcher Papers are
an important link to learning more about the pre-Grand
Lodge era. I would submit that to the best of my
knowledge, this research has added the following
information to what has been published about Belcher in
Masonic or other literature:

Peripheral ancestral and biographical information;
Belcher's references to The Duke of Wharton; his son's
present to The Duke of Montague; his correspondence to
John White from London in 1704; his 1704 Journal; his
large number of English associates; his father's
implication with Belcher's success; his mention of "The
Temple Coffee House", "Dicks" and the Rainbow coffee
house; his "patron" correspondence to Second Viscount
Townshend; his old relationship with the famous English
families of Envoy Stanhope at the Hague, to Charles
Townshend and to a lesser degree with Bridges, Walpole,
and Pelham. This research adds some of Belcher's
significant correspondents in England; his letter to an
English Freemason on the 1723 list, Martin Bladen; and
the various letters that are relevant to both Freemasonry
and pre-Revolutionary War history.

The puzzling question to me is the pre-Grand Lodge era.
My conclusion is that Jonathan Belcher was sitting in a
London tavern in 1704 (See Journal expense account for
July 8, 1704, Pg. 124). He had letters of introduction
from men in London in his luggage. He was talking to John
Joe and Lloyds. They loaded Jonathan's luggage into a
double ended "wherry" boat on the Thames River, July 8,
1704, and they began the journey down the river, from
Tower Hill stairs, to Greenwich...

August 16, 1704, he met the heir to the English throne.

September 9, 1704, he met the Queen of Prussia.

On September 20, 1704, Jonathan Belcher, Mr. Watkinson, Mr. Stratford, Mr. Foster, Mr. Strickland, Mr. Colt, the Resident of Denmark, The Danish Admiral, A Burgomaster, and four of ye senate, some gentlemen of ye town, some of the Chief of the Hambro Company, listened to the treasurer "began to Everyone's health present in order as they Sat, Which lasted 'till dinner Was done, after that the Queen's health, and the rest of the Crown'd healths (as they call 'em) in Bumpers..."

By December 27, 1704, there is additional evidence from the White letter that Jonathan was a Freemason. Because of that letter, and Belcher's 1741 statement, of his being a Freemason thirty-seven years ago, it is my opinion that Jonathan's English associates, in the 1704 period, and in the 1730s, were among the pre-Grand Lodge era Freemasons.

The most likely associates are Richard Partridge (1681–1759... in London after 1701); John White (1669-1721); Andrew Belcher (1646-1717); Charles Townshend (1676-1738); Mr. Stanhope (1673-1721), "Envoy Extraordinary" at the Hague in 1704; James Brydges (1673-1744); The various "English Company" at Hamburg on September 20, 1704; particularly Mr. Watkinson, Foster and Dangerfield. Rev. Isaac Watts (1674-1748); Thomas Coram (1668-1751); John Campbell (1678-1743); Archibald Campbell(1682-1761); John Bull (died in 1731); Governor Shute (1653-1732); and James, John, and William Belchier, (Belcher relatives in London) are also noteworthy. The mysterious John Joe; "Chamberlin"; Mr. Van Schaick; Mr. Bluthwait and "Lloyd" are also significant in the important 1704 period. As of this date, not any of these men have been identified as Freemasons, much less pre-Grand Lodge era Freemasons. But all were of age within the time frame, all were associates of a known pre-Grand Lodge era Freemason, several had sons or close relatives that were Freemasons, one had a son who was Grand master, and most fascinating of all, excepting for a letter of 1741, Jonathan Belcher would not heretofore have been verified with new evidence, in London, in 1704.

Regarding pre-Revolutionary War history, because it is my thesis that Belcher's dominant personality created conflict with opposing ministers, in England, one of the curious personal interests that I have experienced in this research, is an attempt accurately to define Belcher's complex personality. There is often a temptation either to overestimate or to underestimate his characteristics.

The Governor's correspondence provides several insights to his personality traits. One example is his derogatory nick names for those he opposed:

"Fuddle cap" for Elisha Cooke; "Taffy and Sancho Panza" for David Dunbar; "Plague of Israel" for Theodore Atkinson; "The linen draper," "Toby and Cadiz Pedler" for Benning Wentworth; "Scotch Loon," "the Hound," "Hero of the mob", "Don Quixot", and several others.

Other ideas are derived from the painstaking and detailed Belcher letters to his Lt. Governor, David Dunbar. After the King's ministers had informed Belcher that Dunbar would remain as Lt. Governor, Belcher attempted to respond to Dunbar's complaint about their lack of understanding in a letter of December 21, 1733. Belcher wrote for over thirty lines on the subject of understanding. He detailed French definitions and other painstaking elaborations to proclaim his meaning of "understanding" in previous letters. A wiser Governor might have brushed aside their misunderstanding with an apology and then gone onto more significant matters.

Belcher occasionally used thinly veiled threats. His letter of Sept. 17, 1733, to Dunbar, is one example: "I sometimes fancy I don't abound in ill nature, tho' I may be mistaken... when any one unreasonably injures me, I am apt to return it when in my power."(B. P. VI, 368).

Jonathan's frequent use of "old sayings" provides an insight toward his rather controlling nature: "Gratitude to our friends and justice to our enemies," "Curst cows have short horns," "a request from a superior was the strongest command," "when people say they care the least they care the most," "If the mountain can't go to Mahomet, I believe Mahomet must come to the mountain," "King William's advice to his Parliament at a difficult juncture was, Steady! Steady!" and another favorite, "They that are out will Pout."

His tendency toward controlling details, when unjustified

for a Governor to bother with, is seen repeatedly. One minor example, among dozens of others, is that he carefully weighed and measured a bushel of walnuts he ordered from England. Finding them one and one half peck, versus four peck; and thirty-six pounds vs., eighty-four pounds. He not only wrote to his brother-in-law and London agent, Richard Partridge, informing him he was cheated, but he insisted on satisfaction. As usual, the Governor was justified in being upset. But from a practical point of view, the consequences of a walnut investigation were hardly justified in exchange for "satisfaction" of a half bushel of nuts. What was Partridge to do at that point? Accuse the nut merchant? Certify weights and measures of nuts? Have an attorney take depositions from all parties involved in the 3000 mile journey? In spite of reasonable care, anyone could be responsible for the missing walnuts. The trivial problem could barely be solved by Scotland yard, not to mention the harm created by an investigation. But once again, the Governor would be reckoned with, in spite of the consequences.

This righteous, but trivial trait, more than any other concept in Jonathan's ten year administration, eventually created serious trouble for the Governor. However, as we will later observe with irony, in spite of my curiosity, Jonathan's personality problems are not the point.

Belcher, like other successful individuals in history, was very ambitious, detail oriented, and hungry for approval. It is unfair to state that he lacked compassion, for there is ample evidence he sincerely cared about others. On the other hand, his letters seem to indicate a frenzy of emotional pleading and defensiveness, rather than calm independence and inspiration. I would conclude that his management technique did not visualize or accept the world of others. He seemed to be focused on controlling behavior and events which were beyond his compass. This is particularly evident with Dunbar, his son, in London, and the Board of Trade.

As far as his ability to learn, as distinguished from his ability to manage, Jonathan was very intelligent. He frequently used Latin, Greek and French phrases, owned a sizable book collection, enjoyed fencing, dancing, bowling, gardening (he imported several unique plants and flowers), and wrote letters on one occasion until two

O'Clock in the morning. He "usually went to bed at ten and rose with the sun." He was fearless with adventure (trips into the wilderness to make peace with the Indians). He would quickly challenge opponents and often battle with significant authority, using eighteenth century charm. One minor miscellaneous point is that he was probably rather a tall man, he grew "8 or 10 inches after the age of twenty-two."

He was a tense boss, but seemed socially at ease. His occasional humor tended to be intellectually spirited observations, although there is evidence that he was on the receiving end of jokes. (see poem with line "For June the twenty-forth was Sunday, And Brother Belcher fasts on Monday" by Joseph Green (1706-1780) in "New England Freemason," Nickerson/Titus, 1874, Pg. 339). Jonathan was structured, a penetrating observer (as seen in his 1704 journal), full of energy and ambition, commonly defensive, often loyal (particularly with his family and friends), sophisticated (certainly in appearance, social contacts, and European travel), more honest than most, and had a take charge personality. His blunders were minor, taken separately, but the collective lack of tranquility created mountains out of molehills. He was removed as Governor because of his exasperated enemies, and recommissioned after his significant opponents, Sir Robert Walpole and Martin Bladen passed away.

Jonathan Belcher and his unyielding ambition, at the age of sixty-five, began again with a new Prime Minister. But in spite of his intelligence, and driving ambition, he would not learn to practise an old idea of Freemasonry: "Peace and harmony are the indispensable conditions under which Freemasons can work and assemble." (Coil, 1961, Pg. 303). Jonathan was even paralyzed in 1750. "From Benjamin Franklin he received an electrical apparatus which was hoped might help him. He remained active until his death on August 31, 1757." ("Sibley's Harvard Graduates," Pg. 448; another Franklin Letter on Pg. 231).

Jonathan has not been identified as the first American born Freemason. His father, Captain Andrew (1646-1717), his old friend, John White (1669-1721), and Partridge are obvious examples, that might be earlier American born Freemasons. Belcher's letter of December 27, 1704, to John White adds to the possibility that John White was an earlier Freemason. It also enhances the 1741 claim that Jonathan Belcher was a Freemason in 1704.

As I reflect on Jonathan Belcher, I would conclude that
the fascinating problems of the American Colonies are
illuminated in his writings. Twenty years after his
death, those problems expanded and led to a Declaration
of Independence.

Jonathan's social, political, and educational associates
linked him with the old and new world. Thus, while other
Royal Governors were imprisoned (Joseph Dudley in the
Revolution of 1689), or rioted against (Thomas Hutchinson
in 1765), or bribed to decline office (Burgess in 1716),
or abandoned the colonies for England (Shute in 1723),
Belcher was a survivor, who attempted to use the only
means at his disposal to solve the problems of the
colonial people: he wrote letters to persuade the powers
that held the reins in England.

It must be emphasized that Belcher was attempting to run
a government without money. The House of Representatives
were generally opposed to the King's appointments, and
they controlled all spending, period. Belcher paid
his own expenses for upwards of eighteen months before
the Assembly would reimburse him. Because of his limited
access to a budget, his frustrations and various schemes
raise eyebrows today. Indeed, the blunder of past
historians (see Sibley, Pg. 153) is they have overstated
his schemes and his personality problems, in contrast to
the far more significant, and insurmountable struggle of
Colonial Governors: serving the King and the people without a budget... with political interference from all
directions... and without elected accountability.

It is true that Belcher was loyal to the King. It is also
true that his loyalty began to reveal his opposition to
policies of the King's ministers.

For example, given his trivial schemes and walnut
priorities, his efforts to enhance the colonies, as a
native born Royal Governor are conceded: hard currency
advocate, fighting the Lords of Trade in their attempt
to usurp his power, resisting tariffs detrimental to
colonial profit, appeals for bounties to improve business
in the colonies (especially regarding lumber and ship
building), defense of forts, paying colonial soldiers,
reform of Quaker taxes to the Church of England, peace
with the Indians, raising naval stores in New England,
and complaints to Walpole about English office seekers.

Although Jonathan's problems were bedecked because of his headstrong personality, the point of focus is the struggle for power between England and the colonies. In a word, like him or not, the ministers to the King were well aware of the needs of Massachusetts, New Hampshire and New Jersey, forty years before the Revolution.

Therefore, in spite of his personality, I think it is objective to conclude that his schemes in the 1730-1757 period, began to illuminate the opposing governmental forces in America and England. Jonathan's writings during the first half century of the 1700s, reveal that struggle and the evolution of our accomplishments. In brief, administration of the colonies before and after Belcher, was fought because of arrogance of power from England, and the Royal Governor. Indeed, two decades after his scorned motives to enhance the American colonies were passed, and with less than four percent of the population of London living in Boston, that government would inevitably explode in "The Revolution."

In view of the train of unsuccessful Royal Governors, even historians, like Hutchinson, rhetorical questions are tempting: given a system of puppet government, could leaders of England or the colonies do anything productive to solve problems of the colonial people? Moreover, in spite of various colonial diplomats in the 1770s, much less from Belcher's ambitious correspondence in the 1730s... did England's ministers want to understand the problems? And finally, can solutions occur for people's problems unless the King is accountable to the people? (see King of Prussia, line three, 1704 Journal Pg. 98).

The lessons and the problems still exist. Although his struggles were often honorable in a corrupt system, Belcher was no more, or less, a hero than any other government "servant" working for special interests. The lesson is an old one: in order to solve problems, the masses of the people must preserve a level playing field between the King and the people. "You have a Republic," responded Benjamin Franklin, "if you can keep it."

The search goes on for pre-Grand Lodge era Freemasons. I leave for another day, senior evidence in America: the 1704 letter to John White, from the first known, American born, Freemason: "pray remember ye Charge most particularly for shall make particular inquiry of that matter on my return..."

APPENDIX I

The purpose of this appendix is to compile a brief guide
to most of Governor Belcher's associates in England
in the 1731-1743 period. It is compiled from his
correspondence published in the Belcher Papers. Note: The
Belcher Papers do not include correspondence between
April 21, 1735 through August 24, 1739. An asterisks
indicates that the correspondence appeared to be with a
close associate. Volume and Page numbers refer to the
published Massachusetts Historical Society's Belcher
Papers. The term "introduces Jonathan Jr." refers to
Governor Belcher's frequent use of his son, Jonathan,
who attended Cambridge and Oxford, to hand carry the
Governor's mail in England. Regarding page numbers,
volume VI provides complete letters up to page 445, and
volume VII up to page 452. After those respective pages
the key points of Belcher's letters are quoted, and or,
summarized. The Massachusetts Historical Society
apparently used that approach because Belcher frequently
wrote identical correspondence to different individuals.
For a more complete list of correspondence from Governor
Belcher, I refer the reader to the index and text of the
Belcher Papers, and to the other manuscripts, which
are not published, but are in the possession of the
Massachusetts Historical Society.

Ackworth, Sir Jacob, 1740 introduction to James Griffin,
on a voyage to England (Vol. VII, Pg. 507).

Attorney General, see-Yorke, Sir Phillip.

Auchmuty, Judge Robert, Court of Admiralty. 1732
conflict between court in Mass. and Court of Admiralty.
Also David Dunbar issue (Vol. VI, Pg. 468,518).

Belcher, James, from Dublin, secretary to Mr.
Clutterbuck, who was secretary to Lord Cartarett, the
Late Lord Lt. of Ireland in 1731. Distant relative
correspondence. Regarding the following spelling of
Belchier, the Governor wrote to James: "You must give me
leave to correct you in the difference of the words
Belchier and Belcher, the latter being much more polite.
The true significance of Belle is fine & Chier won't bear
to be mentioned in English, but Cher is dear, tho' with
the addition of an e it wou'd be cheer or entertainment.
You will forgive me when I say you'll find yourself

entirely out in interpretation of the word Belchier, if
you please look to the French; and I think you'll agree
with me that Belcher has been a good reformation of the
name, and is, as I find it (at the Heraldry Office) us'd
by my ancestors 128 years ago." -1732 (Vol. VI, Pg. 175,
513,517; Vol. VII, Pg. 465,479,487,495,524).

Belchier, James, relative, inholder at Kingston upon
Thames-1732.

*Belchier, John, relative, cabinet-maker in St. Paul's
Churchyard, London. About Jonathan Jr. planning marriage
to John Belchier's only daughter in the 1732 period.
(James, John and William Belchier are brothers (Vol. VI,
Pg. 513; Vol. VII, Pg. 122). Speculation that Belcher met
him in 1704, as he is Captain Andrew Belcher's cousin and
he is listed on Belcher's 1704 genealogy with his sister,
who Belcher visited at the Hague in 1704.

Belchier, William, relative, apothecary, Covent Garden.
brother of above, 1733.

*Bellamy, George, close friend, helped Jonathan Jr.
1733. Bellamy may have been assisting Jonathan Jr. at
college, at "The Temple." He knew "good friend" Henry
Marshall, Postmaster of Boston. Marshall died in 1732 and
Richard Marshal an upholsterer, in Palsgrave Head Court
(London), was Henry Marshall's agent. Correspondence from
Belcher asks Bellamy to contact Richard Marshall. (Vol.
VI, Pg. 207,236,461,502; Vol. VII, Pg. 467,475,478,482).

Bendish, Henry, one letter 1731, acquaintance with
"Lord Chancellor," asks: "letting my son wait on you to
his Lordship" (Vol. VI, Pg. 456).

Billers, Sir William, Freemason and member of Rummer
Tavern, Charing Cross (AQC 74, Pg. 34). Son of a London
merchant; Lord Mayor of London in 1734. Died 1745. In
a May 18, 1733 letter to Jonathan Jr. "I will introduce
myself to the Mayor & Aldermen of Coventry, and to Sir
Wm. Billers, at London (if you think the last may be of
service)..." (Vol. VI, Pg. 286).

Bishop of Lincoln, see Reynolds, Richard.

<u>Bishop of London</u>,   see Gibson, Rev. Edmund.

<u>Bladen, Martin</u> (1680-1747), Early Freemason, The Rummer at Charing Cross (AQC 40, Pg 33). On Board of Trade in 1731. Supported Sir Robert Walpole and David Dunbar. Belcher felt he was betrayed by Sir Robert Walpole, when the King replaced him in 1741. Because Sir Robert Walpole is known to have had an international spy network and was obsessive about plots (see AQC 99, Pg. 189), and because of the Dunbar/Bladen opposition to Belcher, it is interesting to note this alignment against Belcher. Cool relationship after Dunbar problem (Vol. VI, Pg. 61,488,494,507; Vol. VII, Pg. 251,472).

<u>Brundell, James</u>, one of Lords of Trade with Bladen. Dunbar problem (Vol. VI, Pg. 471; Vol. VII, Pg. 472).

<u>Brydges, James</u> (1673-1744), Duke of Chandos, not the known Freemason. James Brydges son, Henry, was Grand Master in 1738. Belcher's correspondence regards real estate which the Duke was interested, in New York. Introduces Jonathan Jr. (Vol. VI, Pg.381,480,500; Vol. VII, Pg. 476). (AQC 21, Pg. 230,241).

<u>*Bull, John</u>, old friend, died in 1731 period. Wife-Hannah Bull (Vol. VI, Pg. 468,490,495,516). All to Hannah Bull. Expresses condolences and promises, in two letters, to pay debt.

<u>*Burchett, Josiah</u> (1666-1746), secretary to Admiralty. Helped Jonathan Jr. Burchett's grandson stayed at Belchers (15 letters 1732-1743).

<u>Burnet, T.</u>, "Before I left London I assur'd Mr. T. Burnet I wou'd very heartily pursue the King's order to me in favor of the children of my late dec'd predecessor,..."(see letter to Abraham Van Horn, Nov. 26, 1733). Belcher made a speech in Massachusetts Assembly and raised 3000 Pounds for the former Governor, William Burnet's, children (no correspondence to T. Burnet).

<u>Byng, George</u>, Viscount Torrington, First Lord of the Admiralty. Mentioned Capt. George Protheroe, who was apparently Captain of the man of War "Blandford." Belcher made a return voyage on that ship, from England in Aug.

1730. Belcher thanked Byng for "greatful sense from this country to all the Kings's goodness", regarding Protheroe and The "Blandford on station" off Massachusetts. Byng introduced to Jonathan Jr. (Vol. VI, Pg. 151, 458).

*Calamy Sr, Edmund, Rev., died in 1732 period, helped Jonathan Jr. (Vol. VI, Pg. 470).

Campbell, Archibald (1682-1761), Earl of Islay, afterwards third Duke of Argyle. In 1732 he was Keeper of the Privy Seal for Scotland, and afterward Keeper of the Great Seal of Scotland. Helped Jonathan with law. Member of "The Society for Propagating Christian Knowledge," in Scotland. Governor Belcher "and eleven other gentlemen to be their correspondent members in these parts... pursuing interest of this noble charity by sending missionaries among the original natives of this country..." (Sept. 19, 1732). Note: Belcher called himself a "perfect stranger" to the Earl. Even for Belcher the letter is extremely friendly to a stranger. Asks the Earl to allow Jonathan Jr. to "pay his visit him and receive his help in the law".... "Particular honor to me, my son, & whole family." This is a curious letter from Belcher (Vol. VI, Pg. 188).

Campbell, John (1678-1743), Duke of Argyle, 1732 gift-white otter muff. Intro to John Jr. in 1732. In a letter to the Duke of Newcastle, Duke of Argyle (John Campbell at that time) and the Lords of Trade, Belcher requested an engineer, Majr. Paul Mascarene, a Captain in Collo. Philips's Regiment "now in garrison at Anna Polis Royal in Nova Scotia" to repair and fortify "Castle Wm" in "this Province." In an unrelated Nova Scotia matter, William Skene was a President of a 1737 Nova Scotia Committee in a land dispute in Belcher's Provinces (Belknap, 1831, Pg. 241). John Skene, who died in 1690 as deputy-governor of West Jersey, some claim to be the first Freemason in America (AQC 91/227-8). Skene was from Scotland, not born in America. Any connection between Belcher and Skene is undetermined at this date (Vol. VI, Pg. 195,484; Vol. VII, Pg. 185,465).

*Carteret, Edward, "...it may ever lye in my power to contribute to his Majesties service in the business of the Post Office under your care, or to do you or your friends any acceptable services in this part of the world..." Mentions Jonathan Jr. (Vol. VI, Pg. 456).

* Caswall, John, "sorry to hear of the death of my old friends Mr. Caswall..." Nov. 1, 1731. This is probably the brother of H. Caswall (no correspondence to John Caswall).

Caswall, H., received three hogshead of Malmsey wine. Helped Jonathan 1731, but relationship cooled by 1732. Belcher had lent funds to his brother in London. The brother had died before September 18, 1732. Related to Belcher's wife's, mother's, "sister Caswell". Governor Belcher's wife's mother was Mary Partridge (?-1739), wife of William Partridge (1655-1729). Their son, Richard, was in London as an agent 1701-1759. Governor Belcher exchanged 23 pr Kidd gloves that were the wrong size for his wife. Caswell was presumably a merchant (Vol. VI, Pg. 470).

Cavendish, William, Duke of Devonshire, 1732. Solicits Commission for Anthony Reynolds as Lt. Gov. of N. H. in 1732. Introduces Jonathan Jr. (Vol. VI, Pg. 471).

Clark, Sir Robert, bought land in Oxford from Mr. Thompson 1731 period. Associated with Commissioners for Indians regarding appointments in 1733 (Vol. VI, Pg. 453, 513; Vol. VII, Pg. 477, 481).

*Compton, Spencer, Earl of Wilmington, 1732, close associate, four presents. Solicits for Anthony Reynolds, and Major Paul Mascarene for help with dispute against Belcher. Dispute was in form of opposition to Belcher mailed to the Privy Council and Plantation Board (Vol. VI, Pg. 456,465,471,494,505; Vol. VII, Pg. 59,75,241,354 443,457,506,525).

*Coram, Thomas, born Lyme Regis 1668, mariner, died in London 1751. Foundling hospital london, "old friend." Solomon quotation (Vol. VI, Pg. 86,111,211,250,297, 391, 454,491,514; Vol. VII, Pg. 231,245,332,411,462,466,474, 478,495,499,522,524,529-32,556-60).

De la Faye, Charles, Under-Secretary of State in England in 1731. De la Faye was a Freemason on 1723 list. Member of the Horn Tavern in Westminster (AQC 37, Pg 112). Belcher asked De la Faye for a supply of paper, sealing wax and pens (Vol. VI, Pg. 469, 516).

Dingley, Robert, introduces his nephew, Andrew Oliver in

1733. "Tell my old friend Dingley he has done the head of the cane nicely." (Vol. VI, Pg. 456,503).

Dunbar, David, associated with Duke of Wharton according to Belcher. Friend of Martin Bladen, known Freemason. Lt. Gov. of Belcher... "my enemy." (Vol. VI, Pg. 318,324,329, 331, 345,351,354,360,366,422,440,493,499,506,511,514,515, 518; Vol. VII, Pg. 44,116,459-61,464,524).

Duke of Argyle, see Campbell, Archibald.

Duke of Argyle, see Campbell, John.

Duke of Chandos, see Brydges, James.

Duke of Devonshire, see Cavendish, William.

Duke of Grafton, see Fitzroy, Charles.

Duke of Newcastle, see Pelham, Thomas.

Earl of Islay, see Campbell, Archibald.

Earl of Wilmington, see Compton, Spencer.

*Edgecumbe, Richard (1680-1758), Parliment 1701, friend of George Selwyn and younger H. Walpole. Lord of the Treasurer. Although very little correspondence, Belcher helped find his land. Introduced his son. Close associate (Vol. VI, Pg. 193).

*Fairfax, Brian (1676-1748/9), one of Commissioners of Customs (1723-1748). Belcher assisted his kinsman in 1731. Helped Jonathan Jr. (Vol. VI, Pg. 63,165,185,202, 240).

Fane, Thomas, Lord of Westmorland, on Lords of Trade in 1731. A kinsman was "Mr. Norton." Correspondence about David Dunbar. Introduces Jonathan Jr. (Vol. VI, Pg. 291,471,480; Vol. VII, Pg. 472,477).

Fenwick, Edward, in 1733 his son stayed at Belcher's house. Helped Jonathan Jr. (Vol. VI, Pg. 461,478,502, 512).

Fitzroy, Charles, Duke of Grafton, Freemason on Feb. 6, 1730 at the Horn Tavern (See AQC 37, Pg. 114). Also Lord

Chamberlain in 1731. Grandson of Charles II, by the
Duchess of Cleveland. Church request in 1731 (Vol. VI,
Pg. 65, 67).

Fitzroy, Augustus, Lord Augustus, son of Charles
Fitzroy. Married Elizabeth Cosby, daughter of William
Cosby. William was Governor of New York. No Belcher
correspondence, information only.

Frankland, Sir Thomas, introduced Jonathan Jr. Belcher
commission request for Robert Barker in Philadelphia,
Franklind's nephew visits Belcher (Vol. VI, Pg. 453,487,
495,516,517).

Gibson, Rev. Edmund (1669-1748), scholar and antiquary,
Bishop of London in 1731. Gibson was a Whig and labeled
in England as "Walpole's Pope" (see "History of England,"
By Keith Feiling, Professor at Oxford, 1963 edition, Pg.
647). Belcher felt Sir Robert Walpole deceived him near
the end of his governorship (see Belcher Papers in 1741
period). Correspondence over Rev. Price Commission at
Kings Chapel, Boston (Vol. VI, Pg. 71,488,512; Vol. VII,
Pg.175,455,457).

Goizins, Mr., Bristol copper ore dealer in 1731/3 (Vol.
VI, Pg. 482,484,491,504,514,518; Vol. VII, Pg. 465,472,
480,493,497).

Governor of the Bank of England, see Holden, Samuel.

Guyse, Rev. John (1680-1761), minister at Herford and
London, "kind mention" of Jonathan Jr. in London (Vol.
VI, Pg. 393,461,491,503; Vol. VII, Pg. 491,540,559).

Hart, William, copper dealer in Bristol, England (Vol.
VI, Pg. 455,461,463).

Holden, Samuel, merchant in London, Governor of the Bank
of England. Died in 1740. Helped Jonathan Jr. (Vol. VII,
Pg. 462,474,478,507).

Jekyll, Sir Joseph, in 1731, gift not identified. Thanks
for "favor and respect" to Jonathan Jr. (Vol. VI, Pg.
456; Vol. VII, Pg. 474).

Jones, Sir Thomas, Freemason of the Lodge at Bedford Head
in Covent Garden (AQC Vol. 7, Pg. 151); In a letter

dated Dec. 3, 1733, Belcher mentions that "Mr. Reynolds is married to Sir Thomas Jones's widow, a young lady of 25..." (Vol. VI, Pg. 437).

King, Peter, Lord Chancellor in 1731, gift of New England law "of some amusement to your Lordship" (Vol. VI, Pg. 455,486).

Lords of Trade, in 1731 were Earl of Westmorland, Paul Docminique, Thomas Pelham, Martin Bladen, Edward Ashe, Orlando Bridgeman, James Brudenell, Archer Croft. Of the above, Westmorland and Pelham were positive to Belcher, Bladen and probably Docminique were negative. (Vol. VI, Pg. 14,67,147,158,226,240,246,248,251,276,286, 294,307,346,428,465,472,489,495,497; Vol. VII, Pg. 19,78, 108, 127,156,179,185,225,253,255,347,357,377,460,461,464, 467, 480, 481, 496,501/3,512,517,519,521,522,527,530,537, 541,546).

Lord Augustus, see Fitzroy, Augustus.

Lord Barrington, see Shute, John.

Lord Chancellor, see Edgcumbe, Richard.

Lord Chancellor, see King, Peter.

Lord Chief Justice, see Sir Robert Raymond.

Lord Harrington, see Stanhope, William.

Lord of the Treasurer, see Bendish, Henry.

Lord of the Treasury, see Walpole, Sir Robert.

Lord of Westmorland, see Fane, Thomas.

Lord Weymouth, see Thomas Thynne, 2nd Viscount of Weymouth.

Lord Wilmington, see Compton, Spencer.

Marsh, John, in 1732, thanks him for "civilities" to Jonathan Jr. (Vol. VI, Pg. 453,469).

<u>Montague, Duke of</u> (1690-1749), first noble Grand Master
(1721-1722). Belcher's agent, Richard Partridge, selected
the prank playing Duke for the Governor's present of an
Indian cannoe and "wolvering skin." Belcher wrote to his
brother-in-law, Partridge, who had been in London thirty
years: "2 little Indian cannoos & a wolvering skin to
be presented in my name where you judge it may be most
acceptable." (Dec. 7, 1731). Belcher's son, Jonathan
Jr. may have been a participant in selecting the Duke,
for Belcher wrote to Jonathan Jr. on Sept. 18, 1732: "The
canno & wolvering, I see, went to the Duke of Montague."
The presents given to the Duke, may provide a clue into
Jonathan Jr. and Richard Partridge's Masonic affiliation,
but not necessarily, for the Duke was also of political
significance. In the 1730s, the Duke was one of "the most
popular officers of the Royal Household." (AQC 79, Pg.
82). From the above correspondence, it appears that
Governor Belcher was an associate of the Duke of
Montague, although there is no Belcher correspondence to
him published in the Belcher Papers. The most recent
research on the Duke of Montague, who was the leader of
Freemasons when the first Constitution was ordered to be
prepared, implies that he was made a Mason privately,
possibly by Dr. Desaguliers (AQC 79, Pg. 72). Friends
of the Duke included many with Belcher: Lord Townshend,
Phillip Stanhope, Sir Robert Walpole, The Duke of
Newcastle, but conspicuously absent, Belcher did not
mention or correspond with the Duke of Richmond, Grand
Master 1724-5, who was a very close friend of the Duke of
Montague. (see Knights of the Bath, from letter estimated
to be in the 1725 period: Montague to Richmond, and 1749
Hoax to Stanhope (AQC 30, Pg. 180-181).

<u>*Morton, John</u>, "respect to" Jonathan Jr. Apparently
Morton knew Rev. Dr. Calamy. Belcher mentions his death
Oct. 21, 1732 letter. Morton assisted Jonathan Jr. in
England regarding his numerous visits to nobility (Vol.
VI, Pg. 459,469,472,486,492,502,503,513; Vol. VII, Pg.
398,464,475,494).

<u>Munday, James</u>, wishes him to introduce Jonathan to Lord
Chief Justice Raymond, Sept. 19, 1732 (Vol. VI, Pg. 484;
Vol. VII, Pg. 464).

<u>*Neal, Rev. Daniel</u>, in 1731, favors to Jonathan Jr.
Belcher mentioned the death of friends in England, no
names mentioned (Vol. VI, Pg. 461,481).

*Newman, Henry, born in Massachusetts in 1670, died in England. Sometimes agent for New Hampshire in London. Newman was a librarian of Harvard at one time. Belcher was an "old friend." Newman provided a home for Jonathan Jr. on his arrival in London in 1731 (Vol. VI, Pg. 57, 74,389,495,502; Vol. VII, Pg. 247,394,411,457,458,466, 467,474,479,498,524,551,560).

Oglethorpe, Gen James E.(1696-1785), Freemason and Master of first Lodge in Georgia in 1735. On engraved list of 1736 it is number 139, the second American Lodge listed, Boston being Number 126 on the 1736 list. Born in London in 1696, member of Parliament in 1722, died in England as the only founder of a Province who lived to see the formation of the United States. Founder of Georgia. "It is a great pleasure to me, Sir, to hear of your health... (now refering to Georgia) I have heard one condition of the tenure of their lands is, in case there be no male heir of the family the daughters are all excluded on the death of the father, and the lands to revert to the Trustees or to the Crown. If this be so, the condition is hard. We have here a fine country, capable of naval stores, grain, swine and black cattle, has lead and copper mines, and perhaps the best fishery in the world... You will, Sir, pardon the freedom I have taken, which I think I have done as a true friend to the new colony. I have order'd Mr Belcher (reference to the Governor's son, Jonathan Jr. ed.) of the Temple to do himself the honour of putting this into your hands, and I shall greatly esteem your favour & countenance to him. I wish you always much health & honour, & am in all our commands, Honoble Sir..." (Vol. VI, Pg. 278,506; Vol. VII, Pg. 69).

Oliver, Andrew (1706-1774), Freemason, St. John's Lodge of Boston in 1740. Oliver was Belcher's nephew and later Lt. Governor of Massachusetts. After Oliver lost his wife and father, he went to London in the late May period of 1733 with several letters of recommendation from Belcher. Belcher wrote on behalf of Oliver to his friends in London: Francis Wilks, Robert Dingley, John Morton, Jonathan Belcher Jr., Richard Partridge, Rev. Isaac Watts, Rev John Guyse, J. Waters, and Evans (probably the Secretary to Lord Chamberlain). Since Freemasonry was not organized in Boston by Henry Price until July 30, 1733,

222   FIRST AMERICAN BORN

apparently Andrew went to London before this time (see
B. P. Vol. VI, Pg. 503). It is possible that many
of the above are Freemasons, as many of them are also
mentioned in the Nov. 1, 1731, letter, that Belcher wrote
to his son, Jonathan Jr., after he had arrived in London
soon after his twenty-first birthday.

Onslow, Arthur (1690-1768), Speaker of the House of
Commons from 1727-1761. Onslow introduced Mr. Shirley
(Gov. Massachusetts 1741) to Belcher. Shirley was
recommended as a pleader to the Courts in Massachusetts
in 1731 (Vol. VII, Pg. 396, 525).

*Partridge, Richard, important colonial agent for several
Provinces. Partridge was the brother of Governor
Belcher's wife, Mary, and he was born in Porstmouth, New
Hampshire. He was a Quaker and also the personal agent of
Belcher. In London 1701-1759. Belcher signed his letters
to Partridge "Your affectionate Brother." Belcher wrote
over 100 letters to Partridge from 1731 to 1743. The
subjects include a wide range of governmental activities
and solicitations to the Board of Trade, Secretary of
State, various members of the Privy Council and other
significant individuals in England. See the Duke of
Montague, and text of this research, Pg. 189-195.

Paxton, Nicolas, 1732 soliciting for Jonathan Jr. (Vol.
VI, Pg. 472; Vol. VII, Pg. 474).

*Pelham, Thomas (1693-1768), Duke of Newcastle, James
Anderson wrote that Pelham became a Freemason at an
"occasional Lodge at Sir Robert Walpole's House of
Houghton-Hall in Norfork..." Anderson's account is
placed between 14 May and 24 June 1731 Grand Lodge
meetings (AQC 37, Pg. 109). Thomas Pelham's brother was
Henry Pelham. Thomas was Secretary of State in
1731. There were two early Pelham Freemasons at St.
John's Lodge of Boston: Peter in 1738, and Charles in
1744. Belcher sent wild geese, a hogs head of Malmsey
wine, another "Indian canno & five paddles" to Pelham
(One canoe went to the Duke of Montague). Belcher wrote
seventeen letters to Pelham between 1731-1733, primarily
in an attempt to replace David Dunbar. One of Lords of
Trade in 1731. Letter regarding Belcher's support for
Pelham's associate, Mr. Shirley. Another for Belcher's
support of Anthony Reynolds, a son of the Bishop of
Lincoln (Vol. VI, Pg. 10,25,100,103,117,132,152,171,216,

309,384,407,455,459,475,500,505; Vol VII, Pg. 57,85,185,
282, 312,337,340,457,460,464,467,477,479,481,495,504,506,
508,510,519,520,530,537,540,541).

Pellet, Dr., probably the Freemason (1671? -1744), in
AQC 40, Pg. 137. Soliciting for Jonathan Jr. (Vol. VII,
Pg. 476). Belcher's letter is dated Nov. 9, 1734.

Popple, Alured, secretary to the Board of Trade in
1732 (Vol. VI, Pg. 113,452,458,469,486.516; Vol. VII, Pg.
148,464,472,479).

Prendergast, Sir Thomas, early Freemason, initiated at
the Horn Lodge, in March 1724 (AQC 30, Pg. 177), in
the presence of The Second Duke of Richmond, Charles
Lennox, who was Master of that Lodge and Grand Master
in 1724/5. Prendergast was a Postmaster General for
Ireland, disliked by Sir Robert Walpole, had a rather
creative sense of humor (see AQC 30, Pg 192/3-letters to
The Duke of Richmond), friend of The Duke of Devonshire
(AQC 30, 207) and also Grand Warden in 1725. Belcher's
correspondence has to do with an unfavorable opinion of
William Shirley's (1741 Governor of Massachusetts and
replacement of Belcher) 1741 management of collecting a
debt due from Robert Auchmuty to Sir Thomas Prendergast:
"What your attorney's reasons were for conducting your
affair with M Auchmuty in the manner he did are unknown
to me, but this I know, that it was unsafe to you, and
what, I believe, no gentleman of his profession would
have advis'd to." In a six month earlier correspondence
it appears Belcher was correct: "It has been generally
suppos'd Mr Auchmuty has 12 or 14 hundred ounces of wrott
plate, which I had a mind Mr Shirley should have in pawn,
in case he did not complye with the first payment..."
Prendergast is in sharp contrast to the usually serious,
religious and loyalist Belcher. Sir Thomas's father, the
first Boronet, and also named Thomas, was a Jacobite, and
Roman Catholic associated with the plan to assassinate
William III in 1696. The son was witty, anti-clerical
and Protestant (AQC 30, Pg. 193, 207). (Vol. VII, Pg.
526,538).

*Protheroe, Capt. George, "Old friend" of Belcher.
Protheroe returned to England in 1732. Interesting quote

from Belcher to Protheroe: "We continue in the old way, and if the King don't save us, I can't see but we will be lost" (June 26, 1732). (Vol. VI, Pg. 475,477,494).

Raymond, Sir Robert (1672-1733), Lord Chief Justice of the Kings Bench in 1731, introduced his son Jonathan Jr. (Vol. VI, Pg. 196,484).

Reynolds, Anthony, son of Bishop of Lincoln. In America from 1731-1732. Belcher appointed him to the Naval Office of New Hampshire. He returned to England in the 1732/3 period (Vol. VI, Pg. 96,143,457,461,462,467,492,512).

Reynolds, Rev. Richard, Bishop of Lincoln from 1723 to his death in 1743. Belcher offered to make his son Lt. Governor May 25, 1732 (Vol. VI, Pg. 53,129,134,235,475, 476; Vol. VII, Pg. 6,138,466).

*Reynolds, Thomas, son of Bishop of Lincoln, a law student or lawyer in London. Belcher's letter wishes Thomas to "to act the part of a brother to my son." (Vol. VI, Pg. 492).

Royall, Isaac (1672-1739), close friend who lived many years in Antigua, returned to Massachusetts in 1737. Note: In 1738, Grand Master Robert Thomlinson of Massachusetts, went to "England via Antigua, where finding some old Boston Masons went to Work and made the Governor and sundry other gentlemen of Distinction Masons, whereby from our Lodge sprung Masonry in the West Indies." (1733-1792 Massachusetts G. L. Proceedings, Pg. 6). (B.P. Vol. VI, Pg. 255,449,463,474,481).

Sandford, Thomas, "desires him to go with Jonathan Jr., to wait on Sir Joseph Jekyll and Sir Philip Yorke..." (Vol. VI, Pg. 456).

Sayer, Dr. Exton, the name Sayer is interesting, Anthony Sayer was the first Grand Master of England, but nothing is mentioned in the Belcher Papers regarding who Exton Sayer is, or where he came from. Letter regards William Shirley and Belcher's recommendation to the Massachusetts Judges as pleader. Introduces Jonathan Jr. Same letter sent to Thomas Pelham, Francis Fane, and John Marsh (Vol. VI, Pg. 452).

Secretary of State, see Townshend, Charles, Viscount; Pelham, Thomas and Stanhope, William.

Sharp, William, Clerk of Privy Council in 1733. "my friend." Letter regarding Governor's wages (Vol. VI, Pg. 411,453,484,488,512; Vol. VII, Pg. 464,474,479).

Shute, John (1678-1734), Lord Viscount Barrington, 1732 office appointment of John Boydell (Belcher spelled it Boydill) for Post Master of Boston after Henry Marshall died (Vol. VI, Pg. 209,458,469,482,512; Vol. VII, Pg. 476).

* Shute, Samuel (1653-1732), born and died in England, Governor of Massachusetts 1716-1723. Governor Belcher's father, Andrew Jr., was a Councillor for Shute until his death in 1717, as was Governor Belcher from 1718-20 and 1722-23. Also close to Jonathan Jr., in England (Vol. VI, Pg. 35,113,221,512; Vol. VII, Pg. 475).

Sladen, Rev. John, introduced Jonathan Jr. (Vol. VI, Pg. 478).

Solicitor-General, see Talbot, Sir Charles.

Speaker of the House of Commons, see Onslow, Arthur.

Stanhope, William, Lord Harrington, Secretary of State. There is only a mention of Stanhope in a Nov. 1, 1731, letter to his brother-in-law, Richard Partridge: "...I see you have an interest in Lord Islay (this means the Brother of the Duke of Argyle) & Harrington and had used it in my favour..." (Vol. VI, Pg. 37). Charles Stanhope, brother of William, was a member of the Lodge at the Bear and Harrow (AQC 40, Pg 235).

Talbot, Sir Charles, Solicitor-General, introduced Jonathan Jr. (Vol. VI, Pg. 456; Vol. VII, Pg. 473,477).

Thynne, Thomas, 2nd Viscount of Weymouth, Grand Master of England in 1735. There is virtually no correspondence between Belcher and Lord Weymouth. Belcher did mention Lord Weymouth to his son Aug. 7, 1734: "As to Ld. Weymouth, if he be a gentm. easy of access & you can rationally hope for his interest I approve of your attempting it..." Jonathan Jr. was planning to run for Parliment, from the bourough of Tamworth, it eventually

failed. This letter combined with several other letters
to Jonathan Jr., implies that Jonathan Jr., had several
acquaintances with Freemasons. I do not know when
Jonathan Jr., became a Freemason, it is estimated to be
in the 1731 period (for above quoted letter see Vol. VII,
Pg. 95).

* Townshend, Charles, Viscount (1676-1738), Secretary of
State and patron of Governor Belcher, his son, Charles,
was an early Freemason (AQC 40, Pg 237). Townshend's son,
Hon. George Townshend, apparently spent time with Andrew
Belcher, the first Deputy Grand Master of New England
(January 8, 1734/5) at the home of Governor Belcher: "my
eldest son is his bedfellow and constant companion..."
important acquaintance of Belcher (Vol. VI, Pg. 90,420,
487,502,508; Vol. VII, Pg. 17,182).

Viscount Torrington, see Byng, George.

Viscount Weymouth, see Thomas Thynne (Grand Master 1735).

*Van Dam, Rip, Dutch family, mariner at least as early
as 1686. Made councillor to governor of New York in 1702
and acting governor from July 1731, to August 1732.
Interesting because of Belcher's trip to Holland in 1704.
Van Dam used Richard Partridge as agent on Belcher's
recommendation (Vol. VI, Pg. 45,99,451,467,473).

*Wagner, Sir Charles (1666-1743), Lords of Admiralty
from 1718-1742. Distinguished English naval officer, warm
relationship. Possible connection between Wagner and the
Duke of Wharton (see Oct. 28, 1739, letter on Pg. 186-7).
Introduced Jonathan Jr.(Vol. VI, Pg. 386,401,417,475,517;
Vol. VII, Pg. 227,253,419,460,479,487,494,506,513,522,
524,531,534,541,556).

Walpole, Horace, brother to Sir Robert Walpole, similar
correspondence to Sir Robert. Present of a pair of geese.
(Vol. VI, Pg. 456,472; Vol. VII, Pg. 264,456,491,508,
535).

Walpole, Sir Robert (1676-1745), according to James
Anderson's account in Grand Lodge meetings, between
May 14 and 24 June 1731, an occasional Lodge was
held at Sir Robert Walpole's House (see AQC 37, Pg. 109).
First Lord of the Treasury and Chancellor of the
Exchequer [Prime Minister] 1721-1742. Dunbar issue.

(see notes on Martin Bladen). Introduces Jonathan Jr. Present of a hogshead of Malmsey wine (Vol. VI, Pg. 5, 400,465,472,493; Vol. VII, Pg. 167,223,351,506,534).

Waters, J., introduced Andrew Oliver, nephew of Governor Belcher in 1733. This was apparently a business association as Belcher also wrote to "Messers Waters" about their business relations with Foye, Belcher (Andrew?), and Lyde. Foye and Lynde were apparently children of Governor Belcher's sister, Sarah (Vol. VI, Pg. 461,503,513).

*Watts, Rev Isaac (1674-1748), poet and devine, born at Southampton, died at Theobald's. Watts is one of the few who is referred to "my son Andrew sends you a great deal of respect & service..." Andrew Belcher, First Deputy Grand master of New England in 1733, signed the original petition which stated: We are a sufficient number of Brothers regularly & duly made so in his Majesties Kingdom's of Great Britain and Ireland..." Governor Belcher and Andrew were in England between 1728 and 1730. Andrew Belcher was twenty-one in 1728. Possibly Andrew met Watts during that period (Vol. VI, Pg. 139,205,503; Vol. VII. Pg. 14,392,475,491,550,559).

*Wilks, Francis, agent for Massachusetts in 1728-1740s period, Wilks was helpful to Jonathan Jr. in England. Wilks died in the 1743 period (forty-five letters between 1731-1743).

*Williams, Joseph, Treasurer of the Society for Propagating the Gospel among the Indians. Belcher was apparently closely associated with Williams when he was in England. Belcher recommended his nephew, Andrew Oliver, to be a Commissioner of the Society, and his son, Jonathan Jr., to be a member. The May 25, 1734, letter ends with unusual affection for Williams: May you, Sir, constantly enjoye a great measure of health, with every other easy circumstance in life, and may you & I at the dissolution of soul & body, thro' the mercy of God, in Jesus Christ, mount with eagle wings to the tree of life, & eat & live forever. This is & shall be the prayer of, worthy Sir." (Vol. VII. Pg. 67; Vol. VI, Pg. 513).

Yorke, Sir Phillip, attorney general in 1732, introduces Jonathan Jr. (Vol. VI. Pg. 456,494).

APPENDIX PART II

The purpose of this appendix is to provide a brief guide to English Kings and the Massachusetts/New Hampshire Governors in colonial government (not including 1641-1689 period). Belcher's father was on the Council of Safety in 1689, and was on the Governor's Council from 1702-1717.

Year in office	King of England	Governor of N. H. / Mass. (birth and death in brackets)
1689	William III Belcher visited King William III birthplace in Holland in 1704. William took over England in the bloodless revolution of 1688. (1688-1702)	Simon Bradstreet (1607-1697) N. H. Simon Bradstreet (1607-1697) Mass. (N. H. and Massachusetts were a united colony until 1679) New Hampshire became a separate province in 1679, Massachusetts became a province by Charter of William and Mary in 1691.
1692	"	John Usher (1648-1726) N. H. William Phips (1651-1695) Mass. (Usher from, and living in, Boston was surprised to be replaced "in his absence" by a 1697 commission to Belcher's future father-in-law, Wm. Partridge, Lt. Governor of N. H.)
1697	"	William Partridge (1655-1729) N. H. William Phips-Mass. (1651-1695) Mass. (Partridge was a fill-in Governor until the New Hampshire "rebellion" against Usher was filled by the Earl of Bellomont. This rebellion was near the end of a nine year war between the "Grand Alliance" of England, Holland, The Holy Roman Empire, and Spain, against France.)
1698	"	Samuel Allen (1636-1705) N. H. William Phips (1651-1695) Mass. (Allen obtained title to New Hampshire from a complicated transfer dating to the 1630s from John Mason, he was commissioned in the King's absence on June, 6, 1696, by the interest of Sir Henry Ashurst, and Partridge was the Governor in Allen's absence.)

1699   "   Earl of Bellomont (?-1701) N. H.
                                Earl of Bellomont (?-1701) Mass.
                                (The Earl, very popular in America,
                                died in March 5, 1701, having arrived
                                at his "eastern governments" on July
                                31, 1699).

1702   Queen Anne   Joseph Dudley (1648-1720) N. H.
        (1702-1714)   Joseph Dudley (1648-1720) Mass.
First   Queen of the   (Dudley appointed Capt. Andrew
Joint Kingdom of   Belcher, Jonathan's father as a
Great Britain and   member of the Governor's Council
Ireland in 1707.   in 1702. Thus begins Belcher's
                                journey into politics).

1714   George I   "   "
        (1714-1727)
        First Hanover (Germany)
        King of England. Belcher
        met his family in 1704.

1716   "   Samuel Shute (1662-1742) N. H.
                                Samuel Shute (1662-1742) Mass.
                                (Shute was helped into becoming Governor
                                by three concepts: (1) George I had taken
                                over as King, (2) The peaceful time was
                                an appropriate time to reward valuable
                                service in the past war (3) Jonathan,
                                Dummer, and Ashurst bribed Burgess with
                                1000 pounds not to accept his commission.
                                Dudley retired in Roxbury, Mass.).

1727   George II   "   "
        (1727-1760)
    Son of George I. Shute departed "hastily" for England
                                in June 1723. The Lt. Governor's took
                                over in each province for five years.

1728   "   William Burnet (1688-1729) N. H.
                                William Burnet (1688-1729) Mass.
                                (Burnet died after five months as
                                governor).

1730   "   Jonathan Belcher (1681-1757) N. H.
                                Jonathan Belcher (1681-1757) Mass.
                                (Belcher was replaced, unhappily, in 1741;
                                but he would regain the King's favor in
                                1747 and govern New Jersey until his death
                                in 1757).

1741   "   Benning Wentworth (1695-1770) N. H.
                             William   Shirley   (?-1771) Mass.

1757   "   Benning Wentworth (1695-1770) N. H.
                             Thomas Pownal (1722-1805) Mass.

1760 George III   Benning Wentworth (1695-1770 N. H.
         (1760-1820)   Francis Bernard (?-1779) Mass.
      Grandson of George II
      Disastrous reign. Occasional
      insanity, heavy English debt,
      and determined regulatory
      nature contributed to War
      of 1775

1767   "   John Wentworth (1736-1820) N. H.
                                 Francis Bernard (?-1779) Mass.

1770   "   John Wentworth (1736-1820) N. H.
                                 Thomas Hutchinson (1711-1780) Mass.

1774   "   John Wentworth (1736-1820) N. H.
                                 Thomas   Gage   (? 1787)   Mass.

1776, July 4, Declaration of Independence forms the
             United States
1788, June 21, United States Constitution ratified by the
    approval of New Hampshire. A Province, "Hardly worthy
    of being called a government," fifty-four years
    earlier, in Jonathan Belcher letter to the Board of
    Trade Oct. 2, 1734.

KEY LEADERS OF ENGLAND
DURING BELCHER'S 1730-1741 GOVERNORSHIP.

King George II (1683-1760) King of England after 1727.
Sir Robert Walpole (1676-1745) Prime Minister between
                            1721-1742.

Privy Council to the King includes: (partial list).

     Sir Robert Walpole (Prime Minister).
     Lord Townshend (former Secretary of State).
     Duke of Newcastle (Secretary of State).

Privy Council (continued)

Lord Chancellor (Richard Edgecumbe (Lord of Treasurer).
Lord Westmorland (Also on Lords of Trade).
Lord Raymond (Lord Chf. Justice of the King's Bench).
Lord King (Lord High Chancellor).
Lord Yorke (Attorney General).
Lord Talbot (Solicitor-General).
Lord Jekyll (Master of the Rolls).
Earl of Islay, Archibald Campbell (Keeper of Great Seal
                                      of Scotland).
   William Sharp (Clerk).

Lords of Trade:

Earl of Westmorland   Paul Docminique
Thomas Pelham   Martin Bladen
Edward Ashe   Sir Orlando Bridgeman
James Brudenell   Sir Archer Croft

MISCELLANEOUS BELCHER LETTER TO BENJAMIN FRANKLIN
(Franklin was accepted as a Freemason in Feb., 1731)

"Sir- As you are not only a lover of learning but without
a Compliment an Ornament to it in the Age wherein you
live you will forgive the freedom I take in Recommending
to your Favour and Friendship Mr. John and Samuel
Winthrop two worthy young Gentlemen making a Journey this
Way partly for their Health as also to see this Country
(this letter was written when Belcher was Governor of New
Jersey, at Elizabeth Town, N. J. -ed.) The elder is
Professor of Phylisophy at Harvard College in New England
and the other is an Officer of the Supreme Court of the
Massachusetts Bay. They are descended from one of the
first families of New England and their deceas'd Father
was my particular Friend and Acquaintance and after saying these things I will only add that any respect or
Civility you are pleas'd to shew them I shall take as a
fresh Instance of your Real Regard for Sir Your hearty
Friend and Servant. Jonathan Belcher." (April 26, 1754,
see "Franklin Letters," and Mass. Historical Society
"Belcher Letters."). The above noted John Winthrop (1714-
1779), son of Adam Winthrop, made the first study of sun-
spots in 1739. As a famous astronomer he also made the
first prediction of the return of Halley's comet in 1759.

Adam Winthrop, who was a "particular friend" of Belcher,
married Anne Wainwright. They raised sixteen children.

APPENDIX PART III

The purpose of this appendix is to provide a general guide to the individuals that Jonathan Belcher recorded in his Journal of 1704. The following dates designate the major stopping points, and page references in the text, of the three month journey.

July 8 O.S. to July 24, N.S. (Pg. 23-28), at sea from Greenwich to Rotterdam.
July 24 to July 29 at Rotterdam (Pg. 28-33), Rotterdam summarized July 29.
July 30 (Pg. 34), visited the Hague and passed through surrounding towns.
August 1 to 11 (Pg. 40-48), Amsterdam and surrounding towns. (Amsterdam summarized August 11).
August 11 to 15 (Pg. 48-54), on the road to Hanover.
August 15 to 26 (Pg. 54-65), at Hanover to meet the Heir to the throne of England. Hanover summarized on August 26).
August 26 to 29 (Pg. 65-75), on the road with a minor stop at Lambspring.
August 29 to 31 (Pg. 75-79), at Silver mine.
September 1 to 7 (Pg. 80-84), on road with minor stops.
September 8 to 17 (Pg. 84-99), at Berlin to see King and Queen of Prussia. Berlin summarized Sept. 15-17.
September 17 to 19 (Pg. 99), on road.
September 19 to 28 (Pg. 99-106), at Hamburg with English Company. Hamburg summarized Sept. 27.
Sept. 28 to Oct. 3 (Pg. 106-107), on road to Amsterdam.
Oct. 3 to 13 (new style calender) (Pg. 107-113), in Amsterdam area.
Oct. 4 (Old style calender) (Pg. 114), in London.

Abbess of Lutheran Monastery, August 25, close friend of Electress of Hanover. Played cards.
Abbey Lockum, Chief Clergyman at Hannover, August 26.
Barr, Mr., August 16, 26, one of the principle gentlemen of Hanover who was entertaining English gentlemen on August 16. He lived next door to Chapezeau coffee house. Belcher carried a letter from Barr to Mr. Bouche at the mine.
Barr's daughter, August 23, 25, amused when Belcher slept on the floor at Chapezeau's.
Belcher relative, see Willis.
Bellamont, Lady, August 16, 23, 25, 26, it is unknown if Lady Bellamont was related to the late Earl of

Bellomont, who died in 1701 and was the Governor
of Massachusetts and New Hampshire in the 1699
period. Lady Bellamont was a close friend of the
Electress of Hanover, Sophia.

Bellamont's sister Lady Ann, August 23, at Hanover sent
letter via Belcher to Abbot of Lambspring.

Bellamont's niece, August 23, 25, at Hannover. Belcher
visited with the "pretty handsome" niece.

Benson, Mr. Austin, August 27, Belcher had a letter for
him at Lambspring, expecting to see him in
Amsterdam, and planned on his company to Hanover.

Bennison, Madam, August 23, at Hanover. Played cards with
the Electress of Hanover.

Bothmar, Baron, July 30, and letter of recommendation
to the Electress of Hanover from the Baron, who
was visiting with Stanhope at the Hague.

Bouche, Mr., August 29, 30, 31, operator of the Elector's
four-seventh interest in the silver mine at
Clausthal. Belcher delivered Mr. Barr's letter to
"Mr. De Bouche."

Brown, Mr., July 29, a wealthy English merchant mentioned
in Rotterdam.

Bluthwait, Mr., Aug. 15, probably William Blathwayt (see
Index), an associate of Governor Joseph Dudley of
Massachusetts. Apparently a "friend in London"
(clerk of the King's Privy Council) who provided
Belcher with a letter of recommendation to Mr.
Pooley. Associated with the Electress of Hanover.

Burgomaster, Sept. 20, English Thanksgiving in Hamburg.

Burnett, Mr., Sept. 15, a Scotsman at Berlin, part of the
English company who was a favorite of the Queen
of Prussia.

Charles II, August 27, historical note of the former King
of England (1630-1685).

Chamberlin, Mr., August 15, same as Mr. Bluthwait.

Chapezeau, August 15, 21, a French coffee house in
Hanover, where Belcher dined and met several
Englishmen in Germany.

Cockburn, D.E., August 2, 3, 4, 10, 13, October 4, 5,
the minister of the English church in Amsterdam.

Cockburn, Mr., son of the minister, August 9, 23, 25, 26,
30, September 10, 27, October, 4, 11, hired
travel companion with Belcher from Holland
throughout Germany.

Colt, Mr., Aug. 16, 17, 21, 24, 26; Sept. 20, 27, Colt's
father was the Envoy at Hannover before Mr.
Creket. He welcomed Belcher to Hanover, and

visited with him at Hamburg.

Colt's Secretary, August 16, a German who speaks good English.

Dangerfield, Mr., Sept. 23, Dangerfield married a German, turned Lutheran, had the finest house in Hamburg, where Belcher and others of the English Company dined. His father was a "porter" for the English company, and was buried by them.

Danish Admiral, Sept. 20, at English thanksgiving in Hamburg.

Deplat, Count, August 24, at Hanover, "to see his house."

Desborough, Capt., July 12, captain of yacht "Cleveland."

Electress of Hanover, Sophia, August 16, 17, 19, 23, 25, 26, Sophia was the granddaughter to James I, (1566-1625) King of England after 1603, and his wife, Ann, of Denmark. Sophia (1630-1714) was heir to the throne of England. She was kind to Belcher, card games etc., well read and fluent in several languages. She was the mother to the rarely English speaking George I. Sophia sent a letter to her daughter, Sophia Charotte, the Queen of Prussia, via Belcher (see August 25).

Elector of Hanover, see George I.

Emerson, Mr., September 21, minister at Hamburg.

Ernest, Duke of Brunswick, August 16, 25, 26, youngest brother of George I. "To be the Bishoprick of Osnabrug, and is studious."

Foster, Mr., Sept. 19, 21, 24, 26, 27, at Hamburg, Belcher had letter of recommendation to Foster. He was very helpful to Belcher in Hamburg.

Frederick I (1657-1713), see King of Prussia.

Frederick William I (1688-1740), son of Frederick I.

George I (1660-1727), August 16, 17, 23, 24, 25, 26, 30, King of England in 1714, Elector of Hanover after his father, Ernest died in 1698. The future King spoke English, a rare occurrence, with Belcher.

George II (1683-1760), August 16, 19, 25, 26, King of England in 1727. Belcher first met the Prince who would eventually commission him as governor twenty-six years later, on August 16, 1704.

Hammond, Mr., July 25, 26, 27, an English gentleman, one of Mr. Spranger's acquaintances.

Hobby, Collt., Oct. 4, invited by Belcher's close friend in Amsterdam, Mr. Schaick.

Hope, "the Quaker", July 29, successful merchant is mentioned in Rotterdam.

Howard, Mr. Frederick, August 27, uncle to the 1704 Duke of Norfolk. Howard was a monk at Lambspring.

Huntley, Lord, September 7, 9, 10, 11, 15, at Berlin, a Scot, Roman Catholic, who was associated with the English envoy at Berlin, and showed Belcher the sights in that city.

Joe, John, July 8. Towerhill stairs to Greenwich.

King of Prussia, Frederick I (1657-1713) Sept. 10, 15, Belcher provides interesting insights into the King and his son Frederick William I (1688-1740).

Knightly, Capt., August 27, brother to the Abbot of Hanover. Belcher delivered a letter to him from Lady Bellomont.

Lapenan, Mr., July 29, a merchant mentioned in Rotterdam.

Leibnitz, Gottfried (1646-1716), September 11, 13, famous German scholar and mathematician. Belcher had interesting conversation with Leibnitz.

Lloyd, July 8, Towerhill stairs to Greenwich.

Lord Portland, July 8, 12, October 13, aboard yacht with Belcher, has country house at Susklet, on July 30.

Lord Woodstock, July 8, son of Lord Portland.

Lords of the Admiralty, of Amsterdam Oct. 7.

Manlesfield, Lord, August 26, not a favorite of The House of Hanover.

Maxillian, Prince, August 23, second son of Sophia, Electress of Hanover. In the army during the Battle of Hockset.

Milleson, Gabriel, July 8; 12, 25, 27, Oct. 11, commander of "Katharine," that Belcher sailed aboard.

Molesworth, Mr., August 16, 25, an Englishman briefly mentioned at Hanover.

Montague, Mr., August 16, an English gentleman and his governor mentioned, that Belcher met at Hanover. (unknown which Montague from journal, however, he was traveling to Hamburg, the place where the interesting September 19/20 "thanksgiving" occurred).

Poltney, Mr., August 16, 21, Belcher received a visit at Hanover.

Pooley, Mr., (also spelled Poley); August 15, 16, 17, 21, 23, 26, 24, one of the Englishman at Hanover. Introduced Belcher to the Electress of Hanover, Sophia. Belcher had two letters of recommendation addressed to Pooley, from "Mr Bluthwait and Mr Chamberlin."

Powel, Mr., September 8, 10, 15, nephew to Lord Raby in Berlin.

Princess of Anspach, Sept. 15, 16, daughter of King of Prussia.

Queen of Prussia, September 9, 11, 13, 15, 16, daughter of the Electress of Hanover and wife of Frederick I. Belcher delivered a letter from the Electress.

Raby, Lord, September 7, 8, 9, 10, 11, 12, 14, 15, at Berlin, the English Envoy to the King of Prussia, Frederick I (1657-1713). He was the grandson to the Earl of Strafford, who was beheaded.

Raby's Secretary, September 10.

Ramsey, Captain, July 9, 12, captain of "Bonadventure," and commadore of July 8 fleet of ships.

Reeves, Mr., July 29, successful merchant mentioned in Rotterdam.

Resident of Denmark in Hamburg, Sept. 20, at English Thanksgiving at Hamburg.

Resident of Sweden in Hamburg, Sept. 27, "He was sick where the publick entertainment was" in Hamburg.

Rowland, Sir (Gwin), August 15, 16, 17, 24, 26, at Hanover. Sir Rowland was part of the English party associated with the Electress of Hanover, mother to George I. Belcher mentions that Rowland read Clarendon's History to the Electress.

Sanders, Captain, July 12, captain of ship "Lousdike."

Schaick, Mr. Van, August, 1, 2, 5, 6, 7, Oct. 2, 3, 4, 6, "My priceless friend" in Amsterdam. Schaick was among several merchants who Belcher delivered recommendations from his "friends in London."

Scott, Mr., August 20, 26, showed Belcher some of attractions at Hanover. One of the English gentlemen of the Elector's at Hanover.

Senate, September 20, "and four of ye Senate" at the English Thanksgiving in Hamburg.

Sincerf, Mr., July 29, successful merchant mentioned in Rotterdam.

Sophia, see Electress of Hanover.

Sophia Charlotte, see Queen of Prussia.

Sophia Dorothea, August 19, 24, "She is of a very sweet temper, and very comely." Daughter of the Elector of Hanover, the later George I. Sophia Dorothea married the King of Prussia, Frederick William I (1688-1740), who Belcher mentions.

Spranger, Mr., July 24, 25, 26,27, 30, August 1,4, 5. "A Chiausgeon" of the yacht "Katherine," who showed Jonathan about Rotterdam and Amsterdam.

Spranger, Mr., August 5, October 4, there are apparently two Sprangers associated with Belcher in the Amsterdam area. This Spranger, "a dutch merct to whom I was recommended."

Stanhope, Mr., July 30, Queen's Evoy Extraordinary at the Hague.

Stanhope's Secretary, July 30, showed Belcher the Hague.

Stone, Mr., July 25, 27, an English merchant, offered to do me any service in his power.

Stratford, Mr., Sept. 19, 22, 24, 25, one of the English company in Hamburg. Belcher went hunting with Stratford. Mr. Stratford went to see the English army and was present at the battle of Hochstet, where he met Lord Marlborough and was given permission to give money to the French prisoners.

Strickland, Mr., Sept. 19, 23, governor of Dangerfield, and one of the English company at Hamburg.

Sweat, Mr., August 4, the Queen's paymaster general of the army.

Thomas, Mrs., July 24, a passenger on the "Katherine." She invited Belcher to stay with her family at Rotterdam.

Thomas, Mr., July 24, an English broker, a comical little drunken fellow. "His eating is mean & yet dear enough."

Tibson, Mr., September 8, 15, secretary to the Envoy, Lord Raby in Berlin.

Vandermoulin, July 24, 25, 26, 30, "recommended by my friend in London for anything I might have occasion" at Rotterdam. "I took what money I wanted" in July 25 entry.

Vandermoulin, Peter, July 25. showed Belcher Rotterdam.

Van Rincom, August 5, October 4, 7, a partner of Mr. Spranger, the merchant who Belcher delivered recommendations in Amsterdam.

Van Schaick, see Schaick.

Vincent, Mousieur, Sept. 7, a French ordinary that Belcher was recommended in Berlin.

Wadsworth, Capt., July 28, captain of New England ship called the "Industry."

Watkinson, Mr., Sept. 19, 22, 24, one of the "chief merchants" in Hamburg. Belcher delivered a letter of recommendation to Watkinson and he invited Belcher to the "English Thanksgiving for Hochstet

Victory" on Sept. 20, 1704, and provided Belcher
with a horse to go hunting.

Wellden, Mrs., (possibly weeden) August 16, 19, Oct. 10,
an English Lady who "is" a councillors wife and
came there to see the Electress. Belcher's
opinion: "one of the most homely women I
ever saw."

Willett, Mr., Sept. 22, at Hamburg, of the English
company, who carried Belcher in his coach to see
The Resident.

Willis, Mrs. (Belcher), July 30, October 9, at the Hague,
daughter of the brother of Jonathan's grandfather. Mrs. Willis, estimated to be born in the
1640 period. Her father, John Belcher, was born
in England 1615 and died in 1672. Mrs. Willis's
husband was estimated to be "near 60 years old"
in 1704.

Willis, Mr., Sept. 25, 27, in Hamburg, carried Belcher to
see Mr. Stratford's garden. Willis was with
Stratford to visit the English army at Hochstet
battle. This may possibly be Belcher's relative,
the husband of Mrs. Willis.

Wind, Mr., August 15, 16, 23, 24, 25, 26, Belcher met at
Chapezeaus in Hanover. Wind was one of the
Englishmen with Sir Rowland and he took a
fortnight "turn of waiting" on the Electress.
Wind promised to send the Electress's painting to
Belcher in Amsterdam, after it was finished.

Wolfeinbuttle, Duke of, August 30, one of his generals
was at dinner at Hanover on August 25. Belcher
mentioned Wolfenbuttle on August 16, regarding a
George I military victory over Wolfenbuttle.

Wytch, Mr., Sept 27 in Hamburg, "fell a railing against
the King of Sweden...I thought it not very civil
before his Resident."

The purpose of this appendix is to list Jonathan's books, which he deeded to the College of New Jersey on May 7, 1755. (note: "Free Mason's Constitutions." It is unknown which copy of the Constitutions Belcher owned, obviously the first Book of Constitutions was published in London, 1723). Benjamin Franklin printed the first Masonic book in America in 1734, "Constitutions of the Freemasons." There are only seventeen copies in existence. For those interested in rare books there is a sizable research project in this list. Regrettably, only eight books of Belcher's collection survived the fire at Princeton during the Revolutionary War and a second fire in 1802. I have identified six of the existing books on this list (noted with an asterisk). "Catullus, Tibullus and Propertius. In usum Delphini. Parisilis," and Cotton Mather's "Ratio Disciplinae" are unidentified. (See Belcher's deed in "History of Princeton Library" for list and spelling).

Folio's

Pools Annotations
Doct.r Bates.s Works
Basnages History of Jews
Works of the Author of the
   Whole Duty of Man
Burnets History of his
   Own Time first Vol
Bunyan's Works 2: Vol
Le Estranges Josephus
Hows Works 2. Vol
Tillotsons Works 3: Vol
Flavels Works 2. Vol
History of Aethiopia
Burnets History of the
   Reformation 3 Vol
Burnet on the thirtynine
   Articles
Origination of Mankind
Grews Cosmologia Sacra
Mores Philosophical
   Collections
Rapins History of England
   5: Vol
Chamber.s Dictionary 2 Vol
Old Mixons Historical of the
   Stuarts

State Trials 6: Vol
New Jersey Laws
Communitas Fratrium
Trial of the Rebel Lords
Dryden's Works 4: Vol
Crowleys Works
Drydens Poems
The Book of Rates
Savel's History of the
   Quakers
Bucannanon's History of
   Scotland
Guyse:s Paraphrase 3: Vol
Roberts.s Map of Commerce
Poems upon the Marriage of
   the Prince of Orange
   in Latin Ditto
Ditto the Prince of Wales
Massachusetts Laws
The History of N. England
   by Cotton Mather
Visscher's Atlas Minor
Lock's Work's 3: Vol
Sidney on Government
Le Estrange:s Esop
Connecticut Laws

Quarto:s

Fields English Bible
Cruden's Concordence
Wallastons Religion of
    Nature
Dodridge's Family
    Expositor- 2
* Johnston's Psalms
Ainsworths Dictionary
    2. Vol
Abridgement of the statutes
    of Ireland

Silius Italius
Valerius Flaccus
Jones:s Abridgment the 4:
    & 5: Vol.s
Freemason's Constitutions
Newtons Cronology
Shaws Abridgement 3: Vol
Atlas Geographus 5. Vol
Sea Laws 2. Vol
Molloys Jure Maritimo
Boyer's French Dictionary

Octavo

Lidiards life of the Duke
    of Marlborough. 2: Vol
Hoadley's Answer to the
    Convocation
Trade and Navagation
    of Great Britain
Church History of Geneva
The Works of Longinus
Discourse concerning the
    Mine Adventure
Plutarch.s Lives 5: Vol
Neals History of the
    Puritants 4. Vol
Annals of Queen Ann 11. Vol
John Bull
Ciceros Works 12. Vol
Pearce's Vindication
Montagu's Essays 3. Vol
Miscellania Curiosa 3. Vol
Mathers Christian
    Philosopher
Wharton's Works 2: Vol
Echards Roman History
    5: Vol
Potters Antiquities 2. Vol
Debates in Parliament 3. Vol
Chamberlayn's State
Abridgement of Plantation
    Laws

Mayhews Indian Convert
Discription of the State
    of England
Huets History of the
    Commerce of the ancients
Sallust in Usum Delphini
Horace in Usum Delhpini
Le Mercier against
    Detraction
Waterland's Vondication
The Marriners Calender
Gordon's Grammar
Plutarchs Morals 5 Vol
Well.s Georgraphy 4. Vol
Bladens Caesar
* Barclays Apology
Present State of Virginia
Herodotu.s History 2. Vol
History of the Turks 2. Vol
Temples Letters 3. Vol
Annals of King George
Ludlow:s Memoirs 3 Vol
Hickering:s Works 2. Vol
Clarindons History of the
    Rebellion 6: Vol
Annals of Europe
The Works of St. Evremont
    2: Vol
Lex Mercatoria

Octavo (continued)

Bacons Essays
Fields English Bible
Rohaults Physics
Discourse of the Trinity
Hornecks Sermons 2. Vol
Burrishes Batavia illustrata
Rays Wisdom of God in the
    Creation
Mather:s Life
Miltons Works 2: Vol.
Atterbury:s Sermons 2. Vol.
Mrs. Row's Works 3 Vol.
Sharps Sermons 4: Vol.
Antiquities of the Hebrews
    4. Vol.
Watts on the World to
    come 2 Vol.
Epictetus
Smiths Curiosities of
    common Water
The Case of Tyths stated
Roscommon's Works
The History of Holland
    2: Vol.
The History of Jersey-
Life of Col.1 Gardner
Defoe's Works 2. Vol.
History of the Mongul
    Empire
Barcley of Tar Water
* Pemberton's (of N. York)
    Sermons
Dispensary A Poem
Delaun's plea for the
    Non-conformists
Echards Ecclesiastical
    History 2: Vol.
Bradley of Gardning 2: Vol
Works of the Prince of Conti
Le Estrange on Religion
King on the Creed
History of the World
    4: Vol.

History of France 2: Vol
Publius Papinius Statius
Vindicon of the Sunship of
    Christ
Burnets State of the dead
An exortation to the
    Inhabitants of Carolina
Miscellania Sacra 2: Vol.
Flynts Sermons
Mathers Apology
Hows Sermons 2. Vol.
Mrs Row's Letters
Horneks best Exercise
Watt:s Improvement of the
    Mind
Berrystretts Sermons 2.Vol.
Tennents Sermons
Hornek's Crucifyd Jesus
Passages relating to
    Phillips War
Kennets Antiquities
The practical Gardner
    2. Vol.
 The History of Germany 2.
    Vol.
Jenkins on the Christian
    Religion 2 Vol.
Occasional Papers 3: Vol.
Journey thr' Germany
Hoadleys Preservative
Gonson's Charges to Grand
    Juries
Sherlock on Judgement
Chalkley's Collection of
    Works
Gilpin's Life
Doctr William's Sermons 5:
    Vol
Branard's Life
* Fleetwoods Sermons
West on the Resurection
Clarindon & Whitlock
    Compared

Octavo (continued)

King's Primative Church
Colliers Antoninus
Bullocks Sermons
Taylors Establishment
Gambols Maxims
Pemberton's Sermons
Sherlock on death
Rapins Critical Works
     2, Vol.
Hales Contemplations 3: Vol.

Tennent on War
Report of the Committee of
     Secrecy in French
Norris's Letters
Doddridge on Religion
Scott.s Christian Life 5.
     Vol.
Hale on the Knowledge of
     God
Oxford Grammar

Duodecimo

Tennents Discources.
Watts.s Scripture History
Hale on the Magnet
Patrick on the Sacrament
Fire of the Altar
Brightland's Grammar
Castalio.s Latin Bible.
     3: Vol.
Life of Oliver Cromwell
Abstracts of the Acts of
     Parliament relating to
     the Admiraltry
Practice of the Court of
     Admiraltry
* Princes Annals of
     N. England
Turkish Spy 4: Vol.
* Temples Observations
Pomfrets Poems
Telemachus 2. Vol.
Sewel on the holy Spirit
The Spectator 8: Vol.
Steals Political Writings
Journal of the House of
     Commons
Cato's Letters 4. Vol.
Turell.s Remains
Tacitus 3. Vol.
The Guardian 2. Vol.
The Lover

Watts.s Missalanies
Penns no Cross
Cole of God's Sovereignty
Spiritual Retreat
Watts' Sermons- 3: Vol.
Redeemer & Sanctifier
Life of Czar of Moscova
Life of King of Sweden.
Wonders of the Invisible
     World
Mather's Psalms
Triumph of Mercy
Dickinson on Christianity
Kidder of the Sacrament
Shakespear's Works 9 Vol.
Letter to a Clergyman on a
     Sermon preached 30. of
     January
Mrs Mary Loyd's Diary
Persian Letters
Addison's Works 3. Vol.
Pearsals Contemplation
Baxters Call to the
     uncoverted
Popes Homar 6: Vol.
Dryden's Poems 6: Vol.
History of the low Country
     in French 3: Vol.
The Englishman
Hudibrass

Duodecimo (continued)

Tattler 4. Vol.   English, Scotch & Irish
Baronets 3. Vol.   Compendium 4 Vol
The Free holder   The Gazetteer two Vol.
Villar's Memoirs in French   Philip's Poems
Description of Paris   De immitatione Christi
Life of Pomponius Atticus   Whitefields Sermons 2. Vol.
Tully's Offices   Coleman on the incomprehen-
Popes Essay on Man   sibility of God
Horneck of the day of   Shaws Immanual
   Judgement   Fragments of Seneca in
                                 Latin-

Belcher also included in this deed a "pair of Globes"
(probably world maps); "a large Carv'd Guilded Coat of
Arms" (probably the Belcher Coat of Arms, which had the
motto "Loyal au Mort," which he claimed was the original,
but on his coach he used "Loyal Jusq' aula Mort." (B. P.
Vol. VI, Pg. 176); in addition "Heads of the Kings of
England in ten glas'd Frames, My Picture at full length
at present standing in what is called the blue Chamber in
my House." The Governor wrote a deed and accepted ten
shillings for his library and noted other gifts. He is
considered the first major donor to the College.

As a brief assessment of Jonathan's books, it reveals an
obvious interest in religion and the classic authors of
history. The occasional other books are often more
interesting insights into his apparently insatiable
curiosity: gardening, law, grammar, mining, a variety of
religions, antiquities, "smiths curiosity of common
water," secrecy in French, "The Lover," various
biographies, novels, Freemasonry, history, Indians,
trade, etc. For such a collection of books by an
American, twenty years before the Revolutionary War, was
more than an indication of wealth and bold curiosity,
Belcher was a serious book collector.

Regarding inscriptions of existing books:

1. Barclay book: "London, April 12, 1745, The gift of
   Mrs. Benjamin Partridge." (probably Belcher's brother-
   in-law's, Richard Partridge (1681-1759), son's wife).
2. Pemberton's Book: Autograph presentation to Jonathan

Remington, Boston, November 27, 1727 (This would be Captain Andrew Belcher's sister's son, Jonathan Remington (1677-1745), who was Governor Belcher's life long friend, going back to the "Blue Anchor Tavern" days.

3. Temple Book: "The gift of the authors brother, London, May 3, 1699." (This may be a book brought back from London by Captain Andrew's shipping days, Jonathan was at Harvard in 1699).

The remaining books have no noteworthy markings other than Belcher's autograph.

BIBLIOGRAPHY

American Council of Learned Societies, "Dictionary of American Biography," 1929, Volume II.

American Heritage Editors, "The American Heritage Pictorial Atlas," 1966, New York.

American Lodge of Research, "Transactions," Volumes 1-16, (1936-1988), New York.

Belcher, Jonathan, "Journal of My intended Voyage, & Journey To Holland, Hannover & ca: Beginning at London Saturday July 8th: O.S. 1704."

Belknap, Jeremy, "The History of New Hampshire," 1784, (first edition), Volume 1; 1791, (second edition), Volume 2; John Farmer edition, (Volumes I and II combined, with authors corrections and updates, 1831, Dover, N. H.).

"Boston Gazette," (newspaper, 1730s).

"Boston News Letter," (Newspaper 1730s).

Boston Records 1700-1728, "Record Commissioners," Vol. VIII.

Brewster, Charles, W., "Rambles about Portsmouth," 1859, Portsmouth, N.H.

Clark, William, Bell, "Naval Documents of the American Revolution," 1964, Volume I.

Coil, Henry, Wilson, "Coil's Masonic Encyclopedia," 1961, New York.

Drake, Samuel, "New England Genealogical Register," 1850, Volume 4.

Feiling, Keith, "A History of England," 1963, London.

Foss, Gerald, D., "Three Centuries of Freemasonry in New Hampshire," 1972, Somersworth, N.H.

Hudson, Alfred S., "History of Hudson, Mass.," 1889.

Hutchinson, Thomas, "The History of the Colony and Province of Massachusetts Bay," 1765 (1936 Mayo edition), Harvard University Press.

Johnson, Melvin, "Freemasonry in America prior to 1750."

Jones, Bernard, E., "Freemason's Guide and Compendium," 1988, London.

Knoop, Douglas; Jones, G.P.; and Hamer, Douglas; "Early Masonic Pamphlets," 1978, London.

Massachusetts Historical Society, Committee of 1893, "Belcher Papers," Volume VI, VII., and "Belcher Letters 1704-1757 period."

Paige, Lucius, R., "History of Cambridge, Massachusetts," 1877.

Pick, Fred L. and Knight, Norman G; "The Pocket History of Freemasonry," London; and "The Freemason's Pocket Reference Book," London, (both volumes revised by

Frederick Smyth (member of, and present editor of "Quatuor Coronati Lodge No. 2076 Transactions," 1983, London).

Quatuor Coronati Lodge No. 2076, "AQC Transactions," Vol. 1-103, 1886-1990, London.

Sewall, Samuel, "The Diary of Samuel Sewall," (two volumes).

Shipton, Clifford K, "Sibley's Harvard Graduates," Cambridge, Massachusetts, 1933, Volume 4.

Saint John's Lodge, Boston, "History of St. John's Lodge," 1917, Boston.

Stackpole, Everett S., "Old Kittery and her Families," 1903, Lewiston, Maine.

INDEX

This index refers to: 1. The text; 2. The transcript of
Jonathan Belcher's 1704 Journal in this research, and 3.
References to individuals in appendix I. Appendix I (Pg.
212-227) includes further details of other Governor
Belcher correspondents in England, which are not included
in the text of this research. See also appendix III (Pg.
232-238), for a brief guide to individuals in 1704
Belcher Journal. AQC refers to the transactions of
Quatuor Coronati Lodge No. 2076 (Pg. 159).

Belcher, Jonathan (Continued):

258 FIRST AMERICAN BORN

Edgecumbe, Richard, 217
Elector of Hanover, see George I.
Electress of Hanover, see Sophia.
Emerson, Mr., 1704 Journal, 100
Erasmus, statue of, Rotterdam, 1704 Journal, 29
Ernest, Duke of Brunswick, youngest brother of George I;
    1704 Journal, 57,64,66
Fairfax, Brian, 217
Fane, Thomas, Lord of Westmoreland, (appendix Pg. 217).
Farber, John (1695-1756), Freemason, London engraver of
    Belcher, 199
Fenwick, Edward, 217
Fitzroy, Augustus, 218
Fitzroy, Charles: 203,221
Foss, Gerald, D., Grand Lodge Historian Emeritus of New
    Hampshire, ii; and St. John's Lodge of Portsmouth,
    162-163. Author of, "Three Centuries of Freemasonry
    in New Hampshire."
Foster, Mr., 1704 Journal, 99,101,102,103,206
Foye, Sarah (Belcher) (est. 1688/9- ?), sister of
    Governor Belcher, married first to Byfield Lyde,
    married second to John Foye, 6; see Sarah Belcher.
Foye, John, married to Sarah (Belcher) Foye. Lived in
    Boston. While Governor Belcher was in office, there
    was a business of "Foye, Belcher and Lyde." The
    Governor's son, Andrew, apparently ran the business
    with Foye and Lyde. Governor Belcher was not
    involved in business while he was Governor.
Foye, William, mentioned in letter to John White, 1715,
    136.
Franklin, Benjamin (1706-1790), i,2,158,209,211,231,239
Frankland, Sir Thomas, 218
Frederick I (1657-1713), see King of Prussia.
Frederick William I (1688-1740), father of Frederick the
    Great and son of Frederick I, see 1704 Journal, 96
Freemasonry, and giving of gloves, 12; toasting, 22;
    and Boston Freemasons in 1736, 164; and Goose
    and Gridiron and Lodge No. 4, 20; and Hamburg in
    1704 may identify English Freemasons, 17-19;
    see Watkinson, appendix Pg. 237; and John White
    letter of 1704, 137-139; and old Charges, 138-139;
    and St. John the Evangelist, 139, 201; and John
    White, 141, 209; and "Bunch of Grapes Tavern" in
    Boston, 155; and Boston and London Freemasons,
    160-164; and letter to Waltron regarding Lyde
    staying at Henry Sherburne's House, (First Meeting
    place of Freemasons in Portsmouth, New Hampshire),
    170, and see AQC references and appendix.

www.ingramcontent.com/pod-product-compliance
Lightning Source LLC
Chambersburg PA
CBHW061720270326
41928CB00011B/2049